Social History of Africa

SACRED TREES, BITTER HARVESTS

Recent Titles in
Social History of Africa Series
Series Editors: Allen Isaacman and Jean Allman

Making the Town: Ga State and Society in Early Colonial Accra
John Parker

Chiefs Know Their Boundaries: Essays on Property, Power, and the Past in Asante, 1896–1996
Sara S. Bèrry

"Wicked" Women and the Reconfiguration of Gender in Africa
Dorothy L. Hodgson and Sheryl A. McCurdy, editors

Black Death, White Medicine: Bubonic Plague and the Politics of Public Health in Colonial Senegal, 1914–1945
Myron Echenberg

Vilimani: Labor Migration and Rural Change in Early Colonial Tanzania
Thaddeus Sunseri

"God Alone Is King": Islam and Emancipation in Senegal: The Wolof Kingdoms of Kajoor and Bawol, 1859–1914
James F. Searing

Negotiating Development: African Farmers and Colonial Experts at the Office du Niger, 1920–1960
Monica M. van Beusekom

The Bluest Hands: A Social and Economic History of Women Dyers in Abeokuta (Nigeria), 1890–1940
Judith A. Byfield

Colonial Lessons: Africans' Education in Southern Rhodesia, 1918–1940
Carol Summers

Poison and Medicine: Ethnicity, Power, and Violence in a Nigerian City, 1966 to 1986
Douglas A. Anthony

To Dwell Secure: Generation, Christianity, and Colonialism in Ovamboland
Meredith McKittrick

Genders and Generations Apart: Labor Tenants and Customary Law in Segregation-Era South Africa, 1920s to 1940s
Thomas V. McClendon

SACRED TREES, BITTER HARVESTS

GLOBALIZING COFFEE IN NORTHWEST TANZANIA

Brad Weiss

Social History of Africa
Allen Isaacman and Jean Allman, Series Editors

HEINEMANN
Portsmouth, NH

Heinemann
A division of Reed Elsevier Inc.
361 Hanover Street
Portsmouth, NH 03801-3912
www.heinemann.com

Offices and agents throughout the world

ISBN: 0-325-07095-4 (cloth)
ISBN: 0-325-07097-0 (paper)
ISSN: 1099-8098

Library of Congress Cataloging-in-Publication Data

Weiss, Brad.
Sacred trees, bitter harvests : globalizing coffee in Northwest Tanzania / Brad Weiss.
p. cm.—(Social history of Africa, ISSN 1099-8098)
Includes bibliographical references (p. 191).
ISBN 0-325-07095-4 (alk. paper)— ISBN 0-325-07097-0 (pbk. : alk. paper)
1. Haya (African people)—Economic conditions. 2. Haya (African people)—Commerce. 3. Coffee—Tanzania—Kagera Region. 4. Value—Cross-cultural studies. 5. Kagera Region (Tanzania)—Economic conditions. I. Title. II. Series.
DT443.3.H39 W453 2003
382'.41373'096727—dc21 2002027294

British Library Cataloging in Publication Data is available.

Printed in the United States of America on acid-free paper.

06 05 04 03 SB 1 2 3 4 5 6 7 8 9

The author and publisher gratefully acknowledge permission to reproduce the following:

Figure 2.2 on page 66 of this volume is reprinted from Edmond Césard, "Le Muhaya (L'Afrique Orientale)," *Anthropos* 31 (1936): 100. Permission kindly granted by the Anthropos Institute.

Figure 3.1 on page 90 of this volume is reprinted courtesy of the White Fathers' libraries in Rome.

CONTENTS

Illustrations

FIGURES

PHOTOS

ACKNOWLEDGMENTS

Writing is always a struggle, but having the chance to thank your friends and colleagues for their efforts to lend comfort in that struggle is an honest pleasure. I am fortunate that so many have seen fit to help see me through this book; whatever merit it has certainly reflects their efforts on my behalf. In the first place, I must thank the people I came to know in Northwest Tanzania, the Haya men and women who shared their thoughts, and sorrows, and laughs, and lives with me while I was living in Rubya and Rwagati. My many discussions with them about everything from the black market to banana husbandry are the inspiration for this work. I have tried, above all else, to be true to the understandings they emphasized in our conversations, and I hope that I have never misrepresented these views or betrayed the trust they placed in me. I owe a special thanks to Severian and Anatolia Ndyetabula for the chance to live in their home among their friends and family, to Ma Carolina and Ta Gregory and especially Kyabona, and to our late friend Mzee Juma for making me feel so fully welcome. *Bakasinge Waitu!* My research in Tanzania was funded by a Fulbright-Hays doctoral dissertation fellowship, and the Tanzanian National Institute for Science and Technology (UTAFITI) enabled me to live and work in Tanzania.

Writing this book allowed me to travel to some most hospitable places, whose appealing qualities helped make it possible for me to complete this work. I must thank both the archivists at the White Fathers' libraries in Rome who greatly facilitated my work in the summer of 1996, and the Sisters at the Villa Fatima across the street who made my family feel utterly at home. My research in Rome was funded by a Faculty Summer Research Grant from the College of William and Mary. I was fortunate to spend a year writing at the School of American Research. I must thank Doug Schwartz and the expert staff at the SAR for providing me with the opportunity to work in a spectacular setting. I am grateful for the collegiality and friendship, in particular, of Ned Blackhawk and Val Carnegie who were in residence with me at the SAR.

Jackie Urla, whom I first met in Santa Fe, is not only a dear friend; she also offered cogent readings of substantial portions of this manuscript.

Audiences at the School of American Research, the University of Helsinki, the University of Chicago, and Harvard University offered many helpful comments at the early stages of writing. The members of the Satterthwaite Colloquium were remarkably supportive and insightful in 1998, and again in 1999. I am so glad that Dick Werbner has welcomed me into the fold there, and thankful to all who have attended his colloquium over the years. The conference on revisiting the *Social Life of Things* held at Amsterdam in 1999 was a tremendous source of inspiration for me. I am thankful to all who attended, and especially to Peter Geschiere and Wim van Binsbergen. Their close reading and editorial rigor has clearly improved chapter 2.

Any number of friends and colleagues have read drafts, chapters, or parts of chapters. In particular I owe tremendous thanks to Laurie Lewis, Diane Mines, David Dinwoodie, Peter Pels, Birgit Meyer, Rijk van Dijk, Nancy Munn, Ralph Austen, Jonathan Sadowsky, Katie Bragdon, Hylton White, and Eric Gable. It should come as no surprise that Jean Comaroff was remarkably generous with her time and energy at a number of critical moments. Discussions with her helped me craft the focus of this project and saved me from pursuing innumerable dead ends. Danny Miller has been a great support as well, not only for his remarkably lucid and unbelievably speedy assessments of this project, but for his invaluable encouragement. Tim Burke has read this manuscript more times than anyone should have to! I owe him plenty, and hope I can repay the many favors some day. Bill Fisher has been a great friend and colleague. My respect for his work, and especially his deep intellectual and social commitments, has served to shape my own endeavors. As always, my closest colleagues, Adeline Masquelier and Misty Bastian, have offered their time, their intellect, and their deep friendship. I am lucky to know them.

Jean Allman and Allen Isaacman offered critical but generous commentary on the manuscript. I am grateful for their efforts to tailor my anthropological imagination to matters historical. I can honestly say that this book would be languishing on my hard drive were it not for Jim Lance. He has been an amazing advocate for this project, shown profound integrity in working with me, and above all been so enthusiastic that I felt as though I had to finish the thing! I am sincerely thankful to him and to Heinemann.

Last, never least, I am so glad that Julie Corsaro and Ezra Weiss have been willing and able to come along to so many of the places that this work took me. Knowing that they have been there—and here, and everywhere—for me has made everything possible. Dedicating this work to them is a small gesture for gifts too wonderful to tell.

Introduction

In his history of the Haya Kingdom of Kiziba, Francis X. Lwamgira, the eminent translator and scholar, advisor to kings and colonial officials, describes a very precarious—even touchy[1]—meeting. The encounter in 1891 was between the Muziba king—or *mukama*—Mutatembwa and the first European, Wilhelm Langheld, to meet Baziba royalty. According to Lwamgira,

> The European did not enter the palace because the King thought that he would bring an omen to it as they had never seen Europeans before. When the people saw him they stood on guard to prevent him from entering the palace. Each man came with two spears or a gun to protect the King. (1969: chapter 24, p. 75)

In response to the omen portended by Langheld, Mutatembwa chose a strategy that was part and parcel of the magico-political repertoire of both royalty and commoners in Africa's Great Lakes Region: "Mutatembwa asked the European to have blood relations with him. Some people say that the European accepted and the King gave him his son Musikura to perform the ceremony with him." The success of this strategy was demonstrated after Langheld's departure the next day: "When [the King's attendants] found him gone, they gathered at the palace and gave the King cows, goats, and clothes congratulating him on getting rid of the European."

By an ingenious practice, Mutatembwa was able to create a new relative and send him packing in a single stroke. Perhaps this apparent incongruity is explicable by reference to the fact that blood brotherhood in East Africa is a highly enigmatic relationship (White 1994; Schoenbrun 1998). As White has demonstrated, blood brotherhood provided the potential of elective affinity, an opportunity for men (and men alone) to forge a wide range of relations—it might secure clients for long-distance traders, or acquire heirs for a patriline in need of descendants. Blood brotherhood is, further, not only concerned with inclusive connections; it might also serve to erect barriers of exclusion in relationships—specifically the barriers that precluded sexual relations among blood brothers and one another's female kin. Schoenbrun makes the further central point (1998: 182) that, in the Great Lakes, blood brothers were *abakago* (pl.; *oumkago*, sing.), literally, "those who are protected by means of medicine," and so "the exchange of blood was also the exchange of a type of medicine." The social intimacies at issue in blood brotherhood were ineluctably, constituted by material transformations in the brothers' living bodies. To this I would add that, like blood itself, the term "medicine," *omubazi*, needs to be grasped as a relational matter, its value—"protective" or otherwise—derived from the context of actions and intentions to which it is applied. Thus, Haya today make it clear that "*omutambi n'omulogi*," "the healer is also the sorcerer," and so *omubazi* is simultaneously "medicine" and "sorcery substance." Uzoigwe notes, then, that blood brotherhood was a common practice among long-distance trade partners in Kitara (Bunyoro in Uganda today) and that a violation of its terms caused one's stomach to swell, which led to a painful death (Uzoigwe 1974: 448). All of these instances indicate that blood brotherhood could certainly generate bonds of intimacy and obligation, but this may be precisely because the force of intimacy and obligation so often lends itself to the conveyance of highly mixed messages and thus to duplicitous ends.

In the historical record of Bahaya encounters with German, British, and French colonial officials—from missionaries to military men—such acts of blood brotherhood are a commonplace, especially in the earliest years of the twentieth century. As the original example of Mutatembwa and Langheld demonstrates, this gesture is at once a willing embrace of new powers and a concerted effort to constrain the same. The content of this double-edged form of sociality is further embedded in the concrete form through which this relationship was established. Blood brothers imbibed one anothers' blood in rites of "drinking one another" *okunywana* (see also Beattie 1958), and they did so by means of a very specific medium of interchange: coffee cherries. Coffee cherries, grown in the Great Lakes for the past several centuries (Jervis 1939), were, and continue to be, cooked for chewing in Buhaya. In rites of blood brotherhood, each man coats the coffee cherry with blood incised from his navel, and each then eats one of the two seeds contained within the cherry's husk. In this way, the two seeds within the single pod provide an agricultural icon of the brothers' assertion of bodily and social unity, the creation, as Haya always stressed to me, of "one blood" out of two different men.

By creating one blood, though, blood brothers impose regulations that restrict and delimit further circulations of blood. That is, one of the principle effects of blood brotherhood is that it establishes exogamous prohibitions, not only for the "blood" relations of the two men who enter into blood brotherhood, but for all members of their two clans. Marital and sexual exchanges extending to persons quite distant from the blood brothers themselves are, thus, *cut off* through this exchange of blood (Weiss 1996c). From this perspective, the bodies of blood brothers are not simply united, for their union becomes an obstacle to further physical attachments. Indeed, the *presence* of bodily attachments can itself prevent the fabrication of new blood relations. Thus, one man explained the decline in blood brotherhood in contemporary Buhaya to me by saying that it was no longer possible to be certain that your potential blood brother had not already slept with your sister—a prior condition that would have destroyed these different bloods were they ever unified. The intimacy and separation that Mutatembwa successfully achieved via his blood brotherhood with Langheld, it would seem, accomplished exactly what blood brotherhood was meant to do. The two seeds in the coffee pod are, therefore, doubly iconic, exhibiting both a unity among differences, and a differentiation within unity.

It is coffee, the medium of this, and many more, complex and changing social connections in Northwest Tanzania, that is the subject of this work. The place of coffee in blood brotherhood, as just described, merely exemplifies many of the enduring qualities of this valuable substance. A central claim of this work is that the articulation of attachment and separation, inclusion and exclusion, intimacy and restraint is a critical process in establishing the symbolic and material dimensions of precolonial, colonial, and postcolonial relations. Coffee intended for chewing, like that once used in blood brotherhood, is still grown and prepared today in Haya villages with harvests taken from *robusta* varieties. Both *robusta* and some *arabica* varieties, introduced into the area early in the twentieth century, are also harvested and processed for sale on an international market. Coffee in Buhaya, then, is at the heart of this history because it has been made to serve as an effective vehicle of this articulation. The characteristic dialectic of participation and separation, often of participation as a means of separation, embedded in coffee's place in the social life of the eight Haya kingdoms at the end of the nineteenth century should not be taken as a model, or template, for all subsequent uses of coffee under successive colonial regimes.

The transformation of coffee and of the Haya sociocultural order is not merely a matter of reproducing a set of persistent structural contrasts. Yet, precisely because the transaction of Haya coffee in social life is *always* concerned with articulation—with reconciling hierarchical and even extractive relationships, with the flow of valued resources, and the recognition of proper authorities—the centrality of coffee in (post)colonial worlds has powerfully informed the shape of (post)colonial relations over the past century. German and British projects intended to transform Buhaya by means of promoting coffee production were themselves incorporated into Haya social practice in keeping with long-standing local understandings of the place of coffee in this regional world. The forms of meaningful sociality embedded in Haya coffee came, therefore, to shape the meanings of social relations as they emerged historically in this milieu.

DETERMINING THE "GLOBAL" AND THE "LOCAL"

Given coffee's prominence in the Great Lakes area, and in Buhaya (or Bukoba as the region was known in the colonial era, Kagera as it is known today) in particular, it is important to point out that the oppositional title of this work, *Sacred Trees, Bitter Harvests*, is not meant to be read as a simple narrative of the (post)colonial degradation of a once venerated material. This is not a chronicle of local gifts losing their luster on a global commodities market. Coffee has been revalued, not devalued, in Bukoba in the course of the past century. It would further be a mistake to presume that coffee's value need be expressed as wholly positive, or negative—or even as one thing as opposed to another.

In the course of this discussion I aim to show how Haya farmers and traders have used, and continue to use, coffee to participate in a global order of commerce and capital, while in their very participation they also attempt to retain a critical distance from global forces when they threaten to overwhelm local orders of value. Coffee can be both a blessing and a scourge, a source of assertion as well as dependency. Thanks to profits from the coffee trade that were fairly widespread during much of the postwar period, the Haya were able to achieve extraordinary levels of education, such that the first African Cardinal and the first African Lutheran Bishop would come from this corner of Tanzania (Hellberg 1965). There is also good evidence to suggest that crashing global coffee prices in the 1930s contributed to the conditions that sent many women from Buhaya off to Kampala and Nairobi in search of the means to pay back the exorbitant bridewealth demanded by their former husbands, a search that has given Haya women a reputation for prostitution that is notorious throughout East Africa to this day (White 1990; Larsson 1991).

Coffee that was once essential to the sacrifices required for ancestral blessing, might also forebode the death of the farmer who cultivated it. Today, when coffee for chewing is offered to guests in every respectable home in Kagera, the most prized coffee is that which tastes most acrid—"Its sweetness is bitterness" as many men and women told me. Sacredness and bitterness, then, are less categorical contrasts, or a schema that might be used to organize a total system of oppositions (e.g., gift and commodity, status and contract, ritual and economics, tradition and modernity), than they are ever present potentialities that may be realized—at times in tandem, at times in discord—in any particular practice that makes use of coffee. I am inclined, therefore, to assess the social life of coffee in Buhaya with attention to what might be called the "double" possibilities of this substance; Haya enthusiasm for "modern" methods of coffee production and trade often veils an ongoing indifference to these techniques, while apparently "traditional" uses of coffee are only possible because of fundamental changes in Haya economy and society. Over the past century of globalizing processes, coffee in Kagera has been deployed by those concerned to retain the plenitude of its possibilities, and it makes little sense to reduce its meaning—which is to say, its value—to a single underlying system, cause, or source.

The possibilities of coffee are always situated in zones of contact, of transaction and motion, a point that will prove absolutely central to my discussion of the ways colonialism and its attendant globalizing procedures reconfigure the forms and pathways through which this agricultural medium moves. An offering to ancestors and kings; hospitality provided to neighbors, affines, and honored guests; a harvest, winnowed and cleaned, shipped to a state-run cooperative; or even a mere bud on the branch offered in speculation to money-lending traders, in all of its guises coffee travels between and among persons and places. This ingrained mobility makes coffee an appropriate medium for an analysis that participates in ongoing discussions about the nature of "global" and "local" relations. It has now become something of a commonplace to study "global flows" through the lens of a concrete substance that makes a circuit through various locales (Mintz 1985; Sahlins 1989; Hansen 2001; Burke 1996; Howes 1996). The present work draws on the themes of such studies, although it makes a somewhat different claim about globalization than is often the case. Rather than focusing on the remaking of objects as they shift from one region to another, this analysis is grounded at an ethnographic level in a specific place, but it is a place that is itself the site of trans-regional connections. I do not, therefore, conceive of the "global" as a multiplication of dispersed "localities," but instead understand globalization as a set of techniques for generating relationships. It is the orientation and scale of these relationships—whether they are attuned to the transmission of coffee trees between successive generations of farmers or to the collapsing price of *robusta* at the end of the twentieth century—that make globalization *and* localization co-present dimensions of all social fields.

Thus, even without fully tracing the trail of coffee to consumers in Europe and the United States (or Zanzibar and Dar Es Salaam), it is still possible to insist that sociohistorical practices such as the measurement of coffee volumes and the management of agricultural practice have become global aspects of coffee's value as it is firmly situated within Kagera. The practices and discourses surrounding coffee in this corner of Tanganyika may appear distinctly "remote" from those of coffee markets, roasters, and retailers in the so-called consuming nations, but they are no less "global" for that (Piot 1999). I am interested in coffee in Buhaya, then, less out of the empiricist's concern for following a material substance through a series of "local" positions in the "globe" (a method that, in any case, would unduly fetishize coffee and attribute to it some abstract, universal essence), than I am for the sake of understanding, in the phenomenological sense, how this specific substance organizes and is organized by social action.

Of course, it would be absurdly narrow, to say nothing of politically naïve, to suggest that the value of coffee in Bukoba is exclusively a matter of the lived experiences of the Haya farmers and families who cultivate, cook, and chew it. Coffee production was central to British administrative rule of the region; indeed, the success of colonial rule in Bukoba was in many respects measured by its success in producing coffee for export. The directed, and as I will discuss, coercive enforcement of coffee planting campaigns under putatively "indirect rule," to say nothing of the explosive and continuous development of mass markets for Third World products like coffee over the course of the last century, have forcefully contributed to the density of experience that is embedded in coffee in Kagera. Yet, I must make it clear that one of the principle claims of this work is that it is *not* possible to reduce the significance of coffee to its *determination* by these broad and powerful historical forces if we hope to understand the many and varied processes through which coffee has been made meaningful and valuable by Haya people.

The perspective offered here therefore differs from the approach of many exemplary studies that look at people like Bahaya through a lens trained principally on their position as producers of commodities consumed elsewhere (e.g., Mintz 1985 on sugar; Roseberry 1995 and Bunker 1987 on coffee). When cultural practice is held to be but a reflex of production, "locals" may then be understood to resist or accommodate themselves to the demands of a process to which they are marginal; but such options clearly tell us very little about how persons and objects and the relations between them are valued and acted upon in actual practice. Moreover, the study of global commodities tends to generate a division of global labor into "producers" and "consumers" that has often understood the place of culture and meaning as epiphenomenal, or derivative. Consumers, in this view, have the luxury of giving value to the things of their world, while producers are enchained to the dictates of an overarching system (cf. Mintz 1985, Roseberry 1996, but compare Coronil 1994 for a critique of this approach to global history). On empirical grounds alone this division does exceedingly rough justice to Haya farmers.

Haya farmers' coffee production is distinctive, although by no means unique. There are no plantations in Kagera, no laborers who toil for wages earned by tending to the growth of coffee trees. Further, coffee has a very long history in this region. Its precolonial uses are still relevant in many ways a century after colonization. When talking about "consumers" it is necessary to distinguish between a wide array of consumption practices (many of which have nothing to do with drinking coffee) even in just Buhaya, and when describing coffee "production" it is necessary to recognize that coffee is not a unitary "thing" to be produced. Indeed, as I have argued elsewhere (Weiss 1996c), the complexities of cultivating distinct forms of coffee for a diverse set of "consumers" introduces important ruptures in a putatively coherent, and determinant system of production. When Haya men and women asked me in 1989, "We Haya grow this coffee, we harvest it, and then we sell it to you in Europe. But what do you Europeans do with it?" they were not expressing their ignorance of international markets, but rather demonstrating the limits to such markets' capacity for constraining the consciousness of those "dependent" on them.

AGENCY AND VALUE

Aside from the real, material specificities pertinent to the place of coffee in Kagera, there are important theoretical reasons to critique a view of Haya coffee that conceives of it—*simply*—as the peripheral product of a global system of capital. The questions with which to propose such a critique are among the most vexing in an ethnographically grounded social theory today: how is it possible to assess complex sociocultural orders in ways that recognize that while social beings are always powerfully constrained by a host of forces (as Haya coffee farmers most certainly are), they also understand and act upon their world in terms that cannot be reduced to those constraints? How, that is, is it possible to locate and acknowledge the meaningful agency of all social actors even in the face of systemic oppressions and inequalities? The central purpose of this book is to explore the historically shifting potentials of coffee in Haya communities, and thereby to illuminate these pressing theoretical questions.

Examining the history of relationships between material forms (commodities foremost among them) and social actors, within the context of overarching historical movements like colonialism, globalization, and the making of modernity has been a hallmark of much contemporary research, in Africa and elsewhere. The best of this work demonstrates the ways that the peoples caught up in often wrenching processes make use of such material objects, both novel and enduring, to articulate altered capacities for participating in the worlds in which they find themselves embroiled. Certainly the Comaroffs' seminal work on the "civilizing mission" to Tswana communities in Southern Africa (1991 and 1997) places conflicts over the meaning of such material forms as money, agricultural technique, and pastoralist practice at the center of the "dialectics of modernity" characteristic of these colonial encounters. Sharon Hutchinson's moving account of Nuer society presents a detailed discussion of the manifold possibilities that cattle markets have created in the Southern Sudan. Far from simply reacting to, or withdrawing from the commodification of these iconic beings, Nuer men and women have imaginatively developed highly innovative categories of both cattle and cash, categories that bespeak both the historically shifting meanings of age, gender, and marriage in Nuer society and the often brutally oppressive political–economic conditions the Nuer confront (Hutchinson 1996).

Using a rather different framework, Jonathan Glassman's study of popular rebellion and "class conflict" on the Swahili Coast of Tanzania at the apex of the caravan trade makes comparable claims (Glassman 1995). Glassman's work is attuned to the way that the expansion of commercial opportunities and availability of commodity forms were shaped by a highly contentious structure of status relations, exchanges, and social obligations, even as they contributed to an intensification of the most repressive forms of slavery. Emmanual Akyeampong's engaging history of drink in Ghana presents certain formal similarities to the present study as well, focused as it is on a highly prized commodity form whose contemporary significance is plainly shaped by the prior meanings of libation, even as "traditional" offerings of alcohol have been redefined by a colonial history of commodification, taxation, and health care (Akyeampong 1996). Like all of these works (and a spate of others), mine argues here that it is possible to grasp the abilities of people to creatively act on their worlds, even when facing intense and sustained sociohistorical pressures, by understanding how they give value to things.

The present book, not surprisingly, is most directly related to my first book on contemporary Haya cultural practice (1996a). In *The Making and Unmaking of the Haya Lived World*, I was also concerned to show how processes of commodification and globalization can be fruitfully explored by grounding them within a lived world of experience and action. In that work I took pains to demonstrate how commodification was never a scourge of meaning, but was rather a potent set of possibilities whose significance was concretely realized in cultural forms of bodily experience (like affliction, satiation and hunger, or modes of sexuality) and inhabited space (like mobility along paths and roads, metaphorized relations between urban and rural locales, or the built form of homes and hearths). These fundamental concerns, and my ethnographic appreciation for the cultural significance of lived experience, unmistakably shape the analyses presented in this work. While the focus of *Sacred Trees, Bitter Harvests* is the single object of coffee, it nonetheless expands and develops the themes and scope of my previous book in several respects. It moves beyond the "ethnographic present" in which *The Making and Unmaking of the Haya Lived World* was firmly situated in order to interrogate how the contemporary sociocultural order of Buhaya, its ways of determining, producing, and representing value, has emerged through its broader connections over time and space. In examining the nature and transformation of these connections I consider coffee as a switchpoint between a range of interpenetrating possible lived worlds, since it is coffee, above all other objects, that has been the sustained focus of multiple projects that aim to generate and signify various forms of value in Bukoba.

In an important contribution to material culture studies in precisely such zones of contact as Haya coffee routinely finds itself, Patricia Spyer notes that the characteristic movement of fetishes across borders facilitates the formation of innovative modes of meaning making and value production. In transit across permeable frontiers, fetishes can (Spyer 1998: 3) "open up novel spaces for the construction of agency," spaces that "invite comparison between distinct social orders, possibilities, and schemes." With respect to the materials at hand, I find it especially useful to think about agency as embedded within these conditions of *motion* and *comparison*. What constitutes agency, in this view, is the capacity to act in a world the social actor confronts as a set of possibilities. This characterization highlights the connection of agency to value, for value, as Graeber asserts in his refreshing account of the question, "the way people represent the importance of their own actions to themselves" (Graeber 2001: 45). I would add (as is implicit in this claim) that value is both a way of determining the importance of activity and, further, that value is created by activity. For these reasons agency itself is best grasped not as a specific *class* of actions (e.g., independent, transformative, collectively oriented, or contingent acts), or a particular intentionality (e.g., as a subject position, or a distinctive "voice"), but rather as a relative capacity for producing value. As value is created by actions, so agency must be defined with respect to the ways it can (and cannot) produce culturally specific forms of value. This, perhaps peculiar, understanding means that agency need not be limited to reactions to encompassing forces; further, it need not be limited to those acts that, either by intent or outcome, contribute to demonstrable change. Recalcitrance and refusal, as well as surviving and suffering, all are forms of acting and being in the world. They all require an active engagement with a reality in terms whose importance will be represented and, so, evaluated.

The perspective on agency entailed in both Spyer's and Graeber's models clearly situates activity in the context of alternative possibilities in which a course of action is pursued. Agency thereby becomes a means of effectively moving between different registers of value and meaning. This amounts to much more than simply making a "choice," but asserting the relevance of particular criteria by which to evaluate social action. Let me offer a brief ethnographic example that illustrates how such movements across terrains of value can constitute modes of agency. In contemporary Kagera, there are, primarily, two ways of using coffee: coffee can either sold to local state-run cooperatives, or coffee (of indigenous *robusta* varieties) can be prepared for chewing. While both of these practices are commonplace, in fact Haya farmers are required to sell *all* of the coffee they grow to the cooperatives, and so the preparation of coffee for chewing is a pervasive, if petty offense. As de Certeau has suggested, such modes of "taking pleasure" within the dictates of an overarching system of value production, constitute a kind of popular tactic from the margins (de Certeau 1984: 24–28). Persons within a dominant "order of things" are able to turn that order to their own ends by a process of *diversion*, a strategy that de Certeau describes as *la perruque*, "the wig,"[2] This economic diversion of a worker's time, or a factory's resources (e.g., de

Certeau describes [1984: 25] "a secretary's writing a love letter on 'company time' . . . or a cabinetmaker's 'borrowing' a lathe to make a piece of furniture for his living room" as examples of *la perruque*), becomes a means of inserting "a sociopolitical ethics into an economic system" (de Certeau 1984: 27).

The French worker who borrows tools, or the Haya farmer who diverts his crops, participates in an encounter between alternative modes of evaluation, and in the shifting between these alternatives—a movement that, as de Certeau notes, may not change, or even disrupt the "actual order of things" (de Certeau 1984: 26)—the social actor defines the value of his or her action. This does not deny the reality of the constraints of this "actual order of things," indeed, a diversion entails a routinized order from which *la perruque* diverges.[3] In withholding coffee from the market to prepare it for chewing, Haya farmers are recognizing a *difference* that revalues the significance of both the coffee they offer their guests, as well as revaluing *themselves* as persons whose relationships to one another are constituted, in part, through this divergence. Agency, in this case, is not reducible to resistance to the coffee cooperatives, for offering coffee to guests has its own logic, but the value of this practice in contemporary Kagera cannot be extricated from this context of divergent possibilities. As I will illustrate, much of the history of Bahaya sociocultural practice in the twentieth century can be characterized as an attempt to grapple with a set of alternative registers for valuing coffee.

ON SOURCES AND METHODS

What follows in these chapters is a frankly idiosyncratic assessment of the history of a particular people as grasped through movements of a concrete substance. I do not offer a recognizably linear chronicle of Kagera, although one could probably be pieced together from the materials presented. I fully admit to the glaring gaps in my knowledge of Haya history and culture, but do not feel that they mean that my analyses are unsubstantiated. I have drawn freely on the excellent accounts of Austen (1968) and Curtis (1989), and Rald and Rald (1976), as well as the works of Cory and Hartnoll (1945, Cory 1949), Rehse (1910) and Cesard (1937, 1938a and b, 1939) produced in the colonial era to provide much of the evidence presented here. Although this is by no means a thorough study of missionization in Buhaya, the principal archival sources I made use of are some fascinating materials gleaned from the annual reports, apostolic letters, and diaries of the White Fathers, which I acquired during two months of research in Rome. Above all, in evaluating all of these sources I have been guided by my own eighteen months of field research in Kagera during the late 1980s.

Considering these sources as sources, though, reveals very little about the methods that have guided my interest in making use of them. The meaningful dimensions of social life—problems of embodiment, lived experience, and reflexively organized, culturally constituted practice—which I find the most anthropologically compelling, and which I have attempted to assess here are notoriously difficult to collect (or to "verify") by ethnographic methods; these difficulties are only compounded when analysts ask the same questions of historical materials. In my view, this is because so much sociocultural meaning, that is, the way that people make sense of the world they live in, is simply taken for granted and appears as self-evident to those who are engaged in the business of living their lives. Because it rarely rises to the level of self-conscious reflection or commentary, the meaningful character of our everyday and ordinary experience is not typically preserved in the kinds of sources to which historians have access. Small wonder, then, that crises, contestation, and rupture are so vigorously examined in some of the best social history, for it is frequently the case that a "crisis" is precipitated when the taken for granted is called into question, and so becomes explicitly articulated, and knowable in novel ways.

There is widespread recognition of the fact that archives and oral traditions tend to privilege rather particular perspectives; but even "the intelligence of everyday life" which a more catholic historical methodology pursues (Cohen 1989) may pay relatively little attention to the quotidian features of social practice. All of the secondary sources on the history of Buhaya, for example, note that the *arabica* variety of coffee was introduced by the White Fathers in the first years of the twentieth century (Jervis 1939). Yet the White Fathers' records from these years scarcely make note of the fact and provide even less insight into the significance of this introduction. How was this coffee distributed? To whom? How was it planted? Where did the Fathers plant their seedlings, and (above all) for what purpose? As I describe below in chapter 4, the Fathers did take an active interest in the growth of trees (of many kinds) in Kagera, but just *how* they did so was not an issue they felt worthy of documenting. Similarly, it was all but useless to ask Haya farmers in the 1980s about the introduction of *arabica* coffee, and not simply because none were old enough to remember that colonial enterprise. Indeed, not only the introduction of *arabica* a century before, but a host of transformations, regulations, and innovations surrounding this crop all carried out in the decades prior to independence were of little historical interest. It is as though coffee cultivation was so commonplace it scarcely registered as a matter worthy of remembering.

All of this is not to say the social actors are simply mute and passive bearers of self-generating meanings. On the contrary, my primary assertion—and guiding methodological principal—is that meaning is an intrinsic feature of our experience because we *make* it in our routine activity. And it is this link of meaning, not to subconscious structures buried in the recesses of "minds," but to *actions* that can provide us with a method for carrying out an anthropologically informed historical practice. To return to the last example, while the events and actions that gave *arabica* its place in Kagera were unremarkable in the view of late-twentieth-century Haya farmers and traders, their pragmatic attitude toward this variety made them quite interested in the many problems that cultivating this coffee entailed. The potentially deleterious effects of *arabica* on their banana gardens, the costs of inputs to fertilize it, the fact that it was so fragile a plant that it was often more trouble than it was worth—all of these were matters that anyone and everyone could discuss with me. These commentaries, in my view, provide a kind of pragmatic history, or perhaps an understanding of "history in practice," for embedded within these meaningful claims are a totality of colonial and postcolonial interventions that have shaped the place of *arabica* coffee trees in contemporary Haya life. It is precisely through such daily practices, I argue, that the meaningful character of historical processes is revealed.

Given this methodological foundation, I have no qualms about reading much of colonial history through the lens of the fullness (but never *completeness*) of ethnographic experience. I freely follow the "hunches" (Pels 1999) I derive from this experience (in ways suggested by my brief discussion of *arabica*) in order to pose questions of the past never quite posed in the same way by those whose accounts of the past are available. Through all this I aim to demonstrate how a fine-grained interpretation of incomplete evidence (as evidence always is) can help to illuminate some enduring problems in the study of consciousness and agency, meaning and value as these are grounded in a context of colonial encounter. Coffee is the medium by which such problems were most directly confronted in Northwest Tanganyika, now Tanzania, in the twentieth century, and so coffee provides nothing more—but also nothing less—than a convenient excuse for reexamining some abiding anthropological questions.

STRUCTURE

These questions are explored in the course of six chapters, organized primarily by thematic concerns. The first chapter describes a kind of template for the way that Haya coffee—or *akamwani*—is understood to embody creative, productive forms of value. While I do not claim to establish a kind of precolonial "baseline" for "local" forms of coffee upon which colonial interventions are imposed (indeed, much of my evidence derives from ritual, agricultural, and exchange practices that were documented in the 1970s and 1980s), I am attempting to provide a set of meanings that relate to royal patronage, ritual offerings, and tree planting techniques that have a constitutive effect on the historical transformation of Haya economy and society in the twentieth century. Chapter 2 considers the consequences of coffee's capacities to store and mediate value in transactions—in short, to serve as a currency—for the ways that other colonial currencies, cowries, and later rupees, were understood and engaged with in Haya communities.

I offer an assessment of currencies in the Interlacustrine world of the late nineteenth century that juxtaposes Haya pragmatic understandings of material wealth with both Simmel's and Marx's analyses of money as a currency form. From this perspective, the colonial growth and marketing of coffee in Bukoba, revalued by new currencies, and Haya people's participation in these processes, are shown to be fundamental to the wider remaking of wealth, the significance of objects, and the attachments of persons and things. Given these new possibilities for defining and producing wealth, I turn my attention in chapter 3 to the consciousness (often contradictory) of value that emerged along with the rapid expansion of coffee marketing in Buhaya. The White Fathers articulated a plainly moralistic and anxious discourse about the dangers of the excessive materialism and deracination ushered in by the growth of coffee marketing, even as their own practices facilitated the ever wider spread of coffee planting, distribution, and marketing. For Haya men and women, moralistic concerns about materialism are also voiced in this era, but in ways that highlight the vulnerability of local farmers to deceptive "outsider" (including missionary) practices.

Chapters 4 and 5 jointly address the transformation of the Haya landscape that commercial coffee production exemplifies. I begin by examining the way in which value and identity are generated through household agricultural practice, considering the spatial and temporal meanings of land holding and cultivation, the gendered character of growth and food production, and the symbolic significance of trees and "fertility" more generally. This provides a framework in which to evaluate the significance of colonial agrarian reforms, beginning with White Fathers' introduction of a vast number and variety of new trees for timber, as well as the massive British coffee planting campaigns of the 1920s.

Finally, chapter 6 turns to a critical dimension of coffee evaluation, namely measurement. The success of coffee marketing in Bukoba in the twentieth century was plainly dependent upon the adoption of new forms of determining how coffee could be measured. The problem is not simply one of introducing new standards of measurement (although this is powerfully important as well), but of recognizing how measures of volume and weight (as well as of "price" and "grade") are both units of standardization and forms of experience that come to constitute the qualities and characteristics of social relations. Rather than unfolding in a chronological sequence, each of these chapters considers data drawn from various moments throughout the twentieth century in order to explore different dimensions of colonial encounters in Kagera, encounters understood as contesting modes of producing value.

NOTES

1. I use this term advisedly, with due consideration of the "tactile" (Pels 1999) nature of the encounters under consideration.

2. I am indebted to David Howes for suggesting the connection to de Certeau to me.

3. On diversions as a strategy of value creation see also Munn 1983 and Appadurai 1986.

1

THE SACRED LIFE OF PLANTS: PLACING ROYAL GROWTH

> In the earliest times the Wahuma of Unyora regarded the lands bordering on the Victoria Lake as their garden, owing to its exceeding fertility, and imposed the epithet of Wiru, or slaves, upon its people, because they had to supply the Imperial Government with food and clothing. Coffee was conveyed to the capital by the Wiru.
>
> —John Speke (1863: 245)

> Karagwah grows according to some, according to others, imports from the northern countries along the western margin of the Nyanza Lake, a small wild coffee, locally called mwámí. Like all wild productions, it is stunted and undeveloped, and the bean, which, when perfect, is about the size of a corking-pin's head, is never drunk in decoction . . . In Karagwah a single khete of beads purchases a kubbah (from 1 lb. to 2 lbs.) of this coffee; at Kazeh and Msene, where it is sometimes brought by caravans, it sells at fancy prices.
>
> —Richard Burton (1860 [1995]: 395)

> That Nyerere, he may have ruined this country; but at least he got rid of those kings!
>
> —Laurean Buberwa (personal communication 1988)

The origins of kingship in the Lakes Region of Central Africa remains a contentious subject. This contention flourishes in spite—or perhaps because—of nearly a century and a half of investigation of this topic by a battery of European and American explorers and academics, to say nothing of at least several centuries of discussion on the subject by the inhabitants of this area's kingdoms and polities. Were the Hinda (or Hima in some areas—the "Wahuma" of Speke's "Unyora") a pastoral people of Nilotic origin who conquered indigenous Bantu agrarians (Speke 1863; Seligman 1966)? Or did royalty and its attendant aristocracy, the Balangila, ascend to their authority from within earlier social arrangements by consolidating control over cattle and arable lands along the lake (Carlson 1989; Schmidt 1978)? Did the successful kings of what became Bunyoro and Buhaya buttress their authority by enshrining their ancestors, the Bacwezi, as deities of collective ritual action; or were these kings able to assert hegemony by appropriating what had long been spirits and spiritual practices recognized by what would become Bairu (the "Wiru . . . slaves" in Speke's account), or "commoner" clans (Berger 1981; Schmidt 1978)?

I pose these broad contrasts, not in order to describe a straw man, easily dismantled by a more sophisticated understanding; nor even, in fact, to enter into these debates and seek an adequate answer to these questions. Rather, I cite these concerns because all the participants engaged by these questions suggest that the establishment of Interlacustrine kingship was fundamentally concerned with a reordering of fundamental relations that were at once material and cosmological. The power of kingship in the region inhabits the land on which its subjects sustain themselves, and becomes embodied in crucial ways through the spiritual forces that allow these royal subjects to heal and reproduce (Schoenbrun 1998).

Of course, simply recognizing that royal power is embedded in a lived landscape and incorporated into bodily practices only serves to bring us to the truly challenging questions: precisely *how* does kingship pervade the organization of a cultural order—and, perhaps more fundamentally, exactly *what is* royal power? In order to pursue just such questions I will consider the specific material forms and practices relating to an apparently commonplace substance—coffee—that had a unique, if not privileged place in the workings and meanings of the Interlacustrine world. The values and actions surrounding the uses of coffee will further be grounded in the particulars of the Haya kingdoms of what is now the Kagera Region of Northwest Tanzania. It is useful to proceed from such a rigorously focused perspective, not because "culture" must be understood as a carefully bounded system of categories and dispositions, but rather because the specific *situation* of subjects and objects—the potential of persons and things in a given field of encompassing relations—reveals the embeddedness of all such positions in a wider world. In the specific character of situated practices, "local" activities emerge *as* "global" process, just as a "global" order comes into being through its manifestation as "local" phenomena.

The purpose of this chapter is to lay a foundation that will allow me to describe this embeddedness of local and global perspectives in the historical transformation of coffee in this region. While I do not claim to establish an original "baseline" against which such transformations can be measured, I will attempt to characterize a kind of template for the Haya production of power and value, a template that is exemplified by royal interests in coffee at the turn of the last century. In the course of this chapter I concretize this productive process by considering the place of kingship and coffee in the construction of the local landscape (especially the cultivation of trees), and the ritual procurement of blessings (especially through sacrifice and royal ceremony) The model I describe here, I would add, resonates in crucial ways down through the course of the twentieth century; it informs the historical transformation of coffee in Kagera even as it has been reshaped by that transformation.

The long-standing interpenetration of local and global dimensions of Haya royal practice is, in fact, suggested by the quotations cited above. A "wild" crop that is cultivated in distant gardens, brought to central royal courts by subjugated laborers, produced for local consumption and sold at "fancy prices," coffee is a product that intrinsically articulates social and material relationships in the Interlacustrine world, in contexts that—even in the mid-nineteenth century—are already inseparably regional and transregional. In describing that process of articulation, I want further to suggest that these early British explorers have—albeit unwittingly—presented a cryptic model of kingship itself. Royal power in the Lakes Region, like such power in many contexts (de Heusch 1982; Sahlins 1985; Valeri 1985), is implicated in the totality of relations, while somehow standing apart from them, is simultaneously "wild" and carefully cultivated. Kings characteristically enslave for the sake of a "stunted and undeveloped" trifle, like coffee.

At least since the earliest encounters between Europeans and Africans in this area, it is has been quite clear that the capacity of kings to exercise the power at their disposal, in different ways and for very different ends at different times, has been closely connected with their control over coffee. Furthermore, my friend's ironic comment about the demise of Haya kings—which expresses a widely shared sentiment in the Kagera Region today—is made possible, from a certain perspective, by the ways in which these kings' connections to coffee were configured and reconfigured by colonial and neocolonial socioeconomic arrangements. As the fortunes of Haya royalty have long been linked to coffee, I will also consider (in subsequent chapters) how the fate of that royalty was equally tied to this product.

Access to coffee was not only one of the prerogatives of kingship, in many respects the social deployment of coffee was vitally important to *constituting* royal power in the Haya kingdoms. This might seem a rather grandiose claim. Yet if it is indeed the case, as most observers have conceded, that royal power depended upon and was manifest in the reordering of material relations and resources that have inherently cosmological implications, it should not be surprising to find that coffee is an integral element in that reordering. Which brings us, yet again, to some complicated questions. Just as it is important to ask what is the power of Haya kings, so too it is important to ask *what is* coffee that it should be so appropriate a vehicle for exemplifying and creating this power? What, for example, are the concrete qualities exhibited by coffee? What kind of substance is it? How does it grow? When and where does it flourish? These are all, I insist, *cultural* questions, part of the situated, contingent character of coffee in this transregional world. To address them I will examine coffee as an icon of agricultural practice and of royal authority, as the preserve of kings and the product of laboring minions. Locating coffee in a concrete world, and tracking its movement through that world, also mean discussing the the sociocultural constitution of place in order to understand the practices through which that world is created, and the kinds of potencies with which it is endowed. In this chapter I offer a way of considering these issues as they are revealed in the dynamic relations between Haya kingship and coffee, relations in which material practices of cultivation, propitiation, and exchange work to generate culturally privileged forms of power and value.

FORMS AND SUBSTANCE: HAYA COFFEE IN THE NINETEENTH-CENTURY INTERLACUSTRINE WORLD

To what, specifically, do I refer when I describe "Haya coffee" or *amwani* in the Haya vernacular? The species of *robusta* coffee is identified as *Coffea canephora*, now known as *Bokubensis* after Bukoba, the port city established by Emin Pasha in 1890 that has since been the administrative capital (no matter the administration) of this region. But this botanical stock grows in a number of regions of East and Central Africa (Jervis 1939: 51–52) and is not the distinctive feature of *amwani*. *Robusta* coffee grown in the Haya region becomes "Haya coffee" through the unique manner of its preparation. To prepare *amwani*, unripened coffee cherries—the technical term for the seed pod, each of which holds two beans—still in their green husks, are boiled along with grassy herbs in large pots. The cherries, perfumed with the herbal flora, are subsequently dried and smoked, but not roasted, over an indirect flame for a period of several days (see Reining 1967: Appendix for a description of this process by a Haya coffee preparer). The coffee cherries prepared in this way are ready to be consumed, not by further grinding, crushing, extracting, or infusing, but simply by chewing the *amwani* whole and spitting out the husks. To state the perhaps not so obvious, then, Haya coffee is prepared to be chewed.

Jervis claims that this method of preparing coffee cherries was derived from Arab preparation of spiced coffees, the local herbs used for Haya coffee replacing the ginger, anise, and cardamom of Arabic coffee (Jervis 1939: 49–50). Regardless of this possible influence, it is certainly clear that Haya communities did not adopt the Arabic habit of *drinking* coffee prepared in this way. Nor have Haya men and women ever eaten coffee, to the best of my knowledge, with any additional embellishments, as, for example, was the case for Ethiopians whose "only food . . . consisted of coffee berries . . . roasted and pulverized . . . which were mixed with grease, rolled into balls, and carried in leathern bags" (Cheney quoted in Jervis 1939: 49). The mere fact of coffee's being prepared and consumed (or, as I shall discuss, transported and exchanged throughout the region) in these ways tells us something about the values it possessed in the Haya kingdoms.

To begin with, while the coffee varieties used to produce *amwani* grew in other regions, these preparation techniques were only practiced in Bukoba. These fully cooked coffee cherries were then traded throughout the region as consumable products.[1] In other words, control over the entire production process, from cultivation and harvesting through boiling and drying, could be exercised within the region, often by the same individual farmers. This process formed a totality with "finished goods" being transacted by producers. If this method of production affords a greater degree of control over the coffee crop, so too, does the particular form of consumption described. Compare, for example, tea that is consumed through infusion. In his account of how sugar came to be a staple of the working-class British diet through the medium of hot tea, Mintz argues that tea is a drink that is readily adaptable by those with limited resources. This is so, claims Mintz, because it can be "successfully adulterated" by diluting it, thereby allowing even the poorest consumers to stretch their supply of tea by ever weaker brewing (Mintz 1985: 112). Haya coffee, once prepared for chewing, is not further processed or added to, and so cannot be "stretched." It is eaten by the handful in individual cherries, a method of consumption that allows of very little economizing. Either one eats coffee or one doesn't. Weak coffee may be less palatable than weak tea, at least according to Mintz, but it is not even a recognized possibility under these regional conditions.

These preparation techniques would seem to create a product whose possibilities for future consumption have been carefully prescribed and delimited. Let me make it clear, then, that I am not suggesting that these methods of coffee production strictly determined the forms and meanings of coffee consumption. It is certainly the case, for example, that coffee was prepared not simply for eating, but for transaction, and the values associated with those transactions—in the nineteenth century, to regions as distant as what is now far Eastern Uganda—are in no way *dictated* by this production process. While I have no evidence to suggest that Haya coffee was ever reprocessed (e.g., ground, mixed with other substances, infused, etc.) prior to being eaten, it is the case that the ways such coffee was consumed—the pragmatic dimensions of its being eaten, the contexts in which it was consumed, and the relationships such consumption instantiated—were no doubt highly varied in the Interlacustrine world of this period (a variation that persisted through the twentieth century). Indeed, one of the central points I hope to demonstrate is that the range of consumption practices needs to be taken into consideration in order to evaluate the significance of such products, commercial or otherwise. What I would suggest, though, is that given the presumption that coffee will be consumed in the finished form in which it is prepared, these productive techniques permit coffee to be understood and treated as a crop that could be used in the Haya world to express and demonstrate an important measure of control. As a product meant to be—if not actually—consumed by itself and not as a component of a more complicated food, as a completed product that could be made to circulate in that finished form, in and of itself the chewable coffee cherry provided a means of asserting and extending control over those contexts in which it would be used.

TREES IN HISTORY

> "[I] told [Rumanyika, King of Karagwe] the history of the creation of man. After listening attentively, he asked what thing in creation I considered the greatest of all things in the world; for while a man at most could only live a hundred years, a tree lived many; but then earth ought to be the biggest, for it never died."
>
> —John Speke (1863: 223)

The importance of coffee as a medium of control is demonstrated, in part, by the extent of Haya royal interests in it. Indeed, coffee trees and the coffee trade are said to have been monopolized by the Balangila throughout the nineteenth century, if not earlier (Austen 1968: 95; Curtis 1989: 54; Hartwig 1976: 111; Lwamgira 1969). Coffee cultivation could only be undertaken with royal permission, and a specified quantity of harvested coffee was routinely included as part of the "tribute" kings and their clansmen demanded of their clients. Again, these arrangements require some specification, since the significance of a "royal monopoly" for a crop that does appear to have been used by both commoners and nobility in this period, as well as the institutional organization of coffee cultivation and collecting "tribute" tell us little about the historical practices through which these patterns are realized. I think it is therefore useful and necessary to attempt to put coffee production in a wider material context in order to appreciate what it might have been that made coffee in particular the focus of this extensive royal apparatus, and the objectification of power that it was.

It is worth noting, as a part of this material context, that coffee is a tree crop. While the consequences of this "fact" has been much debated by agroforestry specialists and others interested in the "development" potential of a host of African communities (Shipton 1994), relatively less attention has been paid to the kinds of value and meanings that trees possess for those who cultivate, harvest, or otherwise encounter them within specific regional contexts. The root for "tree" in many Bantu languages, for example, is the same as the term for "medicine." This identification reflects not only the fact that many medicines throughout Africa and elsewhere are derived from tree products, but it speaks to the kinds of transformative potentials that trees are felt to exhibit across a range of cultural contexts. This potential for growth, agency, and intervention is, moreover, often connected with regimes of power, as trees iconically present the powers of local histories, social upheavals, and dynasties (Schmidt 1978; De Boeck 1994).

In the Haya context, trees are crucial to the processes through which kings and commoners come to imbue the landscape with power, significance, and history. Royal authority is frequently recognized and memorialized by the presence of certain trees, and these tree sites are often associated, even to this day, with the exploits of particular royal, or cosmological figures. Moreover, the land itself can be appropriated and inhabited in categorically different ways once it has been planted with trees. Both the spatial and temporal order of a kingdom are implicated in the growth of trees in a region, while the continuity of the land for those who occupy it as well as the force of kinship and clientship are all made possible through cultural understandings of, and encounters with trees. In short, trees are crucial means by which spatial relations are imbued in Haya consciousness with a sense of "place" (Parkin 1991; Feld and Basso 1996).

Consider the recollected history of Haya kings as recorded by Lwamgira early in the twentieth century (Lwamgira 1969). The hunter and traveler Igaba rests under a large tree on his way to visit Wamala, the last and most celebrated king in the Cwezi dynasty. This tree, he is told, is called Mubito. When Igaba bewitches Wamala, thereby seizing control of kingship in Kiziba (the northernmost of the precolonial Haya kingdoms), he has his royal drums made from this tree; and his clan, that has ruled in this kingdom ever since, becomes the Babito clan taking its name from the Mubito tree (Lwamgira 1969).

The equally celebrated Hinda king of Kyamutwala, Lugomola Mahe, establishes his regime by planting trees with seeds acquired from Mugasha, the powerful spirit of Lake Victoria. Lugomola plants entire forests, trees that mark his iron works, and a tree that demonstrates "he will not be chased" from his kingdom (Schmidt 1978: 317). In particular, trees are planted in order to demonstrate and memorialize decisive acts and judgments, acts that literally transform the landscape by means of the planted tree. Thus, the waters of Lake Ikimba in the inland kingdom of Kianja are held to have receded when the old mother-in-law, who caused the lake to flood in the first place, planted her hoe in the ground and asserted, "I destroy one village and save another." At this very site, on what became the shores of Lake Ikimba separating land from lake, submerged from surviving village, the hoe she planted has grown into a large thorn tree that can still be seen today.

Similarly, Mugasha saves Lugomola Mahe when, after his flooding threatens the king's palace, he plants an *omulumula* tree that causes the flooding to subside (Schmidt 1978: 325). This *omulumula* tree, whose very name means "tree of judgment," is the variety of tree that routinely marks the boundaries of Haya household farms (*ekibanja*, sing.). Royal judgments, as Seitel has pointed out with evidence derived from his extensive knowledge of Haya epics, are characteristically concerned with "setting things straight," instantiating categorical imperatives, and permanently "fixing" rules in place (Seitel 1986). Trees figure prominently in the implementation of such justice, as is iconically demonstrated by the fact that they are characteristically markers of boundaries, between land and water, between neighboring farms and villages, and perhaps even between successive dynasties (as the origins of the Babito suggest).[2] Royal tree planting is understood in the late nineteenth century (as it undoubtedly was for a much longer period of time) to actively reconfigure and redefine the landscape as trees provide enduring evidence of the dynamic practices that produce them.

Named trees in contemporary Haya villages and towns continue to be recognized, even by very young boys and girls, as sites that are associated with such transformative acts. Typically, such trees are associated less with historical figures or activities than with powerful spirits, Bazimu (Muzimu, sing.), or in some parts of Buhaya, Bacwezi.[3] The generic term for such tree sites in Kagera, regardless of the particular species of tree, is *ekigabilo* (*ebigabilo*, pl.). I want to explore different dimensions of social practice that surround these trees, often, and not inappropriately, described as "shrines" in the literature (Cory 1949; Reining 1967; Rald and Rald 1975), in order to consider how processes of empowerment, value production, and historical transformation become embedded in these sites. More concretely, I also hope to show how an understanding of these processes can help to illuminate the significance of trees, kings, and coffee, as well as the implicit connections between them in the precolonial Haya kingdoms.

Even in contemporary Kagera, tree shrines in Buhaya possess an array of important characteristics. To begin with, they are always *named* objects. An *ekigabilo* most frequently bears the name of the Muzimu associated with that tree. The Muzimu may have carried out some action at the site, or the tree may simply be described as a spontaneous manifestation embodying the spirit, or growing from the grave where the Muzimu was buried. The name of the *ekigabilo* may also come to have a wider spatial reference; that is, the farm, or even the village in which the tree grows may bear the name of the tree. In addition to names providing links of the persons, the past, and places, there are other important identifications embedded in the experience of these trees. The land on which such shrines are present ties the spiritual figure embodied by the tree to those who inhabit the land. Even today, families, and successive generations of families who occupy land that includes an *ekigabilo* feel an obligation, of some sort, to recognize these trees as shrines—even if that recognition only entails refusing to uproot the tree.[4] Indeed, the continuous recognition of such trees over successive generations, and the spiritual connections established between landholders, trees, and Muzimu are frequently offered as forceful demonstrations of a family's right to occupy their land, and further generate obligations to *continually* recognize these connections even when former residents leave the land.[5]

This recognition of attachments to place engendered by these trees also has implications for the ongoing experience of kinship relations in Buhaya. Haya today describe their clans (*oluganda*, sing.) as patrilineal and totemic categories. But, as I have described elsewhere (Weiss 1996a), as a means of organizing and recognizing social relatedness, the notion of clan is profoundly dependent on Haya understandings of place and locality. Haya men and women will say they are of one clan, not merely because their clans have the same totems, or even the same names, but because they share common places of origin (*amaiga*, or *ekisibo*). The sense of "origin" people use when referring to the past is usually flexible—it may be the place from which all members of a widely dispersed clan are said to come, or it may be the place from which more immediate relations (e.g., one's grandfather, or great-grandfather) moved before arriving at a current village of residence. When people describe their own origins, they most frequently cite the most recent place from which their antecedents came before arriving at a present locale.

Let us take, for example, two men who are sons of brothers that left their natal homes and moved to separate villages in order to build homes and marry. These brothers' sons would (probably)[6] recognize that they were members of the same clan, and that they shared the same origin. By origin, in this case, they mean the homes from which their own fathers had departed before they were born, and not some prior location from which these brothers' father, grandfather, or other antecedent generation had come. Origins, then, formulate points of connectedness for spatially dispersed relations, but they also serve to differentiate successive generations as they move. This is the case, again, because, once members of a clan have moved, their descendant generations will recognize different points of origin, and thus no longer recognize clanship with those who claim different origins.

Most important about the ways that kinship is formulated in spatial and temporal terms are the implications of trees in defining these relations. Haya family farms (*ekibanja*) have long been the site of intensive, perennial banana cultivation. For at least the past two centuries, villages have been composed of multiple farms, all adjacent to one another, all covered by bananas at various stages of growth. Such farms are clearly recognized to have the potential for extending connections of kin in time and space. The land (*ensi*) itself should pass from one generation to the next, and each generation expects to be ceded access to this land whether as an inheritance or at some other time of bestowal. Trees play an important part in organizing this access. Specific trees could be designated by a household head (*nyin'eka*) to particular heirs;

often daughters, who had no expectation of inheriting land until the mid-1950s, could expect, even in the precolonial period, to be ceded particular trees (notably barkcloth and coffee trees) for carrying out rites associated with the death of senior men and women (Rehse 1910: chapter 9).

This understanding of trees and land planted with trees contrasts strikingly with the control exercised over the grasslands, *orweya*, that surround or border Haya villages. These grasslands, even today, are worked by women, collectively and individually, in small fallowed plots. The land itself is often said to be "unowned" or "empty" *busha*, and acquiring a gardening plot on such land is relatively easy.[7] However, Haya do attempt (as they have for a very long time) to convert open grasslands into land that is planted with trees. In the past only the payment of a nominal fee to the king's administration was required to plant a few trees and establish a woodlot, *ekishembo* (Reining 1967; Rald and Rald 1975). Planting grasslands with trees allows that land to come under clan-based tenure, to become *ekibanja' ky'oluganda*, a farm of the clan. Such land is now definitively different from grassland, a point critical to understanding of the transformation of the Haya landscape in the twentieth century. The presence of trees means that such land is no longer "open," or "empty" (even though open *orweya* may be full of women's crops), it is under the aegis of a recognized clan and has a radically different potential, or trajectory. Indeed, in Kagera in the late 1980s I found that household heads who lived adjacent to large tracts of what appeared to be "open" grasslands would plant a tree or two in these lands—lands being worked by women cultivating peanuts and Bambara nuts—in order to assert their claims to possess these (only apparently) grasslands. Trees give land a depth and complexity of relations and values that are drawn on and invoked over time, generation, and distance.

What is true of everyday trees is especially so of tree shrines. The spatial and temporal horizons of "origins" in shaping relatedness, and the special force that trees, and especially *ekigabilo* have in anchoring Haya households to their farms, indicate that trees are not just fixed, recognized objects, but rather that they are places whose significance extends over space and time. It is not only the families who occupy a farm that contains a tree shrine who validate their attachments to their land through the recognition of these sites, but even the future generations who elect to leave these lands that trace their connectedness to one another by recognizing their common origins. Tree shrines, even in contemporary Kagera, exhibit a power that extends beyond the confines of the ground they occupy. These shrines make possible a "gathering" of experiences, acts, and meanings that characterize and shape a sense of place (Casey 1996: 24–26). They orient ongoing and future actions, allowing places to be known by the names they bear, obligating those who live with them to recognize their significance, and inspiring those who move away from them to remember their origins and retain their connections even as they move across the landscape.

Narrating, naming, remembering, and recognizing. All of these can be thought of as actions that contribute to a process of concretization, in which, to follow Lass (1988), the significance or sense of particular places, texts, or objects becomes actualized in everyday life. That is, these particular ways of engaging with tree shrines are collective acts through which Haya men and women grasp the self-evident meaning of these objects. Through an *ekigabilo* the historicity of the land, the force of kinship relations, or the powers of spiritual forces can all be tangibly grasped, or "experienced as concrete reality" (Lass 1988: 462). The self-evident significance of these tree shrines for Haya villagers, their taken-for-granted force, is an aspect of how, in everyday life, "the world is *given to us* as meaningful in experience" (emphasis added, Lass 1988: 456). Understanding particular experiences of the "givenness" of the world one lives in, the commonplace sense of the self-evident, intrinsic meanings of the ordinary phenomena one encounters, may not only give us insight into the processes by which meaning is culturally constituted, but also to the ways in which those meanings are laden with power. The self-evident character of commonplace experiences suggests that the world is given to us as meaningful, and further, in that very self-evidence indicates that those meanings can have a *hold* over us. Like the mountains and streams that "stalk" the Western Apache who occupy those landscapes (Basso 1990), Haya encounters with trees often reveal the force entailed in meaning.

Fortunately, there is no need to rely exclusively on the language of Husserlian phenomenology to discuss how power and meaning are conjoined in the "givenness" of places and objects in mundane Haya experience. Haya men and women routinely act on precisely such understandings and describe their actions in straightforward terms. When speaking about the "authenticity" of a particular site, object, or even practice, a Haya person will say, "*Nikashangam*"—"I found it (this way)." What makes an experience valid, and I would further say its significance self-evident, is the fact that the person "found it" just as it is at present (in effect, for all to see). This is a mode of authenticating a concretized meaning that is, moreover, not confined to specialized objects like tree shrines. When Haya men and women talked to me about their religious practices, the lands that they cultivated, or their obligations to kin they would say that they had found these things as they currently were. The act of "finding," then, is a way of grasping the meaning, indeed, the truth of such phenomena. It should also be clear that "finding" things as they are also imposes certain constraints, and so embeds a form of power in this process of meaning creation.

Let me specify this connection between signification and empowerment by considering once again *ekigabilo* as "found" objects. One man who was my neighbor, and by his own admission very old, once described to me the importance of a *mukindo*, or palm oil tree, growing at the edge of our farm, that was widely recognized as an *ekigabilo* named for the spirit associated with it. "You see that tree?" he asked. "Since I was a boy that tree has not grown or shrunk at all. That tree is exactly as I found it, and I have over seventy years!" This claim was offered as tangible evidence of the importance, indeed, I would even suggest the sacred character of this tree. The range of ritual observances (discussed below) that were once carried out at such shrines, and were certainly part of the memory of my neighbor, are no longer practiced. But the power of that tree was tied to his immediate experiences of it as an unchanging presence that he had "found" just as I (or anyone else) would find it today.

This understanding of power seems (but only seems) to be tied to an ahistorical, or at least radically conservative vision of social existence. Such assertions sound like claims that authority always lies in the past, and reality is "true" because "things have always been this way." In fact, a Haya practical understanding of what it means to "find" things as they are is profoundly historicized. To "find" something in Haya sociocultural practice is to recognize that the phenomena encountered is the product of some past action that brought it about. In this way, the phenomena itself, whether a ritual, a farm's border, or a style of dress, is evidence of the accomplishment of that prior act. Indeed, Haya men and women will generally describe the antecedent actors who made something available for them to "find" as they did—for example, "My parents were Christians, and so I found Christianity." For my elderly neighbor, then, the existence of our *mukindo* tree was evidence of the fact that something had at some point brought that tree into being. The fact that we could continue to "find" this tree as he had (always) found it was further evidence of the tremendous power of the force that had created it in the first place. To say, then, that a tree is "sacred" because one "finds" it in a particular way is not to say that things must never change, and power lies in those things that are forever unchanged and unchanging. It is rather to say that this unchanging character demonstrates that the acts that created this place were truly, authentically, and self-evidently extremely powerful precisely because they were able so decisively to change the world we find ourselves in. It is because the world is one in which change and the human reconfiguration of objects, the land, and practice are *always* possible, that those changes concretized in places like tree shrines which preclude, or override future attempted changes must necessarily possess a significant force. Our concrete experience, the very evidence of our senses, thus confirms the truth of the powerful, historical transformation that brought about such places. How else could one continue to "find" them as they are?

A VISIBLE SACRIFICE

These acts of concretization—naming, narrating, recognizing, and perhaps above all (because most routinely enacted) finding—are important for understanding how objects (in this case trees) in Haya experience come to have a taken-for-granted significance in everyday life. I have also suggested that such self-evident meanings are often bound to cultural forms of power. To "find" a tree shrine, in these terms, is not merely to recognize the force of the transformation that created it, it is also to acknowledge and thus to *submit* to that force. This recognition and its power are relevant at the mundane level as well as the sacred. In the 1980s, I frequently spoke with Haya women cultivating fields on plots of land that were adjacent to one another and would ask them how they could differentiate their plots from others. Invariably, they would tell me that when they had come to turn the soil they had "found" some indication of another woman's work (in the form of markers, plants, or other concrete evidence) that defined the spatial parameters of her work. Thus, when a working woman "finds" such spatial markers she both knows their meaning and submits to their terms. Acknowledging the value of a tree shrine, even if that means nothing more than refusing to uproot it, has a similar effect. These recognitions continue, in some form, and with regard to certain trees, even to this day in Kagera. But in the past, and as an aspect of kingship and its method of suffusing the landscape, there were yet more elaborate acts attesting to the significance of these sites. The very word *ekigabilo* derives from the benefactive form of the verb *okugaba*, to share, to divide, or (if I may generalize) to sacrifice. And such trees were, and for a very few Haya men and women still are, places at which a propitiator can make important offerings.

Offerings made at tree shrines were presented to the named spirit associated with that place. These offerings contrasted, or at least were distinct from, propitiations that might regularly be made to household, or ancestral forces. In the early part of the twentieth century (and in some Haya households today) each household head preserved a small enclosure (*ihangiro*) toward the rear of the house in which gifts to ancestors, usually the father of the household head, were offered (Rehse 1910: chapter 12; Cesard 1939: 15). Such offerings to ancestors had an element of routine about them; banana beer, for example, was set out at the *ihangiro* every day in order to secure the blessings of patrimony (Rehse 1910: chapter 12). Offerings at tree shrines were different. Some tree shrines were associated with particular Bacwezi figures who were known to overlook certain regions or activities. Mugasha, to whom I have already alluded, was the protector of the lake and of the fishermen who carried out their work on it; Irungu was the Mucwezi of the forest, and hunters made offerings to him to insure their success. Haya men and women often propitiated the spirit of an *ekigabilo* when they were to embark on an important journey, or if they anticipated the arrival of a distant traveler, confirming, yet again, the expansive spatial implications of these particular places (Jervis 1939; Rehse 1910: chapter 12; Cesard 1939: 20). I also found in the late 1980s that the blessings of particular spirits would be sought out after a family had sought the aid of a diviner, suggesting yet another avenue for establishing connections between tree shrines and those who propitiated at them.

The objects offered at these tree shrines could include consumable foods, like banana beer (*olubisi*) and cooked plantains; or grain such as finger millet; or tokens of exchange value, like cowry shells (*ensimbi*); or metallic currencies, like rupees and shillings. And coffee cherries, objects that (as I will argue later) in the regional world of the Lakes Kingdoms, conjoined the qualities of food and currency, and processes of consumption and exchange, were the sine qua non of these offerings. These materials were set at the foot of the *ekigabilo* atop an unblemished leaf (Jervis 1939), much as meals were, and still are taken on "plates" of whole banana leafs in most of rural Kagera. Indeed, Haya men and women I spoke with in the late 1980s described these offerings as ways of "feeding" *okulisa* the spirit in order to acknowledge their presence in social life by means of the primary media of social relatedness, namely food (See Weiss 1996a *passim* for discussion of food and sociality).[8] While people might describe this process as feeding, the term for making offerings in this way at these shrines through these explicit ritual practices is *okubonekya*, "to make visible," to cause to be seen.

Elsewhere, I have described, in some detail, the aesthetic and political dimensions of seeing and visibility in everyday Haya sociocultural life (Weiss 1996a). Haya aesthetics, their interest and attention to the sensory form and perceptual qualities of material objects and especially the spatial dimensions of their presentation, is profoundly concerned with enclosure as a means of assuring control over objects, relations and social processes more generally. Value, I have argued, is incorporated in Haya practice by interiorizing productive processes, removing them from exterior and (relatively) more public relations. Thus, covering, veiling, closing, screening, and wrapping are all routine dimension of productive Haya engagements with their world. They are cultural practices undertaken in order to enhance the value of a given activity. To expose, or to *disclose* in such a world is therefore to offer access to another, to cede power to that other who would otherwise be excluded and removed from the values that one has so carefully enclosed. From this perspective, then, "[b]eing able to see something is to engage it in a profoundly powerful way, to act as a subject with respect to what is being seen, but also, possibly, to be subjected to it. . . . [This makes the capacity to see a] form of power as well as perception, and making things visible is essential to Haya constructions of authority. The right to see and be seen are central means of demonstrating relative rank, position, and privilege in Haya social relations" (Weiss 1996a: 121). Offerings made to spiritual forces must then be understood as means of accessing power in terms of precisely how, and what, and to whom they "make things visible."

Consider the following invocation, one that Ishumi (1980: 71–72) tells us he recorded from a village elder making an offering of thanksgiving for the success that his son had achieved:

Katonda Nyamuhanga ishewange;	God the Creator, omnipresent;
Owa*maisho* nkolugega;	Of the myriad eyes to see everywhere;
Enta*bonwa*, em*bonwa* luboni omurubaya;	The unseen, seen only inside the hidden, secret place
Nikwehongela kakimo hamoi neka yange.	I commit myself along with my household to you.
Iwe mulinda byona; *Boneka* akamwani n'Enkologo ezikagenzileo.	You watch over everything; Receive a bit of coffee and its accompaniments.
Iwe eyatwete omwilu wawe mutabaniwa Akatabaala amwitunda akashuba kutabaluka.	You who have led your servant my son out to seek wealth, and to return with it.
Omuwe amani nobumaza ashube ashubeyo;	Be his strength and courage to return yet again
Abone ebindi ebyokusimisa.	He should see more things with which to thank you.
Iwe ishewanga, *boneka*.	You omnipresent, receive.[9]

In this text I have highlighted the references to seeing and vision, *okubona*, a theme that clearly characterizes both the power of Katonda (one of many terms for God common in a contemporary Christian vernacular) and the relationship of the propitiating father to Katonda.[10] Katonda is all-seeing with "a myriad eyes," yet he remains "unseen" (*entabonwa*), or paradoxically seen only when simultaneously hidden. And the elder's relationship to this deity is instantiated with an utterance "*Boneka akamwani*" that exemplifies this perceptual capacity. Here, this plenipotentiary source of vision is offered a token (the *akamwani* is the diminutive form of coffee, *amwani*) with the stative form of *okubona*, "to see," which I would prefer to translate "Let it be visible." The sociolinguistic form of this propitiation is important, because it shows how the father *establishes* the power of the deity in the very act of invoking it. The invocation, that is, emphasizes the potency of Katonda as a being with extraordinary powers of vision; the entreaty, *boneka*, thereby provides a performative event in which that ability is demonstrated. This father, then, does *not* ask the deity to act, in spite of the term "receive," a poor translation of *boneka* that reflects a notion of prayer and sacrifice in which deities "receive" in anticipation of the blessings they might provide as return "gifts."

Indeed, the propitiator does not even ask Katonda to *look at*, or *see* what has been made visible. Rather, Katonda is acknowledged as all-seeing, and his propitiator, therefore, comports himself in accordance with that divine ability.

The ritual practices of the father do not attempt to act upon the deity, to attract it, to cajole it, to make use of it, to make a request of it, or even, in fact, to *thank* it. Instead, the invocation describes the totalizing strength of Katonda, relates the successes of the son—here, again, the "servant" *(omwilu)* of Katonda's acts—and asks the deity to continue, simply, to *be* (*Omuwe*). To *ask* the deity, even to ask it to "receive," would be to *subject* the will of that supreme power to the will of another, thereby diminishing it. The propitiator of these rites makes virtually no reference to his own action—other than his own *reflexive* action upon himself (*Ninkwehongela*, "I commit myself")—which strengthens the assertion that constructive agency lies exclusively with the spirit. In effect, these ritual acts are designed to demonstrate the pervasive potency of the deity, and then to act in a way that conforms with the definitive features of that evident force. "In the presence of You who *see* all," I would paraphrase, "this offering is *visible*." And it is seeing, *okubona*, this text suggests, which is so encompassing a form of mastery (so encompassing, in this case, that its agent remains unseen) that to be visible to that force is to *participate* in it in empowering ways. The offerings are made effective, not because they transform or otherwise act upon a recipient, but because the form in which they are presented best allows them—and their provider—to be subject to a totalizing dominion.

This discussion of Haya offerings (I would even say Haya sacrifice) clearly owes a great deal to Lienhardt's account of the relationship between "actions" and "*passiones*," the experience of action upon the self, in Dinka "symbolic action" (Lienhardt 1961; see also Kelly and Kaplan 1990: 140–141). What is especially important about Lienhardt's discussion, and what is echoed in the present analysis, is the recognition that the iconic demonstration of the potency characteristic of such totalizing power, or as Lienhardt puts it "the discovery of an image which is the active counterpart of human *passiones*" is in fact a means of exercising *control* over experience (Lienhardt 1961: 151). Dinka sacrifice, for example, achieves its ends not by coercing divinity, nor by *failing* or refusing to act, but by allowing the Dinka "to create their own 'situation as it really is'" (Lienhardt 1961: 250). An "existential truth" is thereby effected and enacted by human actions, a truth that demonstrates human weakness, subjugation, and dependence on divinity. Recognizing the dynamics of such understandings of power as they are actualized in social practice, a dynamic of willful subjugation to a thoroughgoing form of control as itself a means to acquiring, or at least enjoying the benefits of some of that potential force; combined with an appreciation of the concrete sensory and perceptual contours—the potency of seeing, and the visible subject of that gaze—of relations and actions that characterize and make possible this dynamic, can actually go a long way toward helping us grasp the sense of coffee in both earlier *and* contemporary Haya social practices. Coffee needs to be examined as the quintessential medium through which the active constitution of power—exemplified, but not exhausted, by these ritual offerings—is realized as a feature of the Haya "situation as it really is."

The phrase *Boneka akamwani* ("Let this bit of coffee be visible") used to convey the offerings is telling in this regard. Coffee is understood in Haya communities to have qualities that lend themselves to visual acuity, to rendering the unseen visible. Coffee, for example, flowers in the midst of the "dry season" in Bukoba, and this flowering is viewed (and smelled) as an augury of the reinvigoration of the agriculture cycle as a whole.[11] In particular, the whiteness of these coffee flowers is noted as a positive sign. It should not be surprising to find that whiteness is closely linked to visual perception (cf. Turner 1967: 60–90; Weiss 1996a: 119–126), and so the potency and predictive ability of coffee is recognized as something that is powerfully "made visible." Moreover, Cesard notes that earlier in the twentieth century coffee cherries could be used in divination practices in ways that emphasized these perceptual features: "The *mulaguzi* (diviner) in Buhaya ordinarily makes use of a basin of water and some coffee cherries. One divines according to the pattern presented by the cherries and therein finds that which had been hidden" (Cesard 1939: 19).[12] As a divinatory tool, coffee reveals "that which had been hidden," making visible what could not otherwise be seen. The technique of placing coffee in water further highlights these visual qualities, as the transparency of water leads to a clarity of sight. In the late 1980s Haya friends told me of sorcery techniques using bowls of water and coffee in which the image of the person one intended to harm could be made to rise to the water's surface, another more nefarious means of exposing a visible form. Indeed, the verb *okuela* means to be clear, to shine, to be white, to be pure—a semantic range typical of similar Bantu verbs—and the sensory appearance and divinatory uses of coffee flowers and cherries participates in all of these acts. It seems appropriate, then, that offerings "made visible" are presented as "a bit of coffee."

The qualitative forms of coffee transactions—or perhaps conveyance is more appropriate than transaction, since even to assume that they have the capacity to compel a return gives them more credit than the discourse implies—display not only the extremes of power entailed in relations between donors and recipients, characterized by concrete perceptual and aesthetic features, they also suggest the kinds of value that are embedded in the concrete objects so transacted. *Boneka akamwani* is a phrase not confined to encounters with spiritual forces, or applied principally to ritual contexts, for *akamwani* is a standardized term for any token offering to another. Indeed, substantial items, including significant sums of money, livestock, or valuable commodities such as clothing and textiles, can all be presented (in the context, for example, of marriage exchanges, or property disposition at inheritance) by a donor as *akamwani*, a bit of coffee. This characterization of offerings works, in effect, doubly to diminish the donor with respect to the recipient. The diminutive term *akamwani*, a bit of coffee, and never the standard *amwani*, in and of itself emphasizes the meager character of the offering. Further, the categorization of even goats and clothing as "just a bit of coffee" belittles, or at least renders extremely modest the very act of offering. Of course, it is not unusual for a donor to describe his or her offering as *akamwani* as a kind of false modesty, one that ultimately draws attention to the wealth that the donor commands, wealth that is so great that they consider even heads of cattle a mere "bit of coffee." But such description, while it does not really seem to diminish the donor (and may have the opposite effect) confirms the significance of the category *akamwani* in describing an offering. "A bit of coffee" works to establish a pronounced *contrast* (and not just a difference) in values; either the *akamwani* made visible to the deity accentuates the power contrast between propitiator and spirit, or the magnificent bestowal characterized as a meager token draws attention to the wider control of wealth that the donor commands. It should also be clear that one does not "really" need to be wealthy in order to describe a significant offering as "a bit of coffee." The practical significance of this description allows even the poorest donor to imply a wider control of wealth, to suggest even a certain profligacy that demonstrates a *command* over wealth (i.e., that wealth is no issue for me if I can call the goat I give away *akamwani*) even when extreme wealth is not *possessed*.[13]

ROYAL SIGHT, ROYAL STRENGTH

A little bit of coffee goes a long way. The *akamwani* category in Haya social practices generates a sense of value in a number of respects. In the contrasts it invokes, between lowly propitiators and all-powerful deities, apparently modest tokens and the appearance of magnificent wealth, gracious gestures and indifference to their material consequence, a bit of coffee concretely *makes* a highly valued offering. Moreover, it gives that value tangible, lived qualities. The play between the seen and the unseen, the potency of vision and the world made visible are aesthetic terms that have substantial political implications. In the very acts of imagining, as Lienhardt might say, encompassing powers with real perceptual capacities, the coffee donor may place himself in relation to those impressive forces, and thereby give the world a sense of reality so compelling that it exercises a hold over the donor herself. We choose our world, as Merleau-Ponty puts it, and our world chooses us (Merleau-Ponty 1962). Like the acts of "finding" that demonstrate the force of history in Haya experiential encounters with their world, the offerings presented as *akamwani* have a hold over their donors that discloses in their experience the sense and power of the donor's acts.

The modes and terms of value configured in the bit of coffee were further elaborated—and embodied—in the very person of the Haya king, the *omukama*. The king's body, according to precolonial and early colonial reports (Speke 1863; Rehse 1910: chapter 26), is both the subject and object of a complex visual field. Kings are epitomized, even in contemporary Haya communities, as beings who were secluded from contact, and especially secluded from the view of others. A king must not only remain unseen by others while eating (a practice that is actually characteristic of Haya household meals more generally) but he eats by himself, in seclusion. Tanaganyika's renowned governor, Donald Cameron, noted of his visit to Bukoba as late as 1926 that the Bakama always brought their own food and drink wih them (Cameron 1939: 156). The *omukama* also remains unseen while he drinks, never sharing his beer with others; in contemporary Haya villages this behavior is powerfully antisocial, and readily condemned as royalist. In many respects these gustatory acts of the king are stereotypical of institutions of sacred kingship, which allows the king's need for nourishment to be denied, and his sacred character thereby confirmed (Feeley-Harnik 1985; Hocart 1927; Sahlins 1985). This is certainly an important quality of the Haya *omukama,* but the visual character of this denial is also the focus of royal privilege. So that, for example, while the king remains largely unseen, his subjects relate to him as objects to be seen by him. "On [his] excursions," Speke reports of his encounter with Rumanyika in 1859, "no common man dare look upon the royal procession" (Speke 1863: 253). When the royal entourage passes through a public setting his subjects avert their gaze from him and declare "*Kaboneka waitu!*" "It is visible, our lord" a phrase that should be reminiscent of the coffee propitiator. Here, the subject reduces himself with the prefix "ka" the singular form of diminutive nouns (like *akamwani*, a bit of coffee). Haya subjects of kings and spirits make their diminished selves available to the gaze of an unseen potency. Further, Haya men and women to this day swear "on the face of the king," *Obusa bw'omukama*. As with divinatory procedures, the truth of what might otherwise "remain hidden" is authenticated before the very source of a kingdom's visual strength.[14] From the face of the king who sees all no action can ultimately be concealed.

These royal prerogatives of "invisibility" and omni-optical presence are further conjoined with the power of coffee in some of the most important kingly rituals. In particular, the rite of the New Moon (*Omwezi Kwema*, or *Omwezi Kwela*) was the critical calendrical referent for royal ceremony. The New Moon itself "was auspicious both for its visual clarity, as well as for its 'newness,' the fact that it is a phenomena that initiates a process, and is therefore unsullied by the passage of time. As one neighbor put it, 'It is a period that has made no mistakes'" (Weiss 1996b: 142). The New Moon ceremonies carried out by the king were crucial demonstrations of authority, vital to the well-being of the king and kingdom, and configured around the potential for making seen and being seen essential to royal power. According to Rehse, the New

Moon ceremonies in the early years of the twentieth century, while celebrated by the populace of the kingdom as a whole, "is mainly for the chief (*sic*), who on his part on this day does reverence to his ancestors and especially his dead father" (Rehse 1910: chapter 15) Carlson adds that at the New Moon the king propitiates his own royal ancestors at each of their tombs (*amagashani*) as well as the royal Mucwezi, Wamala, the last king in the Cwezi dynasty—who "put an end to darkness"[15]—that preceded the Bito line of Kiziba and the Hinda lines elsewhere in Buhaya (Carlson 1989: 170). In this way the king embodies the totality of his dynasty—I would say of the kingship itself—as he propitiates both his immediate ancestors and the "outsider" ancestral figures that his own ancestors replaced. In making these propitiations, which always included coffee and would have been described as a whole as *akamwani* (Jervis 1939: 50) the king places himself in a compromising situation, but one that is characteristic of sacred kingship more generally. The king seems both the absolute sovereign of his kingdom, and yet himself absolutely subject to the very sources of his own supremacy. As the descendant of more powerful ancestors, and doubly the embodiment of a contemporary royal line that recognizes the supreme power of the Bacwezi, its own antecedents, the propitiations he offers call his stature as a sovereign into doubt. By making himself a subject acted upon by forces acknowledged to exercise supreme command, the king casts doubts on his own capacity for "overseeing" his "visible" subjects.

Not surprisingly, the period surrounding the New Moon was one of tension and uncertainty for the king as his capacity for effective rule was challenged. Yet the form that challenge took provided the occasion for a redemonstration of royal power in ways that make clear the links between subjugation and sacrifice, between visible and invisible forces. Rehse notes, for example, that the New Moon ceremonies have an especially ribald and extravagant character. While each household performs its propitiations to its own ancestors, the mood of non-royals is distinctively celebratory in Rehse accounts. The merrymaking, dancing, and drunkenness he describes might be taken as evidence of the waning powers of the king at this critical period, a threatened collapse of authority characteristic of the carnivalesque in such hierarchical sociocultural orders. I am reluctant to make such an argument (in spite of its convenient "fit" with the dangers posed to royal power that the New Moon portends), largely because of the exoticizing account that Rehse provides, and because Haya men and women in the late 1980s described New Moon ceremonies as more solemn in their intentions than Rehse suggests. Still, one aspect of Rehse's report that seems worth noting (irrefutably objectifying and racist as it is) is the following description:

> At the feast of the new moon the men wear their ox hides, the boys wear goat skins, the women barkcloth, and the girls dance naked, their bodies glistening with grease in the form of rancid, stinking butter. The ox hides

> worn by the men look as though they had just been taken out of butter and on their bodies also is smeared the precious stuff. The long handles of their spears, RUSHABI, shine as though they had been extra specially smeared over, or it may only be that they have become greasy because of the men's buttery hands—one is unable to decide. The smallest quantity of butter is wasted on the boys. The women's barkcloths shine like the finest silk owing to its buttery gloss. (1910: chapter 15)

What might be made of this "rancid," greasy mess? Rehse, with characteristic disgust, describes the Haya practice of rubbing themselves and their clothing with butter throughout his account, so his comments about the extremes of this practice during the New Moon ceremonies suggest that we may at least see them as a time for the relatively more liberal use of this emollient. Haya men and women, even in the current day, when petroleum jellies have replaced butter as the "grease" of choice, recognize that butter was used to coat people and things because it was "precious stuff." Access to butter required access to cattle whether one's own or one's overlord and patron. Still, the power and meaning of these "smearing" practices is no mere reflection of the economic strength and status that its provision required.

As I have described elsewhere (Weiss 1996b: 147–149; see also Burke 1996), using butter, or other oils to coat—*okusiga*—the body and clothing is a cultural practice that Haya men and women appreciate for the pristine appearance it creates. A person's well-oiled skin removes the traces of activity—the scratches and blemishes that accrue on the body's surface; further, this oiling is held to inhibit such marks, preserving the unsullied, smooth appearance of a "new" skin. Moreover, the surface of a properly coated skin is shiny and brilliant, dazzling in its allure. It is not merely clear from marks, but literally "shines" with a beautiful glow. This lustrous beauty that preserves the unblemished appearance of the skin is further tied to Haya notions of time and growth. A person's skin coated with butter is likened to the appearance of newborn children and virginal brides, both of whom are unsullied, vigorous, and new. In all of these perceptual and temporal respects, the shining new surface of the oiled body so graphically described by Rehse recalls the qualities embodied by the New Moon, a concrete manifestation of clarity, visibility, and renewal.

I am arguing, then, that at the moment when the supreme power of the king is in some doubt, a potency grounded in significant ways in his capacity to hold his kingdom in his gaze, his subjects make spectacles of themselves. The brilliance and luster of their shining bodies and clothing create a sight that is eminently *visible*. The sheen of a newly oiled skin, under the glow of a moon that makes its reappearance, incorporates a reinvigoration of the active body. Men and women attract attention and boast[16] of their restored beauty with their extravagant oiling; no amount of butter, Rehse suggests, goes "unwasted." Yet it should also be clear that this vitality and renewal are equally critical to the king's strength and control. For in making themselves so impressively visible the king's subjects make themselves available to him in ways that acknowledge the very form of perceptual force that characterizes his power. The New Moon once again brings the kingdom to light, assuring the continued vitality of an all-seeing force, as all that he commands becomes visible.

STRENGTH, TIME, AND DEATH

This achievement by Haya men and women, the demonstration of their own shining vitality, can be understood as a counterpart to the sacrificial offerings already considered. By making themselves visible to the king, his subjects enable and enact his ascendancy. This revitalization shows that by making their sacrifice they are simultaneously participating in that power. They, thereby, enjoy the benefits of being subjects of a power they have successfully produced. Further, the king's power is restored in a doubled fashion at the New Moon ceremonies. As a revitalized subject he successfully commands a newly visible kingdom; and as a propitiator himself to the graves of his royal ancestors and to the shrine of royalty itself, he—like his own subjects—may participate in the power his own actions produce. In the dynamics of Haya sacrifice, perhaps best exemplified by New Moon ceremonies as they were practiced in the nineteenth century, thus the propitiants authorize the potency they create by their own actions (Valeri 1985). Those who sacrifice reap the blessing of that potency, revitalizing both themselves and the objects of their veneration, not as a "return" for the offerings they "give," but by being incorporated into the reality they reorder, and thereby becoming infused with the very power they construct. If their sacrifices are successful, then the propitiants' own condition must embody the "existential truth"—the "situation as it really is"—of the world they have created.

In all these analyses of power made visible it is important not to lose sight of the place of coffee. Again, the coffee offered at New Moon ceremonies is iconic of the wider processes in which it participates. For example, the coffee variety that is most prized for use in such ceremonies is one that "when ripe, becomes a golden-yellow rather than the normal red and is known for this characteristic as *mibona*" (Jervis 1939: 55), a name related to *okubona*, "to see." Further, the intermediaries of the king who collect coffee tribute from his clients for use in these ceremonies are called Wabona, "those who see" (Jervis 1939: 51). These properties of the coffee crop and its processing, like the qualities of whiteness and clarity embedded in divination and flowering, lend themselves well to the revitalizing appearance of the New Moon and its attendant ceremonies.

There is a still wider, and more specific range of connections between the growth of coffee and the reinvigoration of the king and kingdom that illuminate the significance both of kingship and of coffee. New Moon ceremonies are rites of revitalization, and there is evidence to suggest that the king's vitality was in some danger during the days before this celestial body made its reappearance (Hellberg 1965). As the king's vitality is inextricably bound to the well-being of his kingdom as a whole (surely a minimal feature of sacred kingship), it is not surprising to find that the king's subjects celebrated the New Moon by displaying their own vitality. The vitality restored and displayed at this time, a potency that connected king and kingdom, was called a "life force," or *amagala* (Hellberg 1965). According to Hellberg it was this "life force" that was depleted prior to the appearance of the New Moon, a force that was necessary to the king's—and thus his kingdom's survival. *Amagala*, though, was not an exclusively royal asset. Each person, indeed each sentient being, was endowed with *amagala;* as a "life force" no life could exist without it. In particular, Haya men and women held that a person's "life force" was strongly connected to their coffee trees. The death of a coffee tree, for example, was taken as an omen of its owner's death, and it was thought that no person who planted coffee on his own (that is, without first acquiring royal approval) would live to see the crop (Jervis 1939: 53–54; Hyden 1969: 82).

These dimensions of coffee further illuminate its use as an offering in all of the ritual contexts described, for they suggest that coffee is itself a conduit and icon of the vitality that its offering promotes. I would add that these implications give greater credence to the notion that a donor's propitiation of a mere "bit of coffee" is, in fact, a form of sacrifice, an expenditure (perhaps even an extravagant one) with a highly valued potential that is surrendered as a life-enhancing gesture of one's subjugation.

The links between coffee, sacrifice, and life itself might be better understood if the qualities of this "life force," *amagala*, could be specified. The evidence that might permit us to do so are slim, but at least suggestive. Aside from the tangible interpenetration of life forces as suggested by the king's attachments to his realm, and the coffee grower's entanglements with his crop, there are reasons to think that *amagala* is a source of strength that has a periodic and fluid character. The term *amagala* is no longer (if it ever was) widely recognized in Haya everyday discussion, but a few older men and women were able to recall some of its implications and offer some insights into its workings in an embodied Haya cosmology. The first example anyone offered to describe *amagala* was when a neighbor took a piece of withered banana bast, dry, nearly rotting, and quite malleable, and contrasted that "lifeless" form with the green, moist, solid bast still growing on the banana stem. The latter still had its *amagala*, not simply because it was still "living" but because it had a supple, firm form. Some suggested that this repletion derived, not from some abstract principle, or generalized source in life, but to what one woman described as "the strength that comes from sleeping." Sleep, in these characterizations, was felt to be a period of restoration and renewal.

Haya conversation may not recognize the term *amagala*, but it *is* rife with references to, and concerns for, the restorative powers of sleep. "To spend a day without eating (*okusiga n'enjala*)," I was often told, "is sometimes possible; but to sleep without eating (*okulala n'enjala*, that is, to go to bed hungry) is really hard!" Such an assertion implies that sleep is an active process, that the work of sleep requires nourishment—perhaps even more than the work of waking activity—to be successful. Haya greetings make repeated reference to the quality of one's sleep. One man suggested that the morning greeting "*Agalaileo*" was once taken to mean "How did your *amagala* sleep?"[17] Again, the paucity of contemporary, or historical evidence makes it difficult to draw firm conclusions; but it does seem to be the case that Haya men and women physically feel sleep to be a bodily process that may index a person's general well-being,[18] and that, like the fluid that drains from a dried-out banana stem, well-being is a felt quality that is ever in flux, subject to ebbs and flows, diminishment and regeneration.

These felt qualities of *amagala* embody a set of parallels with the New Moon ceremonies already described. Such parallels suggest that the "life force" of the king, his kingdom, and indeed, all of the living beings that inhabit the region, have a temporal form that is characterized by periodic depletion and restoration. Like the darkness of an absent moon that sets the stage for renewed royal potency with the reappearance of the moon, and the restored possibility of presiding over a visible realm, the active powers of sleep during which the living body lies dormant allow the power of each body to be replenished. The implications of *amagala*, the fact that the king's restoration depends upon—but also enables—the restoration of the kingdom as a whole, which is itself an instance of the clear conjunction of hierarchical relations, "sacrifice," and renewal; or the links between eating well and sleeping well (or productively); as well as the ties between persons and the coffee trees they plant and harvest, indicate that this "life force" establishes profound interconnections between living beings. To have life is to participate in—but also be susceptible to—wider patterns of interchange and of being. Especially important for our purposes are the ways in which coffee is made to objectify the forms and values of these interconnections and their potentials for transformation, for being depleted and replenished. The offerings that *make* time, generating the pattern of revitalization that follows from diminishment are made possible through the medium of this product. A "bit of coffee" invokes the extreme contrasts that are necessary to the establishment of hierarchical order, and so make possible the flow of *amagala* in which subjugated propitiators participate in the potency they produce. If life itself is characterized by the transformative interpenetration of such forces, and such forces are channeled through, hierarchically organized by, and given temporal form by the presentation of coffee it is no wonder that the death of a coffee tree could be held to portend the death of its owner, as coffee clearly embodies the possibility of having life. Recall, as well, the Haya assertion that planting coffee as an *individual* and outside the strictures of royal hierarchy will lead to the death of the planter. Such an act violates the very nature of *amagala,* which is intrinsically relational, achieving its fullest dimensions in the interchange between more and less powerfully living beings. These understandings of the ways in which coffee objectifies *amagala* indicate that one cannot attempt to control life in ways that defy its essential character. The implications of this understanding of power, and its grounding in social relations, can further be seen in the way that coffee trees were planted in the precolonial era, a topic I discuss below.

ROYAL GROWTH, ROYAL PLACES

Coffee's iconic presentation of active and activating potency, its mediation of hierarchical, yet revitalizing relationships, and its objectification of life itself—in short, its value in Haya social practice—made it a prized substance scrupulously controlled by kings and their noble brethren. Growing coffee was a prerogative of the Balangila, a privilege whose violation might lead to disaster. Still, coffee was grown, and had to be grown throughout the Haya kingdoms. Its use was essential to the sacrificial offerings I have explored, offerings that were not confined to royalty, and that, indeed, could not be confined to royalty if they were to be effective. As I shall describe further, coffee figured in an array of practices that were—and in many respects, still are—pervasive and quotidian in Haya collective life. In order to retain its value, a value grounded in hierarchical contrast, coffee had to be carefully controlled, but broadly accessible. These paired requirements were attainable through the methods of coffee cultivation and propagation, and the authorization of those methods as practiced in Haya communities at the turn of the century.

According to Jervis, Emin Pasha, the celebrated German resident of Bukoba, was the first to establish nurseries at the end of the nineteenth century (Jervis 1939: 53–54). Prior to these seedling nurseries planted through generative propagation, coffee was grown throughout the region by means of vegetative propagation. That is, rather than growing coffee trees from seed, Haya farmers would grow new plants directly from living trees. One method involved cuttings taken from mature trees. When branch cuttings were used for propagation, each end would be planted in the ground, and in this way two root systems and subsequently separate trees could be grown. Even more commonly, the Haya propagated new trees directly at the site of living trees by bending down their branches, pegging the branch ends into the soil, and thereby growing an independent root system. The branch with the newly established roots was then cut away from the mature plant and became a separate tree. In some instances, though, the independent root system was not cut away from the parent stock, so that separate trees maintained organic connections to one another. Such coffee trees could spread over a wide region as successive generations of trees had their branches used to create yet newer trees, all of which were tangibly connected back to a single tree of origin. Jervis reported in 1939 that examples of such trees could still be found in Bukoba "producing crops which in quality and quantity is equal to the yield from trees [which would have been grown from seedlings] planted several generations later" (Jervis 1939: 53).

These methods of propagation would surely have permitted the growth of coffee to be carefully scrutinized and restricted. It should be clear, to begin with, that a single branch of coffee might produce several dozen coffee seeds, each of which could become a coffee seedling and tree if planted. Yet, that same branch could only produce one or two new trees if propagated by Haya vegetative methods. These techniques not only limited the total yield of coffee in the region but allowed for royal control that authorized its propagation, thereby limiting the range of people who could grow coffee. To take a cutting from a tree without the knowledge of its owner, especially one as closely guarded as a coffee tree, would have required a good deal of secrecy. Haya practice safeguarded this propagation even further by requiring that each coffee grower be able to provide witnesses who could attest to his authorized cultivation. The supplier of a cutting, generally a person of high rank, would act as a witness as to the source of the coffee; and further, the cutting itself was never planted by the farmer of the coffee, but by another man (a friend or neighbor) who could act as a witness as to its proper planting (Jervis 1939).

All of these techniques clearly served the interest of a royal "monopoly" that could control access to an intentionally limited supply of coffee. It is also important to recognize, however, that these propagation techniques are much more than useful means of restricting the growth of a valued good. The control of coffee had a social form that was never simply economistic in its determinants. To begin with, it is evident that the "monopoly" on coffee established "restrictions" that could never be exclusive, or completely exclusionary. That is, the very act of propagating by these methods established *connections* that linked royal and commoner, patron and client, and even growers to non-growers. Coffee is an intrinsically relational object in Haya social practice, as both its propitiatory capabilities and its propagation plainly demonstrate. No man grows coffee on his own, and no king, even one exercising a royal "monopoly," restricts the growth of coffee to himself alone. The very fact that coffee propagation, like the provision of coffee as royal tribute (*enkologo*), was a means of ramifying royal authority throughout an administrative system reveals the interlinking forces entailed in the "monopoly" that kings exercised over this substance.

The specific techniques by which Haya controlled coffee at the beginning of the twentieth century not only formulate social relations, they also disclose some of the *values* of coffee as a meaningful entity. The particular pattern of growth exemplified by coffee trees grown through vegetative propagation instantiates a wider Haya concern with the spatial and temporal form of growth more generally, and agricultural growth in particular. Coffee grown from cuttings or pegged branches concretely articulates generational relations, as parent stocks become vital to maturing plants. This method clearly contrasts with seedlings, as seeds contain within themselves the potential for a fully independent plant. This contrast is present even when cuttings are planted, for both ends of the branch are buried and rooted so that each root system is initially physically conjoined to one another. Branches may be severed from an original plant, and spatially relocated; but the planted cutting reinstantiates a paired relationship from which each plant must subsequently be separated. The technique of pegging branches from parent stock, which Jervis suggests was even more common than that of replanting cuttings, further emphasizes the spatial connection and physical dependency between generations that makes growth possible.

This form of regeneration parallels in striking ways Haya methods for growing bananas, which were and continue to be the staple food grown on every family farm in the region (see the discussion in chapter 4). Indeed, Jervis reports that different forms of the coffee cherry were known by names for different varieties of bananas, suggesting a conscious pairing of these agricultural products (Jervis 1939: 52). For example, in Haya agricultural practice (since at least the latter half of the nineteenth century, as Rehse [1910] describes exactly the same practices), any individual banana plant is part of a set of three clustered generations of plants. A number of shoots are put out by mature plants, but Haya farmers uproot all but one in order to ensure that it gets adequate nutrition as it grows. The mature plant, at the second level, or generation, will have begun to yield fruit. Once these fruits have fully matured, the stem of the banana plant is hacked through in order to harvest the fruit. This hacked-through stem is allowed to remain standing and act as the third generation, the *ekisibo*, or "origin" which is, in turn, the "parent" of the mature fruit-bearing banana plant. In this way Haya cultivation practices produce a three-generational cycle of plants, from young shoots, to mature plants, to harvested stumps. What is crucial is that Haya engage in this method because they feel that the sustained material connections between these generation are necessary to the successful maturation of each banana plant. Shoots, which are the "children" (*akana*) of "mother" (*nyina*) plants "suckle" (*okuonka*) from the moisture of the mature plant, just as harvested stumps continue to feed (*okulisa*) and support the mature, fruiting bananas with the moisture they contain and the secure anchoring they provide (which helps keep the fruit-heavy plants from crashing down).

The temporal connections between generations of plants are, thus, *substantial* dependencies as parent stocks nurture offspring. The temporal form of this growth pattern has important spatial implications as well. The physical connections between shoots and mature plants place shoots at the periphery of central points of development. In this way, each "origin" or *ekisibo* lies at the spatial center of a developmental process (and each plant, as it goes through this growth pattern and puts out its own shoots, becomes the successive center of new generations). Growth moves out from a central point of origin, but turns back in on itself as outgrowing elements become their own centers over time.

I would argue that this pattern, which thoroughly pervades Haya agriculture since each family farm grows dozens of banana plants, can also be said to characterize the growth of coffee trees. The trees grown at the site of parental branches, especially those that are never severed from these origins, clearly embody such a spatio-temporal pattern, as branches move out from their central "roots" only to establish their own roots and subsequent branches. So, too, do cuttings, that are not only peripheral to but spatially removed from their rooted origins, grow through the process of focusing central roots and moving out to new peripheries. Again, the method of planting both ends of a branch makes this clear, as each end forms a central root that only subsequently—that is, after rooting—is severed in half in order to create a peripheral branch at which coffee can fruit. In effect, the branches cut from original plants become mobile icons of growth, not simply replicating, or copying the parent plant—as seedlings do—but reinstantiating the relational qualities and tangible connections in both space and time that make growth possible. This iconicity further strengthens coffee's claims to potency as it contains within itself the potential for an entire order, a fully realized "emplacement" (Feld and Basso 1996), of developmental relations.

What is more, this icon of spatio-temporal growth presented in coffee branches is equally an icon of the king himself. The fact that coffee circulates by royal edict, even in its propagation, alerts us to the links between royal power, mobility, exchange, and growth. It is crucial to note that this movement is not willy-nilly but rigorously grounded in the particulars of place. Coffee circulates because it carefully adheres to these particulars, to the requirements of substantive connections over time, and the recognition of central origins—and the same is true of kings. Like coffee, the kings' development and reinvigorating growth also necessarily entail dynamic movement. For example, in the nineteenth and early twentieth centuries those sons of the mukama who were recognized as his potential heirs are never raised at the palace, the *ekikale*, of their father. Rather, they are raised "as far away as possible from the capital" (Cesard 1939: 28) by kin, a movement that protects them—and the king himself—from the intrigues of noble politics. When the new mukama assumes his authority, though, he does not reinhabit the palace of his predecessor; rather he constructs for himself a new *ekikale*, an act of self-placement that is always noted and celebrated in the chronicle of Haya kings (Schmidt 1978; Cory 1949; Lwamgira 1969). Moreover, the king not only makes for himself a new home, he also continues to establish new strongholds throughout his reign, and moves among these households throughout the year (see also Beattie 1970). I would even suggest that this ongoing movement is critical to the continuous success of the king. The White Fathers at Kagondo, for example, were perplexed (although they reported their own perplexity in terms of "une chose bien mystérieuse pour les nègres") to find that they could not keep track of the movements of their nemesis, the mukama Kahigi, because "at each new moon [the kings] rush to change residences" (Kagondo, 14 March 1903). The spatial relocation of the king at the period of the New Moon achieves a new centering of kinship, a centralization that is concomitant in temporal terms with the establishment of a grounded point of origin. The New Moon thus would have revitalized the power of kingship in its spatial as well as temporal dimensions.

The spatial form of this renewal has tremendous consequences for an understanding of royal power, and of the place of coffee in constituting the power. Origins and temporal precedence in Haya social existence are enclosed and centralized, not just in agricultural practice, but in a wide range of commonplace, ritual, and political activities (Weiss 1996a: Part I *passim*) The king's actions instantiate this pattern, but they also *encompass* its possibilities. Haya farmers throughout the twentieth century (Cesard 1938a; Reining 1967; Weiss 1996a) have, for example, retained their authority in spatial terms by strengthening their attachments to particular places; by building houses that have a strong interior focus; by farming land so as to generate long-term patterns of growth and generativity; and perhaps most powerfully by "staying by the graves of one's father," occupying land once inhabited by those now dead. The king's activities recognize these concerns with centrality and interiority as crucial to establishing and extending his dominion, as his concerns with carefully enclosing his own body at moments of potential challenge exemplify. Yet kings create these spatial and temporal dimensions, not through fixity, by holding fast to ancestral lands for example, but by embodying a *moving* center.

The king's capacity to invoke the terms of authority, control, and productivity, to secure points of central origin and make them the grounds of extension and regeneration in time and space, is something I would suggest he carries with him. Kings can, therefore, focus their power in firmly rooted places, while simultaneously transcending these fixed strictures and remaking place through their continuous movement. And coffee, as I have indicated, similarly conjoins these bases of power. Always a center, grounded in substantial connections to points of origin, yet possessed of the capacity to recreate that central origin wherever it goes—these are the spatio-temporal qualities and concrete powers common to kings and their coffee.

These persistent and pervasive concerns with centrality and growth, embedded in the apparently self-generative force of Haya kings as well as coffee to embody the productive qualities both of rigorous grounding in place, with those of continuously remaking place, draw our attention to important dimensions of coffee that have thus far only been suggested. These have to do with the fact that Haya coffee, and by implication Haya kingship—itself expressed through and defined by a richly elaborated range of coffee related practices—is intrinsically mobile, and indeed transregional. I have considered a definitive, if relatively narrow, facet of coffee's dynamic mobility—namely its imminently transactable character—through an intensive description of the perceptual and pragmatic conditions through which coffee's meanings are actualized in Haya social existence. The intimate weaving of coffee into the nuances of an inhabited landscape, its condensation of historical valences, sensory immediacies, and constraining potencies, suffuse this substance with a sense of place, and in parallel fashion lends Haya places the tone and texture of the coffee that is made to dwell in them.

I want further to argue, as a means both of enforcing this description and setting the stage for an account of the more expansive horizons in which coffee figures, that these meanings are actualized, that is, the taken for granted "sense" that Haya men and women made, and to some extent continue to make, of coffee, as the value of that object. Coffee works in this place-world as an evaluative medium. The substance and the category of *akamwani*—their form and their content—display in their conveyance a recognition of extreme contrasts, contrasts that are ramified in a bodily, perceptual field (through the dynamics of vision, the play of *passiones* and action) engaged in inextricably relational actions. In the effective demonstration of such extremes, power can be generated and canalized. Life forces are sustained and reinvigorated through the clear enunciation, configured as the offering of "a mere bit of coffee," that they are utterly limited—perhaps even entirely insignificant. At the same time, this expression of diminishment as a relative value, and a relative evaluation of the potency of the lives conjoined in the propitiatory "sacrifice," is itself a self-sustaining power. Substantive, material relations of dependency through which generative, life-giving power can be appropriated are concretely manifest in the propagation of living coffee trees. Coffee, under these conditions, is the acknowledgment of an absolutely abject situation that, because it is always a relative diminishment, is bound to constitute a greater power. Wherever there is coffee there must be something more.

In order for coffee to project this potency—to instantiate these extreme contrasts and thereby evoke tremendous power—it has to be offered to others. I turn, therefore, in the next chapter from this account of the dynamics of power as iconically realized in the substantial form of coffee cherries and trees, to a consideration of the ways that coffee cherries figured in social transactions. Here I consider not only the ways that coffee was understood and made use of as a medium of value at the beginning of the twentieth century, but am especially interested in the historical transformation of coffee through its articulation with other valued currencies. The introduction of colonial forms of money and coinage at the turn of the nineteenth century not only had historical consequences for the value of coffee in Bukoba, but each of these media were entangled in complex process of redefining the nature and meaning of wealth itself.

NOTES

1. A number of sources note that coffee was chewed in other parts of the Interlacustrine region, from Buganda in the East to Karagwe in the West (Burton 1860; Kajubi 1965; Tosh 1970; Uzoigwe 1971). This coffee, though, seems to have been chewed in a raw, unprocessed state, and was harvested from wild, not cultivated coffee trees (see below). In both of these respects coffee outside the Haya kingdoms was distinctive from "Haya coffee."

2. Seitel has also pointed out that uprooting or chopping down trees is a characteristic practice of those who would question the judgments of kings and take issue with the categorical nature of their decision-making processes (Seitel 1986).

3. I do not mean to conflate these two categories, although for contemporary Haya, the distinction between Bazimu and Bacwezi is not significant. Bacwezi are recognized in Ankole and Bunyoro as spirits of an ancient royal dynasty who possess mediums, or *embandwa*, who are often associated with particular clans, or households; while Bazimu are simply the spirits of the dead. For most Haya, if they are at all concerned with such matters, the term Bazimu is used more frequently; the Bacwezi are simply understood to be one kind of Muzimu. As Schmidt points out, Bacwezi are spirits, and whether they were historical persons in the ancient past is not a concern (Schmidt 1978: 62).

4. One man I knew told me that when he decided to become a Jehovah's Witness he had the tree-shrine growing on his farm chopped down. This, I would argue, is an exception that clearly proves the rule; he would not have made a point of chopping down the tree as an act of faith if he had not taken for granted that its existence was held to have some spiritual significance.

5. Cory and Hartnoll note that a family who had moved on to a farm where an *ekigabilo* grew could be fined or sued if the shrine were tampered with (Cory and Hartnoll 1945: 160–161).

6. As I describe in detail elsewhere (Weiss 1996a, chapter 7), brothers of the same father and mother may fall out and decide that they are no longer members of the same clan.

7. The gendered politics of grassland have become quite conflicted in recent years, as grazing rights for wealthy pastoralists and woodland rights for those who farm timber and firewood (all of which activities are controlled almost exclusively by men) have marginalized women's agricultural production on these lands.

8. Ishumi also notes that sticks "representing firewood to cook the edibles" might also be offered, extending the iconic links to feeding and eating. The products, then, are offered not simply because they are valuable in themselves, but because they are meant to provide for the propitiated spirits.

9. I have altered Ishumi's translation of this invocation slightly (cf. Ishumi 1980 71–72) to specify its verbal forms and their implications, as described below.

10. I recognize immediately that selecting an account from the post-independence period in Tanzania in order to illuminate precolonial practices is enormously problematic.

Let me make it clear that I am not asserting that there is a fundamental "historical continuity" in such rites that allows me to use this text. The deity addressed (Katonda), as well as the context for the rite (thanksgiving for having earned "wealth"), while not completely unknown in the nineteenth century, have certainly been subject to enormous transformation in this century. Nonetheless, the terms in which the relationship between the propitiant and spiritual power are expressed have clear historical precedents (cf. Rehse, Lwamgila, Cesard), and it is this "narrow" element of the invocation that is the primary focus of my exposition.

11. Bananas, the staple of Haya cuisine, can be harvested throughout the year, but their yields decline in the late summer months (July–August). The flowering of coffee at this time is taken as an index of the future banana crop.

12. All translations from the French are my own.

13. Compare this discussion to my earlier account of *okulongola*, a "premarital" exchange in Haya communities in which women offer men *akamwani* in return for luxurious gifts (Weiss 1996a, chapter 7).

14. Indeed, the blinding of a king or a contender for kingship is often reported in Haya histories as a fatally disabling event (Cory n.d.).

15. The name Wamala is taken from the panegyric "He who puts an end to darkness" (Rehse 1910).

16. The shiny appearance of spears carried during these ceremonies is characteristic of men's "boasts"—*okwebuga*—as spears are icons of masculine virility, lineal descent, and household authority.

17. This is undoubtedly a "fictive," if still perfectly valid, etymology. The infix *ga* could refer to any noun of the *ely—ama* class, and most Haya people translated *agalaileo* as "What is the *news* (*amakulu*) of sleeping?" The noun for "strength" in the Haya vernacular, moreover, is *amaini*, which also fits these grammatical patterns. The semantic content of greeting in any language are notoriously unrepresentative of any language as a whole. My argument, though, is not that people "really used to" ask one another about their "life force," but rather that the sense of that force was understood through its associations with sleep and rest.

18. The connections between "eating well" and "sleeping well" make the qualities of sleep as an index of one's overall well-being even more explicit, since eating in Haya social life, I have argued, is a means of generating and demonstrating satiation, repletion, and value (Weiss 1996a *passim*).

2

Coffee, Cowries, and Currencies: Transforming Material Wealth

> [T]he Baziba are more itinerant than ever: the four rupee tax, where is it to be found? "We have not yet figured out how to forge rupees," they say.
>
> Rapports Annuels—Bwanja (1906–1907: 127)

The processes of growing, preparing, and consuming coffee in the Haya kingdoms of the nineteenth century were always informed by an interest in transacting this substance. Relations with ancient spirits, regional nobilities, and lineal ancestors were all facilitated by offerings of coffee, and the significance of this material good cannot be assessed if it is abstracted from that pragmatic context. A salient feature of these pragmatics of exchange is the constitution of space and the detailed configuration of place they exemplify. The spatiality of coffee is revealed in the designation and memorialization of particular fixed locations that take the form of trees, tombs, and shrines; in the movement of coffee cultivated in distant gardens and transported to royal courts (themselves characterized by mobility over and fixity on the land); through the generative connectivities across the landscape instantiated in the network of coffee trees grown from royal stocks; and in the constraints and expressions of active bodies, bodies that make themselves available to the sight of others, avert their gaze from all-seeing forces, or exuberantly demonstrate the reinvigoration manifest in sacrifice.

Transaction has powerful spatial implications in all of these conjoined dimensions. These implications, moreover, are demonstrated far more widely and recurrently in Haya and Interlacustrine social and historical practice. The hierarchical, cosmological, and historical dynamics entailed in the royal control and deployment of coffee already described make it clear that even in the fine grain of what appears as to be a thoroughly "local" phenomena, a potentially encompassing field of relations is invoked. In what follows, then, I propose to intensify this description of that encompassing field by looking at the value embedded in coffee in transformation and transition. This entails a movement in space and time, an exploration of the circulation of coffee among the traders and markets of East Africa in the late nineteenth century, and a consideration of the incipient processes of overrule through which value itself would be constituted anew. As I will show, this political process of redefining value was made possible in important ways through the transformation of coffee, which became both the instrument and most ready measure of these transformations.

I want to situate and historicize these encounters over the value of coffee in Bukoba and provide an appropriate vehicle through which to compare colonizing and colonized dispositions toward it. To do so I consider not just coffee through time, but coffee's relation to money. In this chapter I explore the conditions that permitted the development of coffee as a cash crop, developments that were facilitated at the outset of the twentieth century by the introduction of new forms of wealth—like colonial moneys—that brought with them novel understandings of value. In order to show how this articulation of coffee with cash was even possible, I first address the kinds of currencies that circulated in the Interlacustrine world at the end of the nineteenth century. In exploring this range of forms, I focus in particular on the kinds of potentials that were granted to qualitatively different objects in order to specify why *this* object should mediate *these* transactions. What was the value of precolonial moneys in this region, and why were they used in the particular ways that they were? How, in turn, did these evaluations shape the value of novel currencies and the various uses to which they were put? In order to address these problems, I argue that it is necessary to examine the nature of "wealth" in Haya communities as a culturally constituted category in this early colonial era.

The writings of European observers, like Burton and Speke, as well as the living memory of Haya elites recorded by Lwamgira, make it plain that coffee has long featured prominently as a long-distance trade good in the Lakes Region, and beyond in East and Central Africa. Coffee grown in the eastern Haya kingdoms along the shores of Lake Victoria made coffee available to the kingdom of Karagwe immediately to their west (now a district in the Kagera Region that immediately borders on Rwanda to its west and Uganda to the North), and through this powerful conduit, Haya coffee enjoyed a far-flung circulation. Karagwe enjoyed its preeminence among the polities of Buhaya, in all likelihood, because of its command of cattle. Its vast plateau, relatively drier and less forested than the kingdoms on the lake front, provided ample grazing lands for large herds. More important in sociocultural terms, hierarchical relations between nobility and commoners were founded on ties to cattle,[1] a situation (parallel in many respects to the *ubuhake* of Tutsi-Hutu relations of neighboring Rwanda and Burundi) that led to an intensification of livestock breeding.[2] During the nineteenth century, the position of Karagwe can further be seen in the fact that it was the most "cosmopolitan" of the Haya kingdoms, in the sense that it was the most directly connected to circuits of exchange and centers of power that included the Ganda empire to the north, and the Swahili and Nyamwezi caravans that traveled from the Indian Ocean through the interior of what is now central Tanzania. This cosmopolitan position is demonstrated, for example, by Burton's report during the 1860s that coffee said to have come from Karagwe was sold in the Nyamwezi center of Kazeh, now Tabora; and by Speke's encounter with Rumanyika, king of Karagwe, who wore Arab clothing and was readily able to converse with Speke's porters in Swahili, the lingua franca of the caravan trade (Speke 1863: 203).

Given coffee's historical presence in this regional world, a presence that is markedly different from that associated with the modes of marketing and production that would come to characterize coffee's place in colonial and neocolonial contexts, it is important to reconsider some presumptions that continue to characterize anthropological and historical accounts of sociocultural transformation. Haya coffee in the nineteenth century certainly appears, for example, to exhibit all of the qualities of a commodity. It was widely marketed, subject to pricing, produced for the purpose of trade in order to acquire other desired goods (such as bark cloth from Buganda, salt from Bunyoro, ivories and cowries from Nyamwezi sources) equally subject to these market conditions. None of these attributes, however, seem to have prevented coffee from serving as a propitiatory offering—I might even speculate that these marketing possibilities rendered coffee an even more appropriate propitiation. Indeed, the signs, materials, and practices of a global order seem already to have made an appearance of some consequence in a region no European had seen before the 1860s.

Local Haya kingdoms of the period clearly did not lie in fortunate seclusion from a predatory world system waiting to encroach. Colonial authorities undoubtedly established new regimes of marketing, organized production, agricultural practice, and land management in a vastly different way. But I want to suggest, in keeping with the evidence of precolonial coffee just described, that it is worth thinking about these changes under colonialism as something other than complete innovations that introduced techniques and possibilities wholly absent from the precolonial scene; or as elements in a chronicle of the progress (or degradation) of colonized societies marked by shifts from subsistence to marketing, use to exchange values, personal bonds of status to impersonal negotiations of contract and price. It might, instead, be at least as useful to look for grounds of comparison by which to explore the differences between precolonial, colonial, and postcolonial understandings of such entities as exchange, property, and wealth in relation to one another. Such a comparative perspective may allow us to avoid the pitfalls of both normative models, from modernization to deprivation and dependency theories, that describe social orders primarily in terms of what they "lack"; as well as these models' paired tendency toward teleological historical visions, in which global forces and institutions are either ruthlessly imposed upon or readily appropriated by local practices.

History is never merely thoroughgoing domination, nor perpetual reproduction. The potential, value, and meaning of coffee in what is now Northwest Tanzania *did* change, and continues to change over time. But not according to terms that were strictly determined either by the colonizers or the colonized. Indeed, it is in the encounter between colonizing and colonized social and cultural agents that the very terms of their mutual transformation were—and continue to be—worked through, a working-through that is the historical process itself.

POTENTIAL STANDARDS: EARLY COLONIAL INTERLACUSTRINE CURRENCIES

> Let us suppose that two men who otherwise engage in no "social relation"—for example, two uncivilized men of different races, or a European who encounters a native in darkest Africa—meet and "exchange" two objects. We are inclined to think that a mere description of what can be observed during this exchange—muscular movements and, if some words were "spoken," the sounds which, so to say, constitute the "material" of the behavior—would in no sense comprehend the "essence" of what happens. This is quite correct. The "essence" of what happens is constituted by the "meaning" which the two parties ascribe to their observable behavior, a "meaning" which "regulates" the course of their future conduct. Without this "meaning," we are inclined to say an "exchange" is neither empirically possible nor conceptually imaginable.
>
> —Max Weber

From a certain perspective, the early colonial relationship between money and coffee in Buhaya exemplifies a history familiar in much of Africa, and undoubtedly other regions of the Third World, a history of cash cropping and taxation, class formation and market dependency. Haya social history presents no exception to these generalized processes, and coffee was the principle instrument of these institutions. Taxes were imposed by the German colonial administration, first at a rate of three rupees per house in 1898; by the end of the first decade of the next century, an annual tax of five rupees was imposed on all persons over thirteen years of age (Rapports Annuels 1909–1910). The development of coffee as a good to be marketed by colonial institutions went hand in hand with these taxes. Mutahangarwa, the mukama (king) of Kiziba, recognizing the extremely high price he could command through the control of the crop—but also acknowledging his indebtedness to his German patrons who backed his claims to succession—required coffee planting of his subjects in 1905, and enforced his rule with the brutal use of *ruga ruga* troops (Lwamgira 1949; Austen 1968). By 1911, the German administration made coffee planting compulsory throughout Bukoba.

This chronology demonstrates the important connections that colonial agents and Haya elites alike made between coffee and cash. The eventual emergence of this crop as the primary source of monetary income in the region—a condition that persists to the present day—was given a powerful foundation by these kinds of relations. Still, as the marketing of coffee in Kazeh, Bunyoro, and Buganda indicates, this important nexus has historical antecedents as well. Colonialism did not initiate the link of money and coffee, and, given the presence of salt, bark cloth, and cowries throughout the Buhaya region at the end of the nineteenth century, it is not entirely clear that the introduction of local coffee traders and taxes made money a necessity of everyday life as it had never been before (cf. Curtis 1989: 62). What was at stake, though, was the transforming significance—and not simply the existence—of these potent bonds of coffee to cash.

The changing history of coffee's relation to money must take account of the changing forms that money took, and in a relatively brief span, in the Lakes Region. Since the late seventeenth century, the Haya kingdoms, by means of their relations with the ascendant Ganda empire, had some access to the Nyamwezi caravan trade to the Indian Ocean coast. Not just the goods, but the currencies of this trade were highly varied at different periods during its history and across different regions of East Africa. These moneys ranged from cloth and beads, to brass wire and iron hoes, to copper coins from British India and Maria Theresa dollars of the Austro-Hungarian Empire (Burton 1860: 27 ff.; Koponen 1988). Prior to the mid-nineteenth century, it is difficult to say how available all, or any, of these currencies would have been in Buhaya, but it is clear that by the end of the nineteenth century cowry shells—*ensimbi* in the Haya vernacular (derived from *simbi* in Swahili)—had emerged as an important, if not primary means of payment within these polities. There is also reason to believe that this emergence was rather swift. The presence of a significant supply of cowry shells, harvested in and around Zanzibar, as far inland as Buhaya, would only have been possible after the mid-century, following a concurrent collapse in the market value of Maldivian cowries, and a boom in the clove trade in Pemba and Zanzibar. The combined effects of these international processes did increase the supply of

Zanzibari cowries throughout East Africa enormously (Hogendorn and Johnson 1986; Koponen 1988).

Still, as Gregory has ably demonstrated in his reanalysis of just such historical moments, the appearance and apparent ubiquity of cowry shells in the Lakes Region in the late nineteenth century cannot be explained in monetarist terms, as though supply drives the value of a currency, and "bad money drives out good" (Gregory 1996). In order to understand the demand for this particular form of currency—a demand shaped by the value of the sociocultural practices they enabled—and especially the power of political authorities to impose and enforce a specific monetary standard, it is necessary to address the establishment and transformation of these concrete media.[3] It is clear, for example, that in relation to other possible methods of payment present in Buhaya at the turn of the century, including cloth, beads (Speke [1863: 213–224] purchased beads in Karagwe with Maria Theresa dollars at what he thought was an exorbitant rate), and perhaps even mythical "banana seeds" (Rehse 1910: chapter 6), German officials favored cowries as a monetary standard.[4] Carl Peters, as a case in point, founder of the Society for German Colonization, made a treaty with Muanga of Buganda in 1890 that required Peters to solicit a tribute to the Ganda in cowries from each of the Haya kingdoms (Peters 1891). By 1892, German authorities were able to require Haya bakama to give them a tribute in cowries, which could then be used to pay local German troops at a rate of 150 cowries every ten days. These payments would have required, in turn, an even greater acceptance in Buhaya of cowry shells, as troops used their pay to purchase local provisions for themselves (Stuhlmann 1894). It is evident that cowries, already in circulation in Buhaya, were important instruments of German and Ganda overrule at the end of the last century, and so increasingly bore the imprimatur of political—and especially colonial—authority.

The Germans made an effort to establish a standardized currency, a project complicated by the introduction of multiple standards and the accepted use of many different media during the first decade of the century. Yet these attempts did not make them the sole sources of the political authority bound up in the use of cowries. Far from being subject solely to the effects of an expanding market supply, cowries had been appropriated by Haya polities for a number of purposes that shaped the demand for and the meanings of these moneys. As was the case in any number of African contexts, the use of cowry shells for ritual, decoration, and adornment had long been established in the Lakes Region prior to their massive importation from the coast at mid-century. This history has made it extremely difficult for economic historians to distinguish the significance of these shells as a currency from their "ornamental value" (Tosh 1970: 116; Hogendorn and Johnson 1986). In Buhaya, for example, cowry shells, sometimes strung in single strands of a hundred and sometimes as individual shells, were frequently circulated for non-monetary purposes.

Strings of cowries were used as amulets, as appeasements to powerful spirits, and as token offerings of good luck on ceremonial occasions like birth and marriage. As I have indicated the case for coffee, cowries were also important divinatory pieces, their double-sided shape providing a convenient icon of differentiation (see also Bjerke 1981). To this day, a payment of "nine cowries" is usually provided as part of marriage exchanges, although actual cowries are rarely available.[5] The number nine is an especially auspicious one throughout the region. Wamala, the last king of the mythical Cwezi dynasty, received nine cowries, or nine strands of cowries, or nine bundles of cowry strands at New Moon ceremonies, as nine is the number "welcomed everywhere" (Rehse 1910: chapter 12), and cowries combined in this number are especially appropriate expressions of good fortune. Such royal presentations of cowries to Wamala, himself especially associated with offerings of coffee by the living Mukama at New Moon ceremonies, further suggests a powerful political legitimation of this currency within Buhaya.[6]

The meanings of these shells, however, do not arise exclusively outside of a sphere of monetized transactions. The utility of attempting to distinguish the value of cowries as currency from their mere "ornamental" (and putatively epiphenomenal) uses must therefore be challenged.[7] Indeed, the monetary form that cowries took in Buhaya makes plain the cultural connections between their uses as ritual, aesthetic, and economic objects. To begin with, while cowries did operate as a currency, they seem always to have figured as part of a system of multiple currencies, even in the colonial era. Thus, cowries were used as an "all-purpose" medium of equivalence that was, nonetheless, not used for all purposes. Cowries could be used to express the commensurate value of different commodities—coffee produced in Buhaya could fetch a price in cowries in Kazeh or Buganda, and cowries could be taken to Buganda to buy bark cloth, or to Bunyoro for iron tools.

Yet, while a range of currencies functioned in these same markets, certain goods could *only* be purchased by particular currencies—and others did not permit of pricing at all. Salt, which is one of the most important and ancient of trade goods in the region (Tosh 1970: 104; Uzoigwe 1974: 432), was sold only for cowries in Buganda in the 1880s, while cloth was most readily sold for beads in Karagwe. Cattle—which were not infrequently exchanged for grain, or other foodstuffs as well as ritual materials—were almost never "sold" for any currency (Rehse 1910; Tosh 1970: 117; Uzoigwe 1974: 449). Commercial activities in the Lakes Region, then, were not characterized by a rigid segregation of separate "spheres" of equivalence. For currencies did circulate in ways that permitted qualitatively different objects to be transacted in their terms. Nor was the economy defined strictly by market principles according to which all objects could be evaluated by means of a single standard of value that had its expression in a common monetary form. Certain goods lent themselves to monetized exchanges, while others were differentially subject to—or excluded altogether from—sale. Just as important, certain moneys lent themselves only to certain types of transaction and to the evaluation of particular kinds of goods, while other moneys were appropriate to a somewhat broader—but never universal—range of conversions.

WHOLES AND PARTS

I will consider the implications of such diverse object potentials for a theory of currencies below. It should be clear, though, that during the nineteenth century, Haya and many other polities around the lake recognized multiple currencies, none of which functioned in and of themselves as all-purpose coins of the realm. In a certain sense it is inappropriate to consider cowries in isolation from these other forms of money. Still, the history of colonialism in the region—to say nothing of the sheer limitations on our knowledge of media like beads, wire, and iron—provide good reason to privilege the cowry in our analysis, much as the overrulers and administrators of Buhaya did. Cowries were clearly not the only Interlacustrine currency, but the generation of colonial moneys did fix on this form in their efforts to transform its significance and to remake money.

It is important to note that cowries circulated in the Lakes Region at the end of the nineteenth century not as individual shells, but tied in a set of strung bundles. Ten single strands, each threaded with one hundred cowries, were tied together to form a 1,000-cowry-bundle that was transacted for monetary purposes, a form of money that appears to have been unique to Interlacustrine Africa of this time (Rehse 1910: chapter 6; Koponen 1988: 119). There is also reason to believe that these imposing bundles were recognized as single units of currency (Figure 2.1). For example in the late 1960s an older man from Bunyoro, where strung cowries had once been a standard currency, compared the value of rupees and shillings—the colonial currencies that succeeded the cowry—to this thousand-*ensimbi* unit (Uzoigwe 1974: 449); Rapports Annuels of the White Fathers indicate that royal duties on trade goods like bark cloth, ivories, and occasionally slaves were exacted in units of 1,000 cowries; and eventually bridewealth (*amakula*) was payable in these standardized measures.

Of course, if cowries could be strung together in this way, they could be unstrung and restrung, as well. This much is clear from the use of single strands of cowries as amulets, nine strings of cowries as propitiatory objects, and even individual shells in divination. The practice of bundling long strings of cowries, and the understanding of this bundle as a single standard unit, is important because it suggests that these smaller cowry groupings need to be seen in some relation to this unitary bundle. To use cowries as currencies, amulets, and offerings in the precolonial Haya world one must either collect together or else unravel a single totality. In other words, the multiple practices

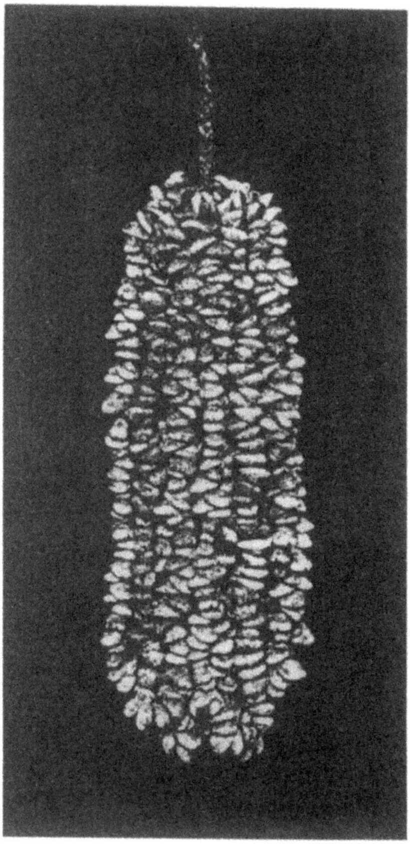

Figure 2.1. Ten strands of 100 cowries were tied together to form a 1,000-cowry bundle. These bundles circulated as single units of currency around the Lakes.

in which cowries were transacted always entailed a relationship between units made up of component elements, wholes and parts.

The relationship of wholes to parts in cowry bundles is significant because these formal features of the currency unit also appear to have been pragmatic dimensions of monetized actions. The cowry bundle was a constructed—and deconstructed—object, one that had to be created through social practices. Printing bills or minting coins are equally social activities that impress upon money the authority of the state or other agency that produces them. The compilation of Interlacustrine cowry bundles, I suggest, not only exemplifies the power of the sovereign that legitimates the currency, it also iconically reveals something about the character of wealth and property that is evaluated in terms of this standard. The Haya verb for tying strings of cowries, according to Rehse, was *okutunga*, and *okutungula*, its reversive, meant to untie a string (Rehse 1910: chapter 12). This verb may indicate connections between cowries and the Swahili caravans that were their sources of origins, as *kutunga* is a Swahili verb meaning to arrange, or string together (but applied only to cowries in Buhaya, which is not the case in Swahili). Further, the word *omutungi*, the nominative formed from the verb *okutunga*, was the term used to describe a rich man in the Haya vernacular of the late nineteenth century, as it is in the present day. To be rich, in so many words, is to be well strung, to be one who can not only amass but also assemble such complex wholes. The cowry bundle was, therefore, both a standard by which to measure the value of other forms of material wealth (as money) and a measure of the social wealth of their owner (as an *omutungi*). This is a central characteristic of money more generally, to which I will return.

I would further suggest that the composite produced by this process of stringing had intrinsically collective dimensions in Haya practice and experience. This is in an inference I would draw from understandings of wealth Haya men and women discussed with me some eighty years after Rehse's observations. Cowries, as I have indicated, are rarely—if ever—available in contemporary Buhaya, and I never saw or even heard mention of the large strung cowry bundles once used as money. Nonetheless, a rich man was still described as an *omutungi*, and *okutunga* is still a recognized and meaningful term. I have discussed the significance of *okutunga* elsewhere (Weiss 1996a: 126), as a process of creating wealth as a kind of "endowment" or "bestowal":

> The meaning of bestowal is more complex than simply giving (*okuha*, to give). A Muhaya . . . once explained their differences to me in this way: "If I give you something [*ninkuha ekintu*], maybe a hoe, or a bucket, on any day I can say to you, "Return that thing to me that I gave you." But if I say, "I endow you!" (*Nakutunga*!), that is yours completely. I can't say, 'Return it to me.' And you, if it is your wealth, you can take it and endow another (*nomutunga ondijo*)."
>
> This kind of wealth, and the act of endowing is also commonly used by royals and commoners, men and women alike, to describe the passage of land from seniors to juniors, as well as the presentation and provision of a wife for a husband. This connection of affinity to processes of land devolution, as well as the relation between receiving and endowing that is indicated by the verb *okutunga*, suggests that wealth, and wealth production are generative dimensions of social relations. That is, wealth is an objectification that embodies the reciprocal relation between the act of bestowal that creates it, and the future acts of bestowal this makes possible.

There is some evidence from the early years of the twentieth century that suggests wealth was similarly understood as a form of generative bestowal. The White Fathers from Kagondo, for example, wrote of a royal official who accepted a farm from a king and note his claim that he preferred "*kutungwa* mukama que du chef" (to be endowed by the king rather than the [regional] chief; Diare du Poste, Kagondo: 14 September 1906). Oral testimonies from the 1980s confirm this understanding. Landholders often affirmed their claims to land by describing how an ancestor had been "endowed by the king"—*akatungwa n'omukama*—with the farm his descendants continued to inhabit. These recognitions of value created by acts of bestowal, past and especially present, draw attention to the *temporal* qualities of this kind of material wealth, as wealth created as an endowment concretizes a connection between past and future acts of bestowal. *Okutunga*, then, produces wealth by configuring a pattern of social relations, not merely between affines, or patrons and clients, but between persons engaged over time in the acts of endowing one another, whose continuous acts are necessary to the establishment of this form of value. Bestowal both derives from and further generates the wealth-making potential of these agents; as Guyer puts it, such forms of giving "promote a dynamic of growth" (Guyer 1993: 257). *Eitunga*, the material wealth produced by this pattern of bestowal, is therefore simultaneously an objective form, a concrete embodiment of wealth,[8] and the ongoing practical organization and production of social ties.

Let me make it clear that I am not suggesting the metaphorical projection of ideas about valuables onto ideas about exchange partners, that is, that just as cowries were once strung and bundled together, endowed wealth now "strings" together successive temporal acts and relations. If there are any resonances between Haya understandings of *okutunga* as a wealth-creating process at the beginning and the end of the twentieth century these seem, instead, to indicate a shared sense of the composite qualities of wealth, and a further recognition of the ways in which this organized composition invests valued objects with generative possibilities. As a consequence of the nexus of relationships coordinated in and manifested by these forms of material wealth, an abstract, generalizable potential for action is achieved. The core semantic and material attributes of "bestowal" across all of these forms and relations, then, have to do with expanding temporal potentials through the creation of composite currencies (Munn 1986). *Okutunga*, in both historical eras, is never simply a means to accumulate an expanding volume of things, or an ever greater quantity of valuables. Rather, those who assemble these totalities of compound parts realize the potential to *transform* that wealth through the wider array of transaction these composite forms make possible (Guyer 1993). The Haya man who strung and bundled cowries might have converted this bundled unit into bark cloth, iron, salt, coffee, etc., just as the recipient endowed with *eitunga* acquires the capacity to endow absolutely anyone he chooses (and not simply "return that thing" to whoever gave it him). In fashioning a whole out of a mere mass of constituent parts, parts drawn from a diversity of contexts (the single shells and strands derived perhaps from a series of marriages, a healing procedure, or as a royal gift; an object that has been bestowed, such as a hoe or a shirt, may once have been purchased, acquired as payment for labor, or received in marriage exchanges), Haya men and women created forms of wealth that would have transcended any of these particular contexts. These valuables had a qualitatively different potential to acquire, attract, and engender yet more wealth. Such wholes-from-parts further allow those who control this kind of material wealth to enjoy the social recognition of an *omutungi*, and so these composite forms also become measures of estimable social wealth. The agency enabled by these totality-creating acts thus define both the potentialities of the valuables produced and the value of the social persons who deploy them.

The qualities made possible through processes of composition might provide us with insights into the character, not only of wealth and value in the Haya context, but of property and possession. When cowries are bundled, or objects are bestowed in the ways described, what kind of *possession* do they become? These issues are especially relevant to our understanding of colonialism in Buhaya, and in East Africa more generally. For colonial officials here were thoroughly and repeatedly concerned with the "problem" of property in their attempts to establish "freehold tenure" (especially over land), and clearly saw private property as a cornerstone of the "rational self-interests" that would promote civilization and capitalism (see Shipton 1992). But was—and is—the kind of material wealth understood in Haya communities as *eitunga*, wealth composed and transacted through ongoing collective relations and practices, a kind of individual property? Does wealth become a personal possession simply because it "is yours completely," as my neighbor put it?

I have argued that Haya wealth created and held under these specific terms has explicitly collective dimensions, that it articulates past and future actions and persons in a material form of value. In doing so, however, it also acquires new potentials that appear to be liberated from the constraints of social others. The object opens on to an expanded field of possibilities, possibilities not bound by obligatory returns for specific goods, or to specific persons. The freedom that accrues to these valuables further becomes an aspect of the person who controls this wealth. As in the case of private property, it seems as though a profound identification that is highly individualized is established between persons and their wealth—in spite of Bahaya's apparent insistence on this connection's collective foundation.

Perhaps there is really no paradox here; after all even private property is a social category and product. What is important to recognize for purposes of historicizing these relations is that, in the Haya case, the establishment of this individualized identification changes the character of the objects themselves. Cowries strung together become singular *units* of currency, the things that one owns become *wealth* when they are bestowed. These personalized identifications and qualitative potentials, then, do not apply uniformly to all "possessions" in the way that both colonial categories of private property[9] and colonial visions of money as a medium of "unconditional interchangeability" and an "internal uniformity that makes each piece exchangeable for another"

(Simmel [1900] 1978: 441) presume. Rather, they are provisional conditions of subject-object relations that can come to exemplify certain abstract capacities and individualized attachments when objects are configured as totalizing, generative forms through the efficacies of social practice.

WEALTH IN COFFEE

Before moving on to an account of the historical relations between cowries and currencies that were introduced at the turn of the twentieth century, I want to draw our attention to some important parallels between the material wealth of cowries, and especially cowry bundles as I have just described them, and a related feature of coffee as a valued medium in Buhaya. At the time when cowry bundles were in use, coffee was cultivated by means of vegetative propagation. This is a technique that not only permits a scrupulous control over and delimitation on the extensive planting of coffee trees (as opposed to propagation from seeds, which can be easily concealed and broadly distributed), but also rigorously grounds the continuous cultivation of coffee in collective sources. Coffee's (re)generative potential was anchored in collective action. This is demonstrated by the complex of practices that attended the planting of new coffee stocks in the precolonial era. Each coffee grower had to provide witnesses who could attest to his authorized cultivation. The supplier of a cutting, generally a person of high rank, would act as a witness as to the source of the coffee; and further, the cutting itself was never planted by the farmer of the coffee, but by another man (a friend or neighbor) who could act as a witness as to its proper planting.

The use of cuttings as opposed to seedlings, a technique that leads to the development of multiple root systems out of single branches, ensures the connections between new trees and parent stocks, as these new trees retain their physical connections to their sources of origins. This method facilitates the careful regulation of a royally controlled commodity. All of these practical techniques plainly emphasize the attachments of generational growth and iconically manifest the fact that no coffee tree has an independent existence. As in the case of stringing cowry bundles, and "bestowing" material wealth (as *eitunga*) more generally, producing each coffee tree is a process that entails the collocation of spatial and especially temporal relations.

I have further argued that the collective formulation of "wealth" in its many varieties in Buhaya, past and present, is ultimately expressed through highly personalized and individualistic identifications and attachments. The category of "wealth," *eitunga*, is an example of the way that Haya sociocultural practice characteristically activates relations between people in order to make explicit what differentiates them (see Strathern 1991: 588; Weiss 1997b). Material wealth, such as cowries, farmland, and affinal ties, as my discussion indicates, provided some of the more effective means of demonstrating both these relations and differentiations at the beginning of the twentieth century. It is also clear that coffee trees, as crucial elements of royal power, exemplified these dynamic possibilities. These trees were plainly embedded in the relational nexuses of political hierarchy and vegetative propagation; yet these relationships conjoin to create an object that is profoundly individuated. The Haya man who planted a coffee tree in the nineteenth century planted a concrete incarnation of his own "life force" (*amagala*), an entity whose death foretold his own. Moreover, as objects that created social connections, coffee trees could do so in individualizing ways. For example, a man could designate an individual coffee tree to be bequeathed as an inheritance to any heir he chose—including members of a clan other than his own—a practice that persists to this day. Even though she could not inherit land until the 1950s, an elder daughter, or other prominent female clansmen could be named the heir of a specific coffee tree at the turn of the last century (Rehse 1910: chapter 15).

These practices indicate that coffee trees were means of creating generational connections, but connections that were forged out of the *detachability* of these trees from a larger estate, and from the social obligations situated in place. "Rooted" in ongoing collective practice, coffee trees are understood as separate and separable entities, unique configurations of power and value. Coffee trees were—and in many respects still are—wealth that originates in, but can be freed from, the moorings of the attachments of social existence, and through that freedom they provide greater potential. In these ways it is clear that a fundamental aspect of the intensely personalized associations between coffee trees and their owners was the *agency* that these trees provided for their owners, an agency realized in the capacity to hold these trees apart as forms of material wealth whose ultimate disposition could be determined by the will of their possessor. Like the other forms of *eitunga*/wealth, already considered, coffee trees were recognized as powerful, singular sources of personal identity and independence, expressive of an individual's life as well as a means of asserting individual potency. To anticipate Marx's comments on money (discussed below) coffee trees were both a form of material value and a measure of the social power of the person who possessed them.

CONTRAST AND COMMENSURATION

These broad parallels between cowries and coffee as exemplifications of Haya material wealth illuminate some important problems central to much contemporary theorizing about value. Both coffee trees and cowry bundles are totalities composed of component elements. The bundle or tree that embodies "wealth" has a potential greater than the sum of these elements. Such wholes are detachable and mobile and can be passed on to others as an endowment. Generative of wealth, as well as measures of the wealth of the social persons who receive and bestow them, these material forms are exemplary icons of value-producing processes. The elements combined in these forms also must be understood to contribute to the social constitution of Haya value. I have argued, for example, that coffee cherries offered to powerful persons—which may include honored guest, affines, or spirits—carry a particular form of value. The value of coffee in such transactional settings depends upon, but also instantiates, hierarchical contrast. So, for example, one offers such persons *always* and *only* "a bit of coffee"—*akamwani*—a usage that diminishes the donor in the context of the wider framework of offering. Value, in these instances, is defined as a relational contrast, as a *difference* invoked in the relationship the offering, or conveyance instantiates (Strathern 1988; Foster 1990). It is not surprising also to find cowry shells, unstrung from bundles, used in similar ways. Individual shells could be offered, like coffee cherries, in propitiation to spirits, and shells were sewn into the regalia of spirit mediums or thrown in divination (Rehse 1910; Cesard 1937). In all of these practices what is emphasized is the *singularity* of the individual shells, their distinctiveness in time and place (upon which divinatory insight depends). As singular offerings both coffee and cowries highlight a hierarchical contrast between meager prestations and their potent returns.

In addition to these oppositional forms of value, though, it is also the case that both within these contexts of offering and in a much wider set of transactional practices in which coffee participates, other modes of value can be formulated and generated. Coffee can be offered to specify a difference in identities; but the very term *akamwani*, "a bit of coffee," is also a *category* that is appropriate to a much wider range of Haya prestations. It describes more than "gifts to gods," or even gifts to powerful (even godlike) men (cf. Gregory 1982). For, in the Haya context—today and in the past—*any* offering, a cow, a hoe, or even several thousand shillings, may be presented and described as *akamwani*. The category, then, transcends—or simply bypasses—the contrast of gifts and commodities. All objects are potentially subject to revaluation in these terms, as even marketed goods are routinely offered as *akamwani*.

The applicability of the category "coffee" to a wide array of objects deployed in a variety of transactions also raises question of another dimension of value. Value may be concretized by coffee not only as contrast, but also as *commensurability*. That is, coffee is a symbolic medium that permits the value, or values, of different objects (livestock, bridewealth, money, etc.) to be expressed in its terms, and thereby compared to—or made commensurate with—one another. Coffee in Haya social practice was and remains a privileged objectification of the commensurability of values. This capacity, shared by now obsolete cowry bundle currencies, is important. It suggests that coffee and cowries can be understood as media that may conjoin expressions of value based on both contrast and commensurability, difference and equivalence, forms of value that are often felt to be characteristic of distinct regimes of exchange (cf. Gregory 1982; Foster 1990). From a historical point of view, the capacity of coffee, in particular, to express commensurate values is especially significant, as it permits us to raise comparative questions about money and coffee within a changing regional economy and society. Both coffee and money in the region would seem to permit values among different objects to realize their common expression in a distinctive, collectively recognized medium. Coffee, like money, might then be understood as a kind of currency, a circulating standard by means of which objects may be converted into one another.

When commensurability is discussed with reference to monetary systems in many contemporary approaches to value, it is often used to describe the capacity of money to "level" differential values, to reduce the qualitative differences between phenomena to a quantitative expression. Such a capacity is often cited as a bane—or potentially a liberating innovation—of commercialization (Parry and Bloch 1989; Simmel [1900] 1978). But the history of the relations between cowries, coffee, and other currencies in the Lakes Region of the late nineteenth century, and crucially between different *kinds* of money and markets and coffee in this era, suggests, as I have already shown, that commensurability can be understood and organized in different ways for different ends. Money, and its symbolic analogs, is thus best understood as a cultural object imbued with qualitative as well as quantitative values, and potentially subject, therefore, to agentive alterations of its meanings (Weiss 1997b).

In the Haya case, material wealth might be seen to conjoin aspects of both contrast and commensuration, relationships that I would argue are *each* important to an adequate understanding of how value is objectified in these cultural and historical contexts. There is and has long been a market for valuables in Buhaya, a framework that allows the value of objects to be compared, and further to be expressed in terms of specific common evaluative media. At the same time, what makes such commensurations possible, and what permits a given medium to express commensurability, are the sociocultural processes through which significant differences are elaborated on and objectified. Haya material wealth like cowry bundles, bestowed goods, and coffee are forms that incorporate differences, conjoining diverse elements into singular objects, objects that stand apart and become imbued with distinct possibilities. Foremost among these possibilities is commensurability itself. The strung cowry bundle can be converted into—and further serves to express the value of—an array of goods. The bestowed possession can be bestowed in turn to whomever its possessor desires. Coffee grown from royal stocks can be transacted with divinities and ancestral powers in return for extraordinarily powerful capacities, or be used, as *akamwani*, "a mere bit of coffee," to evaluate other offerings. Those peculiarly fabricated valuables that objectify relationships of significant differences thus come to assume the capacity to express commensurability. This potential for the interconversion of values, so prominently associated with currencies, is not a general feature of subject-object relations in Buhaya—of all forms of "property," "ownership," or "possession"—but it is a quality that can be realized and made operative in Haya practice. It is also a feature of these practices that was to undergo significant transformations as different currencies, novel understandings of wealth, and new regimes of value—projects all intimately connected with changes in the nature of coffee—entered this context under European colonialism.

THE VALUE OF NEW CURRENCIES: 1898–1908

In January of 1898, almost a full decade after Bismark's *Reich* interceded to transform German East Africa from a private trading company into an official colony, the colonial administration in Bukoba introduced a new currency, the Indian rupee (Diare du Poste, Kashozi: 3 January 1898). Soon after, and not coincidentally, the administration imposed an annual hut tax of three rupees (Diare du Poste, Kashozi: 9 May 1898). Clearly an effort was made to use these measures to assert the tangible hegemony of a new colonial regime and to stimulate those economic practices that were part and parcel of that hegemony. As the governor of Bukoba himself stated, these first taxes were designed "to spur Africans to enter the cash economy, particularly as European caravan or plantation employees" (Austen 1968: 54). At the same time, it is important to recognize that while these measures may have been intended to buttress the innovations of a cash economy, as well as an innovative form of cash, the tax system itself did not require the use of rupees, or even of money. Hut taxes were payable in rupees *or* cowries, well into the first decade of the twentieth century;[10] and mission records from throughout the region, from Kashozi in the North through Rubya in the South, give the distinct impression that taxes were most frequently paid not in any kind of money, but by corvée labor. Indeed, payments of all kinds continued to be made in cowries for at least a decade after the introduction of the rupee, and cash transactions seem to have been limited to interactions with colonial institutions—that is, the payment of fines and taxes using currencies received from such authorities for labor and other services. In this early period, then, money clearly did not come to pervade Haya sociocultural activity, in spite of concentrated measures taken to promote it.[11]

This apparent marginality of the rupee notwithstanding, it would be a mistake to see the introduction of this currency as a complete nonstarter. While rupees may not have circulated all that widely in these early years, there is, nonetheless, strong evidence to suggest that the possibilities of payments rendered in such a novel currency—to say nothing of the administrative practices in which the rupee figured—did much to transform Haya understandings of wealth. As I have already indicated, cowry shell bundles did serve as a measure of wealth and as a medium that enabled its accumulation and circulation. Rupees, then, did not introduce these possibilities, but I will argue that they did articulate with extant currency forms in ways that led to a reconfiguration of material wealth and a new consciousness of value. The relations between persons and objects, their organization and characteristic qualities, as well as Haya men's and women's understandings of the processes that generated these relations were transformed. Proof of this transformation is demonstrated by the fact that this exotic currency did become an everyday necessity for Haya men and women, so much so that the White Fathers' Annual Report from 1909—a few years *before* coffee planting became compulsory—could describe their "dominant religion" as "rupees" (Rapports Annuels—Bukoba, 1909–1910: 266–267).

What did the reconfiguration of wealth entail, and what made rupees the appropriate vehicle of this process? Could wealth be objectified and assembled in the composite forms already discussed by means of rupees, or was the character of Haya wealth, its potentialities and trajectories, undone by this currency and the colonial processes that animated it? Considering these questions requires an exploration of the place that coffee—and cash cropping—played in remaking Haya understandings and concretizations of material wealth. To begin with, though, I want to examine some of the formal properties of rupees and the symbolic import that these properties might have had. It is worth belaboring the obvious to point out that rupees were metal coins. This fact was certainly made note of by Haya taxpayers, and seems to have contributed in at least some measure to the intractability of this money.

Communities in Buhaya had been smelting iron and producing iron implements since the sixth century B.C., and there appear to have been close connections between iron forging and kingship, as well as iron tools and monetary forms since at least the 1600s (Schmidt 1978). Iron hoes functioned as a kind of trade currency in much of precolonial East Africa (Koponen 1988), and Buhaya was an important source of iron tools in the Lakes Region. These tools do not, however, appear to have served as currencies in Buhaya, but they were clearly a part of important exchange practices. Foremost among their uses was as elements of bridewealth. Many Haya men and women in the 1980s clearly recalled a time when hoes (*enfuka*) were included in marriage payments; even today, the bride's family will stipulate what they expect (usually in the form of cash equivalents) in terms of a set of recognized categories (e.g., a list of requested items might read a goat for the bride's father [500 shillings], a sheep for her father's father [500 shillings], sheets and blankets for her mother [250 shillings]), and one of these categories is sure to be hoes for the bride. These iron implements (at least according to contemporary accounts) were explicitly intended as compensation to the bride's family for the loss of her labor and as an acknowledgment (perhaps, according to some, even as a reminder to the bride) of the labor that she would perform for her husband's clan.

These sorts of hoes, reserved exclusively for women's agricultural activities (Rehse 1910: chapter 7; Cesard 1937: 109), also figured in another set of Haya transactions (see Figure 2.2). I quote in full the daily diary entry from Kashozi for 27 July 1903:

> Among the curiosities of the demonic houses [spirit huts . . .] are found cowries and small hoes. It is not uncommon to find these objects in the same hut; the hoe is usually in the middle of the cowries, strung together on a small stick, flanking the hoe.
>
> Certain natives have the custom of sacrificing a hoe at the death of a household head.

The juxtaposition of strung cowries with hoes—of the very same kind offered as bridewealth and used by farming women—as offerings to divinities indicates that they might share certain capabilities. Without commentary on what are now obsolete practices, it is certainly difficult to determine which attributes of this pair are being invoked by this relation, or indeed the nature of their connection. There do seem to be certain parallels in these objects, which warrant some speculative attention. Hoes are received in bridewealth specifically as compensation for (or at least recognition of) a daughter's activities. Other elements of Haya bridewealth are described today, not as *compensation* for future losses, but as *thanks* for past parental and familial actions that enabled their daughter to be raised into a mature woman. Hoes differ from these other objects, then, not only because they are specifically paired to the bride herself, but because they emphasize her embodied *potential*, an as yet unrealized possibility that is being transferred to others. This concern with objectifying an undetermined potential, as opposed to an acknowledgment of that which has already been definitively achieved, indicates one possible similarity between cowry bundles and these iron hoes. Hoes, however, are unlike cowry bundles in that they do not have an infinitely generalizable potential, but rather are directly linked to the specifically gendered capabilities of a particular type of agricultural activity. In this sense they are clearly not currency—which undoubtedly made them appropriate to bridewealth exchanges that eschew market-pricing mechanisms. They concretize unrealized, but clearly and relatively narrowly defined, practical capacities.

While they do objectify an as yet unfulfilled possibility, these hoes could not in themselves be defined as "wealth," *eitunga*, in the way that cowry bundles can. They do, though, stand in an important relationship to such embodiments of value. Indeed, a bride whose marriage is facilitated by the transmission of these hoes *is* frequently described in Haya discourse, by both men and women, as this kind of "wealth." *Okutunga* was—and remains—the

Figure 2.2. Hoes used for bridewealth and sacrifice.

term commonly used to describe the process of providing a husband with a wife; he has had wealth bestowed upon him. To provide hoes, or bridewealth of any kind, may make such wealth possible, but it is by no means an *equivalence* for the wealth that a bride *is*. A husband does *not* bestow wealth on his father-in-law. In fact the objects given in bridewealth are colloquially referred to as "things," *ebintu*. While this category is not as generic and homogenizing as it may sound (although "things" are given as bridewealth, not just any "things" will do) it does serve to differentiate "things" from the "wealth" that a bride embodies. The category of things unambiguously diminishes the character and value of bridewealth with respect to the value of the bride. Hoes are mere things that, nonetheless, can be made to acquire value, if not the full status of wealth. They are distinct from other marriage payments, as I have indicated, in their direct association with the agency and potential of the bride herself. A father who acquires hoes in bridewealth is thereby able to give evidence of the fact that he has successfully nurtured and matured[12] a marriageable and capable daughter, and has further been able to provide her productive potential to others. A household head thus demonstrates the viable generative capacities of his own household by his abilities to produce and then bestow a new and *separate* generative ability (i.e., that of the daughter/bride) that will contribute to establishing a new household. And it is this characteristically Haya reproductive process that is iconically substantiated in iron hoes.

This understanding of these tools as means of materializing ongoing regenerative processes illuminates their prominence in sacrificial rites—and further indicates some possible implications for the use of metallic coins as a measure of value in Haya social practice. Note that hoes, received by men as bridewealth and used by women in their agricultural activities, are "sacrificed" upon the death of the household head. The nature of this sacrifice is unclear from historical records. Reports from early in the twentieth century indicate that Haya mortuary practice typically included the destruction of a range of personal possessions associated with the deceased (Cesard 1939). Most specifically, hard, durable objects like calabashes and—prototypically—hearth stones, objects associated with the creation of the household as a place of food provisioning (and, thus, social viability and growth) were destroyed upon the death of the household head. Here, then, an implement that displays the generative capacity of the household head and one that further evinces his transmission of such capacity to others (i.e., in the form of daughters for whom hoes were received), is intimately bound up with the life span of this person. What is crucial, though, is that this icon of these powers is removed from circulation (if not actually destroyed) upon his death. In effect the hoe is the manifest personal potential of the deceased, and so it remains identified with him in perpetuity, never to be transacted again.

The significance of this withdrawal from the world of transaction is made clearer when considering the range of objects deployed in Haya social practice, and the different trajectories they had. Any number of possessions were, in fact, made to *endure* beyond the life of their possessor. Coffee trees, for example, were not uprooted when their owner died, in spite of the strong identifications between trees and persons. Rather, they became media for forging transgenerational connections, for "bestowing" wealth upon kinsmen and others. Earlier, I described this feature of "wealth" as its detachability, the fact that it could be made to circulate apart from the particular nexus of goods, exchange relations, and social obligations that produced them. These iron hoes might, in contrast, be seen to have been relatively nondetachable. They did not circulate with greater potential, but rather signified both the successful *fulfillment* of the household head's potency (i.e., the fact that he had raised a married daughter), and (through that marriage) the reestablishment of a new and *different* potential in another household. From the perspective of male household heads, it is *daughters*, as future wives and mothers, that were "detached" as "wealth" from their natal home; hoes, which merely acknowledge that detachment, could never exemplify such value. Hoes, therefore, were part of a *discontinuous* but crucially regenerative cycle of Haya sociality, embodying both the culmination of one household's powers, which is simultaneously the foundation of a distinct household's viability.[13]

What might the implications of these late-nineteenth-century understandings of metal implements be for the introduction of a metal currency? While I have little direct evidence to indicate exactly how this relationship was realized or experienced for Bahaya, I would like to raise certain possibilities drawing on the arguments already raised. I have asserted that metal tools—or at least women's iron hoes—were vehicles of Haya sociocultural transaction made to concretize critical dimensions of personal agency. The agency of an effective household head or an agriculturally productive woman was realized and expressed through the exchange relations mediated by these tools themselves. Perhaps counterintuitively, however, I am further suggesting that while these tools were recognized as objectified forms of value, they were nonetheless *not* forms of "wealth" in the ways that I have detailed this Haya category. Such valued items were closely identified with their owners, and perhaps even substantiated aspects of their being (so much is at least suggested by their ritual possibilities). Yet, they did not secure the sorts of potential that items (or relations) of wealth—like land, trees, or affinity itself—have long been able to provide in Buhaya. Their attachments to the household head at death, their acknowledgment of specifically gendered status and action, their place in a particular nexus of exchange relations, all of these identifications were aspects these objects' value—but they also clearly *delimited* their possibilities to these concrete and determinate contexts. Their value was not generalizable to other transactions or to further cycles of exchange.

For purposes of the present analyses, I am arguing that the strength of these attachments, and hence the *restrictions* on the potential of these objects, meant that iron hoes did not circulate as a *currency* in Buhaya in the nineteenth century. Unlike cowries—and even coffee trees—these tools might have been freely transmitted by their owner to whomever he, or she, chose. Yet they would *not* have permitted the commensuration of objects by allowing them to be evaluated in terms of hoes. Iron hoes were valued items of exchange, but possessing them did not enable their owners to gain access to a diversity of goods, relationships, and similar benefits. They were not, I am surmising, imbued with the potential for action that characterized Haya currencies of this earlier time. The place of iron implements in these offerings, then, suggests that they are *partial* forms of wealth; and the "curious" ancestral shrines described by the White Fathers show how this partiality was *com-*

plemented by the strung cowries to evoke a greater totality. This conjunction of objects in these shrines served to transform the *fulfillment* of a past life into an unrealized regenerative *potential* for the future.

In view of these possibilities and limitations, and given the ways that Haya notions of wealth indexed complex relations between people and things, how might rupees have been attended to? What kind of "property" did they promote, what new actions and relations did they make possible, or perhaps require? Did coins embody the partial and delimited qualities of iron tools or the wealth-laden, detachable potential of currencies?

I have already noted that cowries and corvée labor continued to coexist with rupees as forms of payment and compensation well after the introduction of this colonial money. It is difficult to say whether this coexistence represented a reluctance on the part of Haya to accept rupees as media of value. Given the intentions of German officials, introducing rupees in order to foster Haya wage labor and their further integration into the wider regional political economy of the colony, it seems unlikely that the administration would have happily tolerated the use of cowries, which could be attained outside of these "economic" activities. It does appear to be the case that rupees could be and were used as a currency in this early period. They could be used to make tax payments, be received as wages, and serve as a medium of local and long-distance trade. Certainly the colonial regime did its best to promote the use of rupees, not merely as a special purpose object acquired from colonial officials (for wage labor, portage, piece work, etc.) in order to pay those same officials taxes, but as a generalizable medium of commerce. Indeed, colonial agents, missionaries among them, attempted to establish equivalencies between rupees and cowries and other transacted objects, and further to extend the applicability of "price" as measured in terms of currency values to an ever expanding domain of goods and relationships, most of which had never before been evaluated in market terms.

Throughout the first decade of the twentieth century, cattle, land, and particularly bridewealth were subject to continuous efforts, especially on the part of the White Fathers, to establish clear and stable prices, all of which could be expressed in rupees.[14] In effect, these colonial practices not only encouraged the use of a newly authorized currency, and the attendant expansion of "commerce," they also introduced distinct cultural processes of valuation. The kinds of equivalencies made possible through these pricing mechanisms, the sorts of interconversions they enabled, and the ways in which they concretized the quantifiable *uniformity* of a person's relations to his objects (and, indeed, to other persons—husbands to wives, affines to one another, landholders to their descendants) would all have had a destablizing effect on Haya practical understandings of value in general, and of "wealth" in particular.

This destabilization, though, may have been challenged in Haya social practice. As I have shown, rupees did not simply come to pervade Haya cultural, or even commercial life, but stood in uneasy tension with other media of value in this decade. The perseverance of these alternatives may well have served to contain and delimit the spread of these currencies, and of the perverse subject-object relations they sustained. Again, a bit of speculation may be in order to substantiate this claim. One use of rupees, noted by the oft puzzled White Fathers of Kagondo, provides a possible insight into the value of coins in this period and the sorts of counter reconfiguration of value to which Haya men and women subjected these tokens. It is recorded that "Half-rupees flood into the mission. These last had been exchanged for 50 rps [cents?] the half-rupee. The tax collectors do not want half-rupees. They claim it is an order from Bukoba!" (Diare du Poste, Kagondo: 20 March 1908). This offhand observation suggests that as late as 1908—a full decade after rupees and taxes were introduced—rupees were understood by taxpayers and tax collectors alike (who by this point in the decade were mission-educated Haya clerks—see Rapports Annuels—Bwanja, 1908–1909: 238, and the next chapter) as material forms whose value was not readily partible into quantifiably equivalent units. Single rupees were valuable because they were just that, singular objects.[15] Their value could not be decomposed into component elements that produced an additive set of objects equal in value to the rupee. Perhaps this refusal to adopt the half-rupee was merely the caprice of exacting tax collectors, perhaps it was a more routine feature of the use of half-rupees. The fact that the mission was "flooded" with them does indicate that Haya men and women did not readily accept them in transactions among themselves. In any case, this opposition to half-rupees was a practice that seems to have *made sense* to Haya men and women at the time.

This reluctance to make use of sub-denominations exemplifies, I would suggest, an innovation in Haya modes of valuation. There is neither a continuation of prior understandings of currency units nor an easy accommodation to colonizing visions of property and price in Haya practices at the turn of the twentieth century. Rupees were clearly implicated in a field of emerging equivalencies, and, like cowries before (and beside) them, they embodied an abstract, qualitative potential (see Marx's comments on the "boundlessness" characteristic of money forms addressed below). Like cowry bundles, rupees expressed this potency by their singular character, by the fact that they were discreet units of value, detachable from specific relations and counters with other goods, and "free" to attract other values. But unlike these currencies, rupees were not—at this historical juncture—forms of "wealth." The units they instantiated were explicitly *not* composite forms, wholes made up of parts. Haya practice—or at least their taxpaying—purposefully undermined the implication that rupees could be treated as such totalities Rupees do not seem to have incorporated the socio-temporal connections essential to Haya wealth.

I further suggest that this innovative form of currency as *non-wealth* relates precisely to the kinds of uniform equivalencies that colonial institutions attempted to establish. If rupees were to be currencies, they would not be permitted to diminish the value of wealth objects. Like iron, then, to which these coins were explicitly compared in the Haya vernacular (early accounts [Diare du Poste, Rubya: 28 May 1908] report that coinage was described as *byome*, Haya for iron ore; and see the epigraph to this chapter for a telling commentary), rupees could embody value, but could never be the *equivalent* of the powerful objects and relations—entities like affinal relations or divine strength—laden with generative potential, for which they were transacted. Rupees were prevented from creating these equivalencies by withholding them from precisely the kinds of pricing mechanism—15–20 rupees for a cow or goat, 40 rupees for a "slave girl," one to one and a half rupees per tree—that were never willingly adopted by Bahaya, but which colonial officials worked to impose and enforce. In Appadurai's terms, Haya men and women took pains to "enclave" certain objects (Appadurai 1986: 23–25). What is noteworthy here is that money itself is significantly restricted in its social flows. These colonial coins were remade in Haya practice (as they remade Haya practice itself) into currencies that mitigated the leveling effect of pricing. Introduced as tokens of exchange, rupees were also tokens of a competing consciousness of value, a consciousness that was transformed as it became commonplace.

COINAGE AND COFFEE

The transforming consciousness of value that these currency innovations reveal suggests that "wealth" and "price" were quite distinct values in Haya men's and women's experience early in the twentieth century. Neither opposed to commercial enterprise and the possibility of transacting goods for money, nor willing to permit all objects and relations to be subject to the same standards of evaluation, Haya communities continued to use new moneys in unexpected ways. This chapter has sketched a picture of tremendous variation in object valuation in Buhaya. In the nineteenth century, different currencies had different potential to be transacted against particular kinds of goods. Standardized units of currency, I have argued, were themselves composed of separable elements that exhibited their own distinct forms of value. Haya social practice has long been interested in commercial transaction, even in the production of goods—foremost among them coffee—explicitly intended for trade. Yet Bahaya have also made concerted efforts to challenge the imposition of single uniform standards of exchange often thought to be necessary to "rational" commerce. Clearly there was an uneven range of relationships between these very different currencies.

This very unevenness challenges some commonplace notions about the intrinsic abstractness, and non-qualitative properties of money (in spite of the fact that the use of multiple currencies and the issuing of moneys appropriate to different forms of transaction has historically characterized our own society—see Zelizer 1994). Simmel's assertion that money's "quality consists exclusively in its quantity" (Simmel [1978] 1990: 259) describes both a folk wisdom and a foundational tenet of monetarist economic theory. It should be clear, though, that such an understanding may not be of much use when it comes to assessing monetary systems like the one under consideration. In Buhaya, at least, *qualitative* differences between quantitative measures are clearly recognized. Moreover, the abstraction of currencies, their lack of intrinsic characteristics other than the capacity to express the relationship between different goods, does not seem to be a feature of a money like cowries that could be used for so many extra-commercial purposes. Indeed, it might be difficult to distinguish in any particular instance of exchange whether the cowries transacted are an expression of price, or if the cowries themselves are less a measure of *price* than the actual *goods* being purchased. Again, the "ornamental" uses of cowries cannot be seen as refractory to their economic significance when these categories might well be conflated in a given commercial act.

Marx's discussion of currencies offers a more subtle account, insisting at once on the quantitative and qualitative dimensions of any such form:

> Just as every qualitative difference between commodities is extinguished in money, so money on its side, like the radical leveler that it is, does away with all distinctions. But money itself is a commodity, an external object, capable of becoming the private property of any individual. Thus social power becomes the private power of private persons. (Marx 1906: 148–149)

As both an instrument for the measurement of other commodities' worth, *and* itself a commodity, the very form of money, its existence as an "external object" concretely embodying difference, allows it to express simultaneously the values of quantitative measure (as prices) and qualitative distinctions (as social power). In his discussion of currencies Marx describes a fundamental distinction between "money" and "coin," a distinction that corresponds to the dialectic between the abstract "content," or potential value of money, and the concrete "form," the specific value realized in any particular object. In any given transaction, according to Marx, the object received—including money, when one is selling—is realized as a particular form, while the object given has an abstract potential, a "content" that must come to assume a particular "form." The concrete material currency available in any transaction—"the circulating medium"—has a specific, limited, and quantitative form, which for Marx is the value of a currency as "coin," while the value of currency as "money" is its qualitative abstract and infinite potential for conversion into any commodity at all (Marx 1906: 140–151).[16] Thus, there is an inherent tension for Marx between the "quantitative limits of money and its qualitative boundlessness" (Marx 1906: 150).

The recognition by Marx that money has both quantitative and qualitative dimensions, each of which is differentially realized by the participants in a commercial transaction, provides us with an important insight. If the qualitative aspect of money is its "boundless" abstract potential to be converted into other things, then the Interlacustrine, and specifically the Haya kinds of money I have considered, are both exceedingly and restrictively qualitative. On the one hand, there is an excess of abstract power in a money form like cowries which that has both the potential for commensurating commercial goods and for being converted, not only into other marketed goods, but into divinatory apparatus, ritual paraphernalia, healing amulets, and the like. At the same time, there is a necessary restriction on this abstract potential, as not all objects—not even all commodities—can be purchased by a single type of money.

Within Marx's framework the problem of Haya moneys, given their multiple, interpenetrating contexts of transaction, is to identify, not the infinite, abstract potential of "money" but the particular qualitative potential of certain currency forms. Moreover, the qualitative value of money as the particular potential embedded in it, is not merely a capacity to evaluate the relation between things, but also a capacity that accrues to social persons. Thus, money as a measure of value "measures the degree of its attraction for all other elements of material wealth, and therefore measures the social wealth of its owner" (Marx 1906: 149). This assessment applies directly to those Haya forms of value I have identified as "wealth," material currencies that facilitate the interconversion of different goods, while simultaneously indexing the social position of their possessor. What Marx's insights help to elucidate, then, are the ways in which the potentialities of the money form, in the Haya case potentialities at once infinite and delimited, are configured as particular possibilities for action—and thus as the specific capabilities of social agents—with respect to a historically transforming field of social practices.

How does a focus on coffee in Buhaya at the outset of the twentieth century help us further to get a purchase on this dynamic range of possibilities? Such general features of money, these modes of consciousness, this material history, where do they intersect with this royally sanctioned entity well on its way to becoming a cash crop? I have already suggested that coffee trees could be understood in Haya sociocultural practice as forms of wealth. They were sustained in collective relations, generatively re-created over time, yet detachable from those concrete strictures of sociality. Coffee trees stand apart as independent units whose value can be almost freely converted into an expanding range of valuables. divine and human, and so they embody the kinds of potential and power characteristic of Haya wealth. But coffee also became the principle instrument for the introduction of colonial understandings of wealth and property, value as a very different potential. Part of the status of coffee in Buhaya is demonstrated through methods of propagation that emphasized its collective attachments, and the formal qualities of totalization, a relation between component elements (valued coffee cherries) and singular trees (an index of life force itself). And it is precisely this method that is one of the first aspects of coffee to be transformed.

German administrators in Bukoba established nurseries grown, not from tree cuttings, but seedlings.[17] This transformation (which was not widely adopted by Haya farmers in any community before 1905) not only expanded the possibilities for the dissemination of coffee, thus undermining royal control on coffee stocks, it also entailed a new way of understanding the value of coffee itself. Each seed came to have the potential of mature and enduring trees, trees that were collectively sustained and tangibly connected from one generation to the next. In effect, seedlings made it possible for each tree to become a self-contained entity, an individuated form of property. Thus, the transformation from collective origins into a detachable, bestowable form of wealth—a transformation that gives coffee its specific potential—is diminished, as trees grown from seedlings are *intrinsically* detached, individuated objects. Coffee grown from seeds would no longer depend upon the creation of differentiation through social relations (see Strathern 1991 reference above), as all trees grown in this way are already equally different from one another.

This possibility for creating new kinds of difference, and especially new kinds of equivalencies, is especially important to the development of coffee as a cash crop. Seeds not only made it possible to recognize the separateness and the equality of all trees, they made it relevant to conceive of trees as composed of a homogenous collection of individual and equal units. With the introduction of seedlings in the early twentieth century, each tree would be measured in terms of a quantifiable volume of seeds, a measure that determines the value of the tree itself. This meaningful procedure, quite clearly essential to the effective marketing of coffee as a cash crop, is in fact a significant innovation. As a royal holding and medium of patronage relations, coffee had been evaluated not in terms of a volume of seeds but as the harvest of a given tree. That is, royals received tribute from coffee farmers by collecting the harvest of particular trees set aside for this purpose. Each coffee tree, then, was a unique entity whose value was related to that uniqueness and not to a mass of separate and equivalently valued seeds. The unit of value, therefore, was the tree as a composite whole and not a given measure of individual seeds.

These innovations, like those of colonial currencies conceived of by their minters as quantifiable units of equivalence, made *possible* new forms of consciousness—but they did not strictly dictate their meanings. To this day in

Buhaya, some coffee is withheld from global markets and evaluated in ways that tie the quality of coffee to the particular trees from which it is harvested. Coffee is grown for local consumption (i.e., for chewing) from trees that may be inherited, tied to landscapes of heritage and familial attachment. Nonetheless, the logic of value as expressible through uniform equivalencies was furthered by colonial attempts to transform the production and the very measurement of coffee, attempts that clearly coincided with encompassing reformulations of value as a social form. These colonial projects certainly achieved a good deal of "success"; coffee exports from the region increased in the first decade of the twentieth century from 234 tons in 1905 to 681 tons in 1912. I have demonstrated in this chapter that the colonial growth and marketing of coffee, revalued and remeasured by new practices and new currencies, and Haya men's and women's participation in these processes were fundamental elements in the wider remaking of wealth, the significance of objects, and the attachments of persons and things.

As I will argue in the next chapter, the "religion of the rupee" did convert many Haya men and women, as the market for a host of consumer goods, from American broadcloth to imported clothing, fineries, and bicycles, rapidly grew during this period. I will show that the efforts to incorporate such commodity forms into social worlds without having them deplete, if not obliterate, the generativity of Haya sociality was a concern for Haya men and women, especially as the British administration rapidly expanded coffee cash cropping. I shall also discuss the fact that, well before the transition to British colonial rule, the White Fathers made clear their anxieties about the dangers of coffee commerce for "Africans." The White Fathers' practice—including their anxiety—while grounded in rather different understandings of value than Haya communities would have recognized, would nonetheless have a profound influence on the coffee trade and the struggles (which remain ongoing in Kagera) to come to terms with its implications.

NOTES

1. While patronage relations were linked to cattle in Karagwe, in the eastern kingdoms such relations were founded on royal control of farmland.

2. Such conditions also meant that rinderpest epidemics hit Karagwe especially hard. What was once the most powerful Haya kingdom is now the back of beyond in the Kagera Region, poorly connected in infrastructural terms to the rest of the region and to Tanzania as a whole.

3. In Gregory's development of his "subalternate quality theory of money" he focuses almost exclusively on the ways in which "monetary standards of value . . . are political standards of value," and standardization is best understood to be imposed by force (Gregory 1996: 210). There is much to recommend this perspective as an important critique of monetarism, and in what follows I hope, also, to illuminate some of the coercive mechanisms involved in the standardization of different currencies in Buhaya. At the same time,

Gregory's discussion does not fully explore—as I hope to—the meaningful dimensions of political authority, and the ways in which particular currencies can become especially apt expressions of these meanings.

4. Determining why this was the case is beyond the scope of this study—although I would speculate that German familiarity with cowries on the coast and their increasing interest in consolidating and colonizing East African territories might have led them to this preference for standardization.

5. Cowries, like coffee, are a category of offering that need not describe the specific objects involved. Today, in my experience I found that nine glasses of beer, nine shillings, or small packets of medicine, or even coffee can be offered at marriage as "nine cowries."

6. Cory notes that the upon his installation in his first public appearance a king, the new mukama would distribute cowries to his assembled subjects (Cory 1949: 91). The king's headdress, worn during New Moon ceremonies, a headdress identical to that worn by royal mediums (*babandwa, embandwa*, sing.), may also have incorporated cowries into its design. Such an adornment indicates the links between kingship, possession, and their historical antecedents, with the generalized capacity for interregional commerce facilitated by the cowry.

7. In his recent study of value (2001: 94–104), David Graeber suggests that the "ornamental" aspects of such money—which he describes as contributing to the public image, or "reflection" of the adorned—is in fact a general feature of all moneys, insofar as this "reflection" creates an image that controls the (perhaps dangerous) potential of the money form.

8. The forms of "material wealth" and the "valuables" I refer to in the abstract in this discussion must be taken to include, not only goods and things, but specific social relations—like affinity and filiation—which are clearly forms of wealth that concrete material qualities. Any account of Haya value, or wealth that failed to recognize such social ties would clearly not make much sense.

9. Even the colonial recognition of "lineage property," or "family land" still presumed the stability of the object as a form of property whose ownership was variably collective or personal. What I am suggesting here is that the object's condition as *property* is only defined as a consequence of the specific practices that imbue it with certain qualities.

10. The mission diary of Mugana from 1903 (23 November) reports that one rupee was the equivalent of twelve thousand cowries, but I have no additional evidence to confirm or dispute this rate from another period.

11. It is my impression that Haya labor on behalf of the White Fathers was generally paid for in kind and not in cash for at least the first five or six years following the introduction of rupees. Again, this is only an impression, not the finding of systematic review historical materials—although the diaries are replete with references to goats, sheep, and occasionally cattle, and almost none to cash, as payments (cf. White 1993). The assertion that money and markets never really come to dominate in this part of the world—one that the present argument finds untenable—is, of course, a key tenet of Hyden's now classic claims about the "uncaptured peasantry" of Bukoba (Hyden 1969).

12. The formal term for bridewealth is *amakula*, a noun derived from the verb *okukula*, to mature.

13. Similarly, hearth stones, which are objects essential both to the founding of a new house and to the productivity of a viable, food-processing household are (or were in the living memory of many Haya men and women) destroyed at death. This destruction demonstrates a parallel periodicity, as points of foundation are dismantled, having fulfilled their potential in order to give rise to new foundations. See Weiss (1996a: chapters 3–4) for a more extensive discussion of hearth places and household space.

14. The process of establishing specific rupee levels for bridewealth—in effect, of converting bridewealth into brideprice, a project founded on the European misconception of marriage exchanges in the first instance, is absolutely crucial to the gendered dynamics of Haya political economy, missionization, and the social life of money more generally in the twentieth century. I intend to devote a separate study to an assessment of this process, one that entailed the establishment of specific prices for brides as well as equivalencies between these price levels and the value of cattle and goats that were exchanged in marriage—thereby simultaneously putting a "price" on both marriage and livestock. The White Fathers further devoted much of the first decade of the twentieth century to "liberating" Haya "slave girls"—a category of slavery that the White Fathers "discovered" by a process of invention—which, in effect, proved that slavery existed because money could be used to purchase young girls who had been inherited by the Haya court in the absence of clan or affinal attachments. Again, this history is crucial to an understanding of long-standing Haya concerns about the gendered implications of commerce, marriage, and commoditizatin more generally.

15. In "Northwest Tanzania on a Single Shilling" (Weiss 1997b) I discuss the implications of coins and singularity in greater detail. Part of the argument presented there describes the use of coins, removed from market circulation and from their use as measures of price, as a means of addressing forms of rupture—in particular bodily afflictions characterized by splitting and partition—characteristic of Haya sociality.

16. See Graeber (1996: 9–11) for an excellent, insightful discussion of Marx's understanding of the value of money.

17. Jervis claims that Pasha himself began the process (1939: 53–54), but Cory holds that the evidence suggests it was his successors Langheld and Richter who were responsible for these nurseries (1949: 143).

3

A Religion of the Rupee: Imagining the Coffee Market

> Henceforth, engaging in commerce in the village will be prohibited. In Kashasha they have established a meeting hall (*baraza*), a "sokoni" [marketplace]. The Ihangiro will have his "stock exchange," where merchants and sellers will meet for their business. For the mission, I believe that we will not have much to gain by these sorts of markets. The markets will be in the hands of Indians and Blacks more or less "wangwanisés," the influence of these merchants cannot be favorable to Christianity.
>
> Diare du Poste de Rubya [Ihangiro]: (July 1906)

The complex social and cultural processes that surrounded the introduction of standardized currencies are exemplary, not only of the ways in which innovative relations between subjects and objects were forged in the colonial crucible, but of how unanticipated links of cooperation and conflict were formed among the various persons who participated in these early colonial enterprises. Haya taxpayers very quickly recognized that access to rupees could be a coercive burden; while tax collectors, also Haya men—the products of a French mission education, and agents of a German administration—saw the institution of currency as itself a means to enhance their standing in an expanding social field. It was not only "the colonized" but "the colonizers" who found themselves on the horns of this Simmel-eseque dilemma, confronting the "enigmatic qualities" of money as a source of both alienation and liberation (Simmel 1978 [1900]). The White Fathers themselves were of (at least) two minds on the subject. While they devoted a good deal of energy to standardizing the relationship between cowries and rupees (in part, to facilitate their project of paying the Mukama in order to "liberate" the "slave girls" in his court), they also decried the "dominant religion" in Bukoba—"rupees"

(Rapports Annuels—Bukoba, 1909–1910: 266–267). Money served as the site of uneasy alliance even as it helped establish new kinds of differentiation in this colonial landscape.

Such uneasy alliances between commercial success and material excess are by no means unique to the Lake Victoria frontier. In his comprehensive study of Holland in its "Golden Age," Schama identifies a characteristic anxiety that underlay much of Dutch social experience and practice in this period, namely, a pronounced moral ambiguity that accompanied the phenomenal material success enjoyed (or, perhaps, endured) by Netherlanders in this era. The pivotal conundrum of Dutch life, according to Schama, was how to "moralize materialism" so as to stave off spiritual corruption while simultaneously preserving pecuniary pleasures. While attempts to resolve this dilemma are shown to result in forms of dualistic practice specific to Dutch culture and society (e.g., a recurrent shifting between extravagant feasting and sobering fasts, a scrupulous attention to the boundaries between emerging domestic and public spheres), Schama points toward the ways in which this highly particular "Batavian temperament" was, in fact, the local expression of a global process:

> [W]hile the tensions of capitalism that endeavored to make itself moral were the same whether in sixteenth-century Venice, seventeenth-century Amsterdam, or eighteenth-century London, the social forms and vocabularies generated by them were particular to each community. It can best be summed up as godly patriotism, by definition a general and local phenomenon at the same time. (Schama 1988: 49)

This chapter takes it cue from the recognition that grappling with the moral quandaries of materialism needs to be considered as a salient sociocultural dimension of globalization (see also Miller 1995). In considering these moral quandaries I specifically show how socioeconomic transformations generally associated with global capitalism are inexorably linked to the reformulation of subjectivities, engendering the sensibilities of persons as economic agents in concrete material contexts. Further, I locate Schama's problematic in the context of colonial encounter. Resolving ethical dilemmas posed by materialist pursuits thus also becomes a matter of reconciling alternative moral orders and, thus, modes of subjectivity.

The White Fathers—like missionaries in so many places (Beck 1989; Beidelman 1982; Comaroff and Comaroff 1997; Pels 1999)—were always engaged in both economic and evangelical enterprises. How they reconciled these pursuits, if indeed they recognized a need for reconciliation, was always a matter, to use Schama's phrase, of "the social forms and vocabularies . . . particular to each community." Whether missionaries chose to grease the wheels of capitalist expansion by "sanctifying desire as virtuous ambition and by treating the market as a realm of provident opportunity" (Comaroff and Comaroff 1997: 171–172), or held that the spread of markets rendered good Christians "ignorant of their religious obligations and completely delinquent" (Rapports Annuels—Bukoba, 1909–1910: 267) was in no way predetermined by a universal "Christian morality." Moreover, evangelical attempts to resolve the particular predicaments they envisioned in the materialities they inhabited were equally shaped by the distinct consciousness they encountered. The "social forms and vocabularies" of each African community equally shaped the range of particular opportunities and dangers engendered and imagined in the transforming, colonial fields of material practice. I will show that the White Fathers' attitudes toward commercial enterprise were often at odds with what they perceived to be their evangelical mission—even when, in *practice*, the mission education they provided, and the labor policies they pursued clearly contributed to Bahaya entrepreneurial pursuits. While the paradoxes of the White Fathers' self-conscious vision of their own endeavors are part of a widely recognized moral quandary, familiar to many Christian communities' struggles to appropriate commerce and capital, equally interesting are the ways this quandary shaped the attitudes and practices of the Haya people in the twentieth century. In the first part of this chapter I spell out what I describe as the White Fathers' turn-of-the-century anxieties about "civilization," and then turn to a consideration of Haya farmers/traders concerns as they developed in subsequent decades. My ultimate purpose in this chapter, then, is to address the projects through which specific resolutions to the moral ambiguities of the forms of materialism ushered in by the nascent coffee trade in Buhaya were—and were not—achieved, so as to understand how these undertakings illuminate the complex entanglements of colonizer and colonized.

THE PERILS OF CIVILIZATION: THE WHITE FATHERS' CONCERNS 1906–1911

The White Fathers' diaries reveal the fact that, as early as 1906 (and often in those regions relatively removed from the administrative capital of Bukoba), marketing—especially of coffee—at even the village level had begun to draw the attention of German colonial authorities. This colonial power made rather half-hearted attempts to promote and regulate the coffee trade (Curtis 1989: 89). Yet, the White Fathers noted a brisk business in coffee in the earliest years of this century, putting it ahead of peanuts and beans as crops that provided a monetary income (Diare du Poste de Rubya [Ihangiro]: 19 August 1906). What becomes especially clear in reading the White Fathers' accounts of this earliest trade in coffee was that it entailed the establishment of new modes of sociality whose relations generated new forms of identity. The White Fathers' discomfort with the undue influence of Asians and—perhaps especially—entrepreneurial Africans in Buhaya (evidenced in this article's epigraph—Diare du Poste de Rubya [Ihangiro]: July 1906) may indicate not only the presence of such new identities, but also an emerging awareness of their radical potential. Bahaya villagers also grasped the innovative possibilities of these relations. The White Fathers' own accounts make it clear that "Indians and Blacks" were increasingly drawn together in commercial practices; they further implicate the White Fathers in these entanglements in unintended but essential ways.

What is especially clear in the Fathers' anxious reports is their concern about the influence of those who advance "an active propaganda in favor of Islam" (Rapports Annuels–Marienberg 1906–1907: 123) through the commercial activities that had taken hold in the region. An assessment of this concern, though, must itself be grounded in a broader analysis of these missionaries' understandings of commerce more generally. Such an analysis, to anticipate its conclusions here, indicates that it makes little sense to try to reduce the White Fathers' opposition to coffee marketing to the fact that it was controlled by Asian, Muslim, and Swahili merchants; nor does their anxiety about these communities derive from their association with the unholy practices of commerce. What I argue then is that a multidimensional cultural construction of identity, and not only ethnicity, emerges in relation to the coffee market and its practices. The differential relations of peoples, Haya and Swahili, African and European, with the coffee trade—as well as with marketing more generally—came to be understood as definitive features of identity in ways that resonate even today for residents of rural Kagera.[1]

In any number of ways, the White Fathers were themselves implicated in the development of commerce. They not only attempted to set wages and determine prices—including especially the value of bridewealth—they also worked to standardize colonial currencies as an accepted medium of exchange. The Fathers were clearly not opposed to the use of money in principle. Indeed, the mere material existence of their missions depended upon Haya interests in money, and the missionaries were uncomfortably aware of their dependence on local peoples in this regard. The Fathers in Rubya, for example, were quite proud of their early successes, among them the Central School that became a seminary in 1911. The students at the school were fed with produce grown under the supervision of the mission, but the report of Père Riollier indicates some of the uneasiness of this procedure:

> It might have been advantageous for us to buy this produce [rather than to cultivate it ourselves] from the locals if they had them; but it is useless to dream of this, as they cultivate just what they need, and no more. From time immemorial, there have never been buyers; and they don't change these habits overnight. They would quite like to have clothing, rupees, but to work for them, never. (Rapports Annuels–Rubia, 1905–1906: 160)

This report describes a willingness of the Fathers to engage in commerce, to encourage the use of money for activities that would be "advantageous," as well as an incomprehensible (if already moralized) reluctance on the part of local farmers to do so—or at least an unwillingness to sell food they have themselves produced.[2] At the same time, the conditions under which Haya persons are required to pursue money are persistently cited by the Fathers as "the single greatest obstacle" (Rapports Annuels—Rapport Général de Mgr Hirth 1905–1906: 153) to their mission: "[t]here is the tax, 4 rupees per hut. [The people are always] on a journey in search of the necessary rupees. It is understandable that under these conditions it is difficult to give them a solid religious instruction." Further, the Church was in a position to pay for the labor of Haya villagers, indeed they willingly paid for this labor, if only in order to distinguish these labors from the corvée requirements that they so vociferously denounced in this period; "[T]hose that cannot pay [the tax] must perform corvée under the surveillance of heavily armed soldiers. In order to avoid corvée they come to work for us to earn the necessary rupees. Fortunately, there is no lack of work at the moment: we have a large wall to construct" (Rapports Annuels—Katoke, 1905–1906: 166). And when the Fathers did make work available, they ran the risk that this paid labor might also compromise their religious aspirations: "Many see little in religion other than a means of avoiding the demands of corvée and interminable prestations" (Rapports Annuels—Rapport Général de R.P. Léonard 1908–1909: 229). The White Fathers found themselves on the horns of a dilemma, needing the paid labor of their converts and potential converts, but recognizing that the necessity of a monetary income posed a significant challenge to the very process of conversion. Moreover, in trying to resolve this dilemma by providing work for those who needed to pay taxes, the missionaries might thereby have made themselves seem complicit in the very pecuniary processes they felt to be so detrimental to Christianity.

Beyond the logistical difficulties of a destabilized population motivated by the search for cash, the White Fathers' concerns about commerce were vexed by their own contradictory understandings of the meaning of materialism. While the missionaries were engaged in such activities as building chapels and barracks, developing agricultural projects, and training students in carpentry and other trades, it does not seem that they felt the material dimensions of their enterprises to correspond neatly with their spiritual ambitions. This was not a "civilizing mission" (as I discuss below, the character of "civilization" itself was open to much suspicion by the White Fathers) that conceived of money as an apt medium for "the conversion of wealth into virtue" (Comaroff and Comaroff 1997: 193). It is worth noting, for example, that the Fathers' annual reports offer summaries of activities and events that are generally (although not uniformly) divided into the formal categories of *le Spirituel* and *le Matériel*, the corruption of the latter usually faulted as a barrier to the progress of the former. For example, after describing their excellent relations with Mukama Kassussuro, the missionaries find that

> movement towards our holy religion is very weak. It would be difficult to find a more materialistic people than the Basuwi. The religious principal among them is so poorly developed, above all in the areas around the [royal] Capital and the military fort, where everyone runs after rupees and clothes. (Rapports Annuels—Katoke, 1906–1907: 136)

This materialist impulse is an ongoing source of struggle for the White Fathers, something they sought to overcome directly at times, simply to curtail at others. This proved a most intractable problem, though, in that the missionaries' practice was often seen to contribute to the very materialism they hoped to counteract.

What was especially criticized by the Catholics—in both their initial appraisals of the local communities and their continuous assessments of the effects of the colonial encounter on them—was not the undue constraint that material want imposed on the spiritual improvement of the Haya (there are, in fact, remarkably few reports that express concern for the burdens of poverty borne by the local peoples), but rather the spiritual impoverishment generated by the material *ease* that they enjoyed. Let me quote an early report from Rubya:

> We have found the Banya-Ihangiro rather primitive. Of civilization they know hardly anything save corvée and a few rare pieces of clothing. They live at the mercy of a deprived environment, in a rather irritating climate, with an abundance of food and drink, without any work whatsoever. Imagine that they speak to us of the patriarchal mores, kindness and purity of primitive peoples! I believe that this exists only on paper. Primitive man has a fear of work, of effort, and what can one obtain without these? (Rapports Annuels—Rubia, 1905–1906: 160–161)

This "fear of work" becomes a prominent theme in the White Fathers' reports in the coming years. Occasionally their missionizing endeavors aim to combat indolence, but more frequently the Fathers lament the ways in which laziness has been exacerbated in the contemporary, transformed social order. If the "primitive" condition of the Bahaya promotes a "fear of work," the immediate effects of "civilization" seem only to contribute to these "natural" tendencies to avoid diligence:

> Those who are absent [from the mass] above all, these are the "rouleurs," who, for need or instinct, are in pursuit of rupees and believe they can find what they desire in distant places. The tax, the requirement of those youths planning a marriage to pay a large sum, there are the needs; the desire to

> possess a cow, or some beautiful clothes, even a suitcoat with a pair of worn-out shoes, there are the instincts. Ah! the advances of civilization! (Rapports Annuels—Marienberg, 1908–1909: 233)

The dangers of both material excess and constraint formed a core conflict for the White Fathers, who saw a contradiction in the Janus-faced nature of "civilization," which promises spiritual blessings, but generally provides something less exalted. Père Léonard points to this contradiction when he writes, "Civilization brings them ideas of emancipation and liberty; this is a virtue, but it is also a danger for these poor people, the ideal for a real Negro consisting of rest and pleasure" (Rapports Annuels—Rapport Général de R.P. Léonard 1908–1909: 229). Note here that the destructiveness of materialism lies both in poverty and pleasure, as it is precisely because of his desperate condition that "the real Negro" dreams of a life of idleness. The challenge for the mission lay in inculcating the values of hard work and effort that could only be considered virtues if they were aspired to as ends in and of themselves. The apparent unwillingness of the Bahaya to actually work for the things they desire is deplored by the Fathers, but so too are the very things desired—the cows, shoes, and rupees, that are everywhere pursued. Note, as well, that the material nature of these things pursued subverts the moral character of the activities undertaken to acquire them. Hard work, that is, may be admired by the Catholics, but the unmistakable efforts made by Baziba and Banyangiro to find the rupees required for taxes, clothing, bridewealth, and the like are disqualified as actual "work." Rather, commercial practices are depicted as a kind of mad scramble, in which "everyone runs after rupees and clothes," as trade is dominated by *rouleurs*, "swindlers" whose interest in lucre turns genuine exertion into mere deception.

The effort to distinguish the merits of assiduous enterprise from the vulgar material benefits that accrued to commercial activities, here understood as twinned possibilities given the ascent of "civilization," came to characterize the White Fathers' teachings. Nothing less than the spiritual progress of the Haya as a people depended upon instilling in them an appreciation of the difference between the Providential possibilities of discipline and effort and the destructiveness, if easy satisfactions, of monetary gains. A telling report, which notes that European settlers have "acquired immense properties" in the country, and have begun to "change the social condition of the people," draws this contrast precisely:

> The majority of the youth, the best of them, have found work among the settlers, where they are subject to a ten hour day: six in the morning until four in the evening. It's the true beginning of a social revolution in a country where, from time immemorial, each has done as they please, drinking his "marwa" (banana wine), smoking his pipe, and not even pretending to do

> a bit of work until he was tired of resting. This work brings more than comfort to the population; the people able to become self-sufficient will also be independent of their chiefs, and consequently more free.

The alternative is then presented:

> But, just beside this indigenous world, there is another, less advantageous, but essentially converted; it is a world of Indians, "Wangwana," Baswahili, Baganda, foreigners of all sorts who occupy Bukoba: 'boys,' traders, corvée troops, etc. . . . their dominant religion is that of rupees; the only goal of their life: the pursuit of pleasures. In this cosmopolitan world, especially among the Baganda, the Christian religion also has its adherents, the majority ignorant of their religious obligations and completely delinquent. (Rapports Annuels—Bukoba, 1909–1910: 266–267)

This account not only vividly portrays the difference between the freedom of "self-sufficiency" and the libertine "pursuit of pleasures," it also indicates how important—and difficult—it is to make this difference clear to the Bahaya themselves. That is, it is critical to recognize that the alternative to the world of hard work that lurks "just beside" it is *also* a world of putative Christians—*prosélytes* who are ignorant and degenerate, fallen from the true faith. It is not enough, therefore, to bring the Christian religion to an indolent people, for even conversion to Christianity has a "cosmopolitan" allure that leads all to easily to depravity. There is an implicit understanding in this report, then, of the fact that Catholicism is part of a larger project of social transformation and "civilization," that *le Spirituel* and *le Matériel* present themselves to the Haya people as conjoined parts of a common process. Moreover, and more troubling from the missionaries' perspectives, the White Fathers found themselves confronting dilemmas that the very *success* of their mission helped to establish.

SWINDLERS AND OTHER CHRISTIANS

The response of the White Fathers to this intertwining of their mission with the wider commercial, military, and political changes wrought by colonialism was not to renounce materialism entirely. It is more than evident that the Fathers were convinced that the indolence of the Bahaya needed to be addressed, not by spiritual means alone, but by fostering a love of work. Thus, the aim of the Catholics, in the face of the rapid colonial—and especially commercial—changes that defined the world in which they worked, was to educate Haya men to recognize the proper Christian pursuit of material benefits, to appreciate the values of effort over gain. These aims were realized primarily through education, in both secular schooling and the catechism:

> Surely everyone knows how much the Negro prefers the sweet "far-niente" to labor? We must admit that our pupils suffer as well from the consequences of original sin. All these children, in effect, even those who have received, at birth, the most fortunate character, are thoughtless, and fickle, who stray from desire to desire. It is only little by little that we may manage to overcome this thoughtlessness, and see them faithful to the hours of silence, attentive to their lessons in virtue and science, meditative in prayer. (Rapports Annuels—P. Riollier: Rubia, 1905–1906: 163)

As one station succinctly described it, "The primary goal of our school is the conservation and perseverance of the youth. One aspires therefore more towards a moral training than an intellectual training" (Rapports Annuels—Kagondo, 1906–1907: 129). The religious instruction of catechism—or, perhaps, more accurately, the making of catechumens—was the particular focus of the White Fathers' attempts to emphasize their significant interests in work and effort, while hoping simultaneously to rid those material concerns of their materialist implications. A simple, but thorough (I am tempted to say "economical") regime is described in a brief account of the catechumens in Rubya:

> For those who have begun to understand a bit what it means "to pray" the absences [from catechism classes] are rather rare; they greatly fear the *bubonero* (the strokes that mark an absence); they know that six of these strokes will set someone back three months. We insist a great deal on the love of work. A catechumen who does not work ordinarily becomes a bad Christian. That is why we have suppressed the giving of crosses, small chains, rosaries, etc. Before baptism they must earn at least enough to dress themselves decently and purchase a rosary, or perhaps a cross or a small chain for the beginners. They have understood this, and to this time we have not had any complaints. (Rapports Annuels—Rubia, 1907–1908: 139)

Here is an exemplary account of the White Fathers' understanding of diligence, properly initiated. It is a diligence that plainly reveals itself in material concerns, but is also expressed in the broader conduct of the catechumens, and not merely in their economizing activities. The same Banyangiro who only a few years ago possessed a primitive "fear of work" now "greatly fear" being marked absent from the catechism. It should be evident, as well, that this insistence on proper attendance is implicitly connected to a reordering of time, and the consciousness of time discipline; to accumulate—carefully enumerated—absences is to lose time. Crucially, the newfound "love of work" must not be motivated by material gratification and is willingly accepted—at least no complaints have yet been received. The "rouleurs" may seek rupees and European fashions, but the catechumens must be dressed "decently"—although decent dress did not, apparently, include shoes. This is a decency, moreover, which is not to be *given* to these new converts, but which must be earned by their own efforts. The entire educational procedure seems designed to make the love of work its own reward, as the meager purchases of this work are of no *material* consequence. Indeed, they are devotional objects, normally given away—objects that can be acquired but scarcely *accumulated*—and so they embody the very antithesis of commercial forms. In this way, these tokens become all the more emblematic, not of the "need" or "instinct" they satisfy, but of the work through which they were acquired, and by which they *qualify* as Christians—that is, prove themselves worthy of baptism.

The broadest educational mission of the White Fathers reveals a tortured effort to encourage work while diminishing the material significance of the benefits accrued from work. Promoting a "love of work" by means of which one should only aspire to a Spartan degree of "decency" seems a narrow path to pursue, but it was a way in which the missionaries hoped to acknowledge and accommodate the material consequences of the social reformation they participated in, without allowing the totality of this new order to exercise dominion over the Church. The great danger of this uneasy reconciliation was not simply the enormous temptations of a transformed world in *opposition* to Christianity, but the risk that the teachings of the Church would themselves become diluted, perhaps even subverted as the materialism of this world came to infiltrate the mission. It is for this reason that a figure who comes to generate profound worry in these early years is the catechumen who becomes "a bad Christian." The converts in commerce, the bad example set by Baganda "adherents" to the faith who become "delinquent," these are the sources—even in the earliest years of the twentieth century, well before the expansion of coffee marketing under British rule—of the White Fathers' deepest anxiety. This is an anxiety rooted in what the missionaries themselves perceived to be the paradoxical nature of their own project, one that was intrinsic to the very idea of "civilization" even as it struggled to offer a critique of its threatening possibilities. It is from the perspective of this ambivalence about the colonial process as a whole, and their *own* place in it, I would argue, that the White Fathers' ambivalence about Asian, Muslim, and Swahili merchants has to be approached.

The terms in which the Fathers articulated their misgivings about "bad Christians," catechumens who were instructed by the missionaries and yet departed from their teachings, present very clear parallels to the ways in which the Fathers described those engaged in commercial activities in the region. These traders, for example, are contemptuously dismissed as "Indians and Muslims *of all colors*" (Rapports Annuels—Rapport Général de Mgr Hirth 1906–1907: 120, emphasis added), a pointed critique premised on an antagonism toward what is manifestly perceived as the unruly combination of people. The clearest counterpart to the apostate Catholics that troubled the missionaries are the Africans frequently described as "Wangwana." This name is a Francophone elision of the Kiswahili term *waungwana* (*mwaungwana*, sing.), an identity that came into fashion in the nineteenth century in conjunction with the caravan trade (see Glassman 1995: 61–64). Glassman describes the cultivation of this *waungwana* identity on the East African coast of the nineteenth century, especially by slave porters in the Bagomoyo caravans. He writes:

> Although today *mwaungwana* is often taken to mean a freeman as opposed to a slave, a more exact translation would be "gentleman." In the nineteenth century, the word was used to connote not any particular social status, but rather the general qualities of urbane gentility. Thus, a person identifying with the urban culture of the coast, slave or free, might presume to call himself *mwaungwana* as opposed to an *mshenzi* (pl., *washenzi*), a "barbarian" or "bumpkin" from upcountry. (Glassman 1995: 62)

These connotations of sophistication and independence engendered through one's association with trade would certainly be seen as evidence of the kinds of decadence the White Fathers associated with the worst of "civilization." I have no evidence to suggest exactly how Bahaya understood this term, or who if any would have aspired to such an identity for themselves. By looking at the ways in which the missionaries used this term, however, it is possible to can gain some important insights into their take on the consequences of colonialism for an African politics of identity; in turn, this evaluation of the identities promoted by commercial, military, and other colonial enterprises did have a profound effect on colloquial (and contemporary) Haya understandings of these questions.

The term *mwaungwana* may have been used by porters in the caravan trades to mean "gentleman" as Glassman suggests, but the White Fathers' appreciation of this identity seems less noble. It is worth noting that etymologically this term is derived from the Kiswahili verb *kuunga*, to join, to come together, used in the passive (-ung*wa*) and reciprocal (ungw*ana*) form. Thus, *Waungwana* are those who are "joined together" with one another, an apt assessment of the Nyamwezi and other porters that Glassman describes who chose to identify themselves by this term. The autonomy and solidarity that Glassman argues this identity connoted at the coast might well have had very different implications in the far Interlacustrine interior of East Africa, most especially from the missionary perspective. The Fathers' critical evaluation of the very idea of joining together is evident in the various contexts in which the "Wangwana" are described in missionary accounts, always in cahoots with a motley crew of social types—Indians, "Baswahili," Muslims, Baganda—who engage in commercial practices. The point is not simply that the identities of merchants are always quintessentially "others" who entice "real" locals like Baziba, Banyangiro, and Basuwi into their trade, but that the

"Wangwana" are those whose very existence is the product of serial connections among and between a wide variety of kinds.

I would further suggest that "Wangwana" identity in the White Fathers' discourse is less "other" or alien, than it is alien*ated*. The "Wangwana," that is, are those who have departed from, abandoned, or lost some prior condition with aspirations—or pretensions—to something else. Note, for example that the hardworking youth whose praises are sung by the missionaries constitute an "*indigenous* world," which lies "just beside" the world of "foreigners of all sorts" (Rapports Annuels—Bukoba, 1909–1910: 266–267) now so active in Bukoba—foreigners who the (*newly*) hardworking Bahaya may yet become. It further seems telling, and simultaneously unremarkable, that the missionaries describe "Black" merchants at the turn of the century as "wangwanisés" (as in the epigraph above). The use of this named identity as an adjective permits it to be understood as a process to which a broad spectrum of social identities can be subjected. Baganda and "Baswahili," Blacks and Muslims "of all colors," even Bahaya and (especially?) Christians may not describe themselves as "Wangwana," yet they may all be described as "wangwanisés." Further, the Francophonic rendering of this identity as a transitive verb objectifies this condition of being as a state of becoming, or transformation. It is as though a "mwangwana" is less who one is than that into which one has been made; it is a deformation, or corruption of character.

This idea of "Mwangwana" as an acquired identity that deviates from an "original" condition is the base from which the Fathers are able to orchestrate an assault on a host of suspect qualities, all of which are characteristic of incipient commercial practices and relations. Such a construction, for example, would seem to lurk behind the educational mission of the Fathers that stressed the "conservation" of the youth, as though their fidelity to *themselves* were at stake. Given this Catholic characterization of transformation as "deviation" it is also worth reconsidering the Fathers' concerns about the newfound movement of Haya villagers. The incessant travels of the Bahaya—now "more itinerant than ever" (Rapports Annuels—Bwanja 1906–1907: 127)—not only posed a significant challenge to the missionaries' attempts to proselytize and educate a localized community. More important, the routinization of mobile practices were seen to promote both a departure from "true" ways of life and the appropriation of "false" ones. The persistent tropes and images of speed and motion that saturate the White Fathers' characterizations of the corruption of "civilization" suggest that they saw in an expanding potential for rapid transit and transport an equally rapid *distancing* from an indigenous identity.

The now displaced "real Negro" may have been constitutionally idle, but the stability of his "primitive" existence made him more subject to the possibilities of redemption than the already altered and inherently unfixed "mwangwana." The "Wangwana" also indulged in the evils of smoking

Figure 3.1. Mobility was a potent trope for the moral ambiguities of modernity.

cannabis, which became a rage among young men at the turn of the century. The Fathers repeatedly lamented the shift from habitual drinking to habitual smoking (the latter more frequently added to—but never replacing—the former), a tell-tale characteristic of an insidious process of socialization, the idle native transformed into the fast-moving "rouleur."[3] Ever faster mobility became iconic of a powerful and dangerous emerging condition; it was both a *means* that made the creation of new forms of identity possible, and a defining *feature* of the new identities so acquired (see Figure 3.1).

CATECHUMENS AND COFFEE CLERKS: THE MAKING OF MARKETERS IN THE EARLY TWENTIETH CENTURY

The anxieties "joined together" in the image of "wangwana" identity—the threats of sensual, material gratification without disciplined effort, of indiscriminately mixing different kinds of persons, of deracination, and of uncontrolled motion—are apt expressions of the White Fathers' misgivings about the transformed world through which they hoped to shepherd the Bahaya. These misgivings are certainly compounded by the fact that the commercial enterprises—especially the caravan trade—in which the "wangwana" identity was forged were strongly associated with the Swahili coast. The trade epitomized the quest for pleasures that the Fathers would have to undermine if their efforts to reform Haya work habits were to succeed. Asians and Muslims who arrived in Bukoba as emissaries of the coast bore testimony to the fact that its circuits of transport and transit were now more accessible than ever to the Lake Victoria frontier. The Swahili coast was not only the port of entry for most regional commerce, and so the epicenter of these suspect undertakings, it was also the cosmopolitan heart of those processes of combination and interconnection that led to the acquisition of inauthentic and deceptive dispositions. And so it is with some dismay that the Fathers at Katoke report that even among their most successful converts:

> it is the style here, as in the other posts, of making a small tour of the coast and returning after a year with a thirty sous umbrella and a pair of ragged slippers. They've seen Dar es Salaam, the ships, the sawmills, many Europeans, they've learned four words of kiswahili, and they are utterly transformed; they scorn their own hut, they no longer speak their mother tongue! Exactly like the bumpkins in France who spend twenty-four hours in Paris; they see the Eiffel tower, a car with a driver; returning home they no longer know the provincial ways they suckled with their mother's milk! The coast is the Paris, the Babylon of all the blacks. (Rapports Annuels—Katoke, 1908–1909: 243)

Apart from revealing the (anti)shoe fetish the missionaries appear to have indulged, these accounts—combining ridicule and distress—are especially noteworthy for their reflexivity. The up-country Muhaya is akin to the provincial Frenchman, bedazzled by a mere fleeting glance of urbane life that is still somehow sufficient to sever his ties to his natal custom. While an adequate social history of the White Fathers has yet to be produced, my reading of oversight evaluations of the missions undertaken by administrative leaders of the order also suggest that significant number of fathers "in the field" in Buhaya came from the border zones of France, especially Alsace and Flemish-speaking regions in the north. Nielsel (1971) also found that White Fathers' mission stations were frequently staffed by Alsatians. If this was, in fact, typical, it strengthens the reflexive character of these comments. Indeed, it suggests that the White Fathers may well have been describing *themselves*, or those very much like them, in these disparaging accounts of "touring" Bahaya.

More significant, I think, than the analogy between the peripheralized at home and abroad, is the fact that this Fathers' report is specifically concerned with *Christian* Bahaya. Clearly, for newly converted Bahaya the mission is embedded in a world of seductive innovations, so that a successful adoption of a Catholicism entails the "small tour," a reformed material culture, and a new linguistic competence. Note, then, that the Christians at the coast present a nearly exact *parallel* to the "Wangwana" whose origins are also perceived to lie at the coast. The *waungwana* porters sought to assert their capacity for independent and collective action in a new context of commercial enterprise, and similarly, the White Fathers expressly hoped to develop the self-sufficiency of Bahaya Christians so as to liberate them from the oppression of their autocratic bakama. In each case, though, the autonomy generated by novel social forms emerging and fomenting in the ecumenical practices of the coast produced what was from the Fathers' perspective, an intractable form of identity, disdainful of its "native" ways and transparently inauthentic.

"Wangwana" agents of trade and tempted Christian converts are conjured up as counterparts in the White Fathers' imagination revealing a grave ambivalence on the missionaries' part about the materialist prospects of "civilization." This ambivalence, I would further argue, is greatly complicated by the fact that the Fathers were soon aware of the fact that they were deeply embedded in the very same processes that they saw as obstacles to the Church. This becomes apparent when turning from the anxieties of the White Fathers to the practices of the Bahaya. Again, in the very earliest years of the twentieth century, young men began to engage in the kinds of business activities that have been definitive of Haya economy and society right down to the present day. Moreover, these business activities were clearly facilitated by the mission education they received:

> In this Vicariat as everywhere, [our difficulties] seem more often to increase than diminish. We cannot complain too much about our neophytes;

> they are almost all young in the faith, and they have all of the generosity of youth. As for the catechumens, everywhere it has become more difficult to recruit them and to make them persevere: they are drawn in so many ways to put their hopes somewhere other than religion! The Indians and Muslims of all colors, that arrive in great numbers, seize the youth, and the most intelligent run after them. (Rapports Annuels—Rapport Général de Mgr Hirth 1906–1907: 120)

This alliance of Swahili and Asian capital with the skills of a mission education engenders a new commercial figure:

> Unfortunately we must note a weakening of the ardor of the youth: they continue to visit the catechists, but they are just as interested in the company of certain tax collectors who have left government schools and are now found in different villages gathering the revenue in rupees. There they find books to read and paper for writing. The love of reading and writing is equal at least to that of the words of the catechism: once they learn to write, they go to find a position in business among the Indians. . . . It is thus that we have had to suffer, this past season, the loss of most of our catechumens. (Rapports Annuels—Marienberg 1906–1907: 123)

This "loss" persists, and in consistent ways through the rest of the decade:

> [D]uring this past year many of the young Bahaya . . . have gone to work on the railroad whose terminal is now in Kilossa. The death of a number of them has not eroded the élan, and everyday new recruits depart. If only they would return after their six month contract! But the majority of those who have gotten a taste of travel press on to the coast, and so remain several years absent from the land. Still others go to Rwanda to work in the beef and goat business, or to put themselves to work for the Indians who send them to cover the land to buy them coffee. (Rapports Annuels—Marienberg 1909–1910: 269–270)

These reports suggest that the wayward Christian is not merely a phantasm of the White Fathers' mission, a minion of such infamous alien types as the "Baswahili" and Baganda. Rather, entrepreneurial uses of the catechism *did* become commonplace as Haya young men began eagerly to participate in the new economy—and especially the coffee trade—which was only beginning to flourish at this point in the new century. The business skills and social relations developed through this fledgling trade provided these youth with significant opportunities, opportunities that would greatly expand under British rule, as coffee became the quintessential concern of colonial policies. I would suggest, in fact, that these lapsed catechumens are the direct precursors of some of the most important—and economically successful—traders in East Africa, the *wachuluzi* (*mchuluzi*, sing.).

Who were the *wachuluzi*? Essentially, *wachuluzi* worked as middlemen for the produce markets in a highly decentralized order of production. Individual Haya farmers might produce only a few kilos of coffee each year, but by employing *wachuluzi* who could bulk the harvest of many of their neighbors, the Asian traders could effectively funnel exports through their offices. What made this practice especially profitable, and what further permitted it to proliferate widely in every Haya community, was the system of credit, or crop mortgaging. By means of this mortgaging, *wachuluzi* could make substantial profits by paying out advances to coffee growers strapped for cash between harvests. They would thereby receive the right to harvest and market the grower's coffee crop, often at a rate of two to three times the amount of the cash advance. It was surely these meager advances relative to the great profits taken that contributed to the appellation *wachuluzi*, "the tricklers" (from the Kiswahili *kuchuluza*, "to trickle").

In matters of produce marketing, Asian traders had the kinds of extensive, long-standing commercial and kin ties that bound together interior regional markets with coastal exchanges, and truly global overseas traffic. As Mamdani describes the situation in Uganda, "Trade was for the import-export market and its very structure—centralized, hierarchical, externally oriented—assured the dominance of the established Indian retailer over the incoming African retailer" (Mamdani 1976: 168). It may have been the case that Asian traders, especially in the German period, were able to "dominate" trade in Buhaya, but the *terms* under which Bahaya entered into trade with these Asians generated specifically local forms of practice that make the question of domination and subordination more complicated. These terms suited Haya interests in both participating in the emerging coffee trade and retaining control over the kinds of generative values embedded in landholding as a source of "wealth" (as discussed in chapter 2) and cultivation (to be discussed more fully in chapters 4 and 5).

As coffee prices rose steadily up through the 1920s, and with coffee planting becoming more extensive through compulsory planting regimes (see chapter 4), the opportunity for Haya men to profit from their neighbors with capital offered by Asian patrons was tremendous. Moreover, given the system of crop mortgaging, inflationary pressures, and ever increasing coffee prices, even Bahaya with relatively little capital could advance cash to farmers in need and realize substantial profits. In effect, anyone *with* cash could convert it into profit given access to clients *without* it. This potential continued down through the early 1990s, exacerbated no doubt by structural adjustments that, at one point, caused the Tanzanian currency to drop to 25 percent of its value in less than a year. The effects of these devaluations were recalled as devastating by all Haya that I knew; but it was also recognized that some *wachuluzi* could receive up to ten times the price that they advanced for a farmer's coffee harvest in a single six-month period.

THE DANGEROUS MSWAHILI

The potential of this pattern of practices to exploit micro-differences in economic circumstances, coupled with the thorough decentralization of coffee production, would seem to account for the sheer number of Haya men who pursued such commercial activities in these early decades of the century. From this perspective, the profitability of trade and the relatively minor inputs of capital needed to sustain it appear to have made this sort of enterprise an inevitability. The White Fathers' laments about the "religion of the rupee" must surely have been drowned out with the rising tides of colonial crop mortgaging. While it is certainly the case that coffee commerce was enormously successful by any measure, I think it is not possible to grasp the significance of these transformations if they are seen primarily in the utilitarian terms of the self-interested pursuit of material gain. Indeed, I want to argue that the White Fathers' admonitions about the dangers of material excess and the threat of social forces centered on the coast did not go unheeded by Haya coffee farmers and traders. A close reading of the way in which commercial activities were pursued and evaluated within Haya communities reveals that a dynamic politics—and poetics—of identity informed their purposive efforts to disambiguate the benefits of profit from the perils of avarice, one that often parallels the White Fathers' efforts to address similar quandaries.

In order to assess the multiple meanings of Bahaya participation in the coffee trade, and the forms of identity it generated—and imagined—it is important to address questions of motivation. The problem of motivation can be approached, I would suggest, by a number of different paths. Beyond asking what did Haya young men hope to gain by becoming *wachuluzi*, I also hope to spell out some of the possible meanings that attended to the activities of trading. In particular, I aim to explore the value of trade by looking at how its benefits and liabilities were—and are—imagined in Buhaya. These images of value, and certain imagined figures that personify these values, were as central to Haya discourses of commerce as they were to the White Fathers'.

As an initial tack, I would note that the White Fathers' observations about Haya sartorial pursuits—in spite of their condescension—seem fairly well founded. A number of reports from early in the century indicate that Bahaya did readily incorporate new styles and forms into their clothing practices (Bakengesa 1974). One Muhaya recalled his childhood in the flush 1920s by saying, "I was only young at the time, but I already wore a shirt, and shorts, and a *kanzu* split down the side so people could see the shirt and shorts" (Joseph Mwikilia to *Engoma ya Buhaya*, 17 June 1954, cited in Curtis 1989: 92–93). Moreover, clothing in the form of bark cloth figured as a prominent trade good in the Interlacustrine world prior to the rise of colonial markets; in many ways the exchange of Haya coffee for valuable, imported clothing was a pattern with deep roots in nineteenth-century Kagera. Indeed, I found in my discussions with Haya men who had traded in the black market (*magendo)* during the post-independence period that coffee continued to be linked to clothing. In their near standardized accounts of *magendo*, coffee from Kagera might fetch a better price in Rwanda and Uganda; yet the purpose of transporting coffee to these markets was not to receive a better price for coffee, but to exchange that crop for the finer clothing—and bicycles—that could be procured outside of Tanzania.

The use of clothing as an index of personal status, social position within a hierarchical political economy, and quintessential media of the exchanges by which social bonds are forged has been amply demonstrated throughout Africa (Friedman 1994; Martin 1996; Hendrickson 1996). In precolonial Buhaya, various grades of bark cloth, skins, and plaited grass skirts could be worn to demonstrate one's standing as a noble, *mulangila*—or commoner, *mwiru* (Rehse 1910). Clothing was bequeathed as a royal form of prestige and further marked the inheritance of familial status, as heirs wore the clothes of their predecessors, literally assuming the mantle of authority upon their installation (Cesard 1939). Even today a senior Haya man may anticipate the powers he has attained by noting that upon his own death, his corpse will be wrapped in shrouds provided by his children's spouses (Weiss 1996b). Jonathan Friedman's celebrated account of the "La Sape," or elegant dress in postcolonial Brazzaville, might provide an apposite comparison (Friedman 1994). For Friedman such sartorial devotion is best understood as a mode of appropriating the well-being (or "life force") of powerful persons in a hierarchical order. In this way, the consumption of clothing under French rule exemplifies how "a colonial regime maps onto an already existing hierarchical praxis" (Friedman 1994: 174). In the Haya case as well, clothing was and is a potent medium for constituting and exhibiting hierarchical relations of royalty and affinity, and so their interest in umbrellas and kanzus, slippers and suit jackets, must be seen as more than just the inevitable expression of commodified desires.

I would further note that clothes in Buhaya, whether elaborately painted bark cloth or secondhand cotton T-shirts, not only demonstrate the force of hierarchical relations, they also reveal the interpenetration of local and global relations. The best bark cloth, perhaps the most prized form of clothing in the precolonial era, was attained from Buganda by Haya traders.[4] Even everyday clothing for commoners was prepared from heavy grasses that were harvested in the open savannah (*orweya*) beyond the limits of the agricultural villages (*ekyaro*) in which Haya families live. Fine clothing for Bahaya is iconic of their efforts both to identify with and to distance themselves from the articulation of inside:outside connections (see also Friedman 1994). Thus illiterate farmers in the late 1980s could sport nonprescription glasses in their attempts to command a sign of what they knew to be especially powerful forms of knowledge; Catholics, Lutherans, and Muslims alike could don kofias with a nod to an alternative yet similarly powerful circuit of knowledge. These identifications, though, are always at risk if they suggest an abrupt—or dangerous—departure from Haya sociality. Thus, the genteel father of the groom I accompanied to bridewealth negotiations was ridiculed for "wrapping on a tie" by his future affines who felt his finery asserted an inappropriate inequality between the parties. More pointedly, in the earliest years of its presence in Kagera, AIDS was known as "Juliana" for the style of polyester dress said to have been worn by the Ugandan barmaids frequented by wealthy Haya businessmen—or else purchased and imported by these same men to be worn by their wives and girlfriends at home.

Imported clothing was and is an index that persuasively reveals whether one has mastered—or been mastered by—one's encounters with globalizing forces. Not surprisingly, then, Mwikila notes the disastrous effects of the depression in this way, "The price of [coffee] went down quickly. . . . Our clothes became ragged and torn because we could not buy new ones" (Joseph Mwikilia to *Engoma ya Buhaya*, 17 June 1954, cited in Curtis 1989: 153). If, as the historical record suggests, Haya men and women rapidly and eagerly sought to adopt European and Coastal fashions with the tidy profits they made through coffee marketing, these purchases tell us more than just how materially successful the Bahaya had become. Rather, the specific interest in registering these successes in the form of clothes—and especially imported clothes—bespeaks a concern for engaging with the forces that produce the conjuncture of local and global relations that make such clothes available. In clothing themselves, Bahaya traders aimed to *control* the transformations they would participate in.

Important as these motivations may have been, it would be disingenuous to suggest that Haya youth flocked to the coffee trade simply to enhance their wardrobes. Indeed, I would argue that the significance of clothing is manifest less in the desires it reveals than in the order of relations in terms of which it was organized. Clothing, that is, was not a thing in itself with a self-evident allure for Bahaya, it was the expression of contrasting possibilities. The poetics of imported clothes permitted Haya men to share in new possibilities of a world they might benefit from; but those very same clothes could also be grasped as marginalization and loss, not sharing in a new world but becoming dominated by it. It was this understanding of the contrasts that globalization (best exemplified by the coffee trade) presented, that structured Haya social endeavors in this process. Moreover, as the potential of coffee commerce exploded under British rule, Haya evaluations of these contrasts would reveal striking parallels with the White Fathers' assessments of the contradictory possibilities of "civilization" of which they were a part.

It is noteworthy, for example, that the coffee traders working in conjunction with Asian trading houses were known as *wachuluzi*. This was a term of self-identification, one that promoted these marketers' vision of themselves as conduits for profits that could be drawn down from those with greater resources and made available to those with less. But the exploitative nature of this diffusion of profits was not lost on Haya men and women who depended on the infusion of capital the *wachuluzi* provided. Many of my neighbors in Kagera of the late 1980s, for example, told me that the traders had been called *wachuluzi* because they made tears (not profits) "trickle down"; even more disparaging, Iliffe notes that the "trickling" of *wachuluzi* is "a word with the implication of blood seeping from a wound" (Iliffe 1979: 284). Every bit as important as the ambivalence embedded in the content of this term is the form that it took. The term *wachuluzi* is derived from a Kiswahili and not a Luhaya verb, even though this trading practice had its origins in Bukoba. At a time when Luhaya was certainly the lingua franca in this region (as it is to the present day) the use of a Kiswahili deverbative would have conveyed a clear set of allegiances. The appeal of a new world order, one centered on the Coast, removed from the regional powers of Buhaya—and even Buganda—are made plain in this term.

The allure of Kiswahili harkens back to the White Fathers' condemnations of "the Babylon of the blacks" and the nefarious *waungwana*. The term *waungwana* emerges, as I have indicated, out of the nineteenth-century context of trade and mobility. The missionaries' familiarity with, and application of this term to the social forms they witnessed in Bukoba further suggest that it had some currency in the Northwest. The term fades in importance for either the Fathers or the Bahaya, to my knowledge, after German rule. But over the course of this century an identity emerges that is characterized by much of the same uneasiness about "civilization" and its materialist underpinnings that the Fathers' attribute to the *waungwana*. This new—or newly understood—identity is simply *mswahili*, "A Swahili."

Even a cursory reading of contemporary scholarship on East Africa makes it clear that the meaning(s) of "Swahili" identity is a vexed question, encompassing matters of race and class, land and labor, ritual purity and economic enterprise. The term *mswahili* in Buhaya, though, is distinctly *not* an ethnic label. It is rarely used in reference to people who come from the Coast, practice Islam, or share a particular kind of descent. Rather, it is a category that has come to be applied in a much more general way. In Buhaya, an *mswahili* is quite simply a charlatan. To call someone an *mswahili*—and it is never (to my knowledge) a term of self-identification in Buhaya, as it has become in much of the rest of Tanzania[5]—is to suggest that they are eminently untrustworthy, and above all self-interested. An *mswahili*, unlike a "thief" (*mwizi*) or a "gangster" (*jambazi*), acts through deception, creating the illusion of sophistication and cleverness in order to dupe the unsuspecting. The *mswahili* is all appearances and the personification of instability. Indeed, the term *mswahili* itself implies instability and deracination for many Haya with whom I spoke. The designation is said to derive from the fact that urban peoples lack attachments of sociality (and so act in a self-interested way), and this loss of sociality is revealed by the fact that they only speak Swahili. The image of the *mswahili*, according my Haya friends and neighbors, was of the wayward youth who abandons his home and kin for the pursuit of money and the purportedly easy pleasures of a shiftless urban lifestyle. But to be an *mswahili* was less a mode of personal identity that one could adopt than a kind of cultural style grounded in a social situation. Anyone who took advantage of others—even one's own friends and neighbors—could be described as *mswahili*. The *mswahili* is not a member of a specific class of people, rather he exhibits a characteristic way of treating people, that is, exploiting them.

It is difficult to trace with any precision the origin or usage of this derogatory "ethnic" label. Sundkler notes that Luhaya was not only the lingua franca in Bukoba during World War II, and again in the 1960s when he worked in the region, it was also prized by elites even in public discourse where one would expect Kiswahili to be spoken (Sundkler 1980: 4). It is further interesting to note that, in contrast to Sundkler's and others' (Brumfit 1980, Eggert 1970) view that the German Administration discouraged the use of Kiswahili in order to limit the influence of Islam throughout the colony, Austen finds that the German Administration (quietly) promoted the use of Kiswahili, even diverting funds for Kiswahili language learning (Austen n.d.). Thus, the antagonism toward Kiswahili, embodied in good measure by the *mswahili* insult, requires that communities of Luhaya speakers actively worked (in everyday interaction, at least) to differentiate themselves from Kiswahili speakers. Virtually every Haya person today is fluent in Kiswahili, but it remains a language whose *spoken* use is exclusively limited to a narrow range of (usually vaguely "official") contexts.

However its contours were molded over time, it is clear that the imagined attributes of the *mswahili* identity have made it a potent oppositional category in contemporary Haya discourses of identity. The socio-spatial dynamics of this category are especially important. The *mswahili* is not only typically distanced from his rural home and local ties, he is essentially itinerant. The urban scene of the entire nation is the milieu through which he circulates, rather than inhabiting a specific region or place. As a linguistically coded identity as well, the person of the *mswahili* could readily be contrasted with people who spoke a language grounded in the sociality of a specific region, as opposed to a language that belonged to no identifiable community. Indeed, in vernacular Haya uses of Kiswahili, the term *Kiswahili* "Swahili language" is most frequently opposed, not to *Oluhaya*, the Haya term form "Haya language (and culture)," but to *Kilugha,* which I can best translate as "the Language of Language" (*lugha* is the Kiswahili for "language/tongue" and *ki*—as in

*Ki*Swahili—is the noun prefix for "way, manner, style," hence "language"). Following this logic, Kiswahili is understood as a language that, in effect, is a departure from language itself, a deviation from an authentic mode of existence.

The linguistic formulation of this opposition also permits a none too subtle critique of the nation-state to be voiced. In a polyglot world where all official "national" discourse is conducted in Kiswahili, where Radio Tanzania broadcast in Kiswahili is "so tiresome we only listen for the obituaries," and schoolteachers "will beat you if you don't speak Kiswahili," the assertion that the *mswahili* is a shameless and alien character is also a cogent political challenge. Moreover, this image of untrustworthiness is tied especially closely to the *social* use of language (and not simply to a formal code), so that one need not speak Swahili to be considered an *mswahili*. The *mswahili* is anyone who uses language in a flattering, long-winded, and deceptive way—so even speakers of the Haya language can refer to one another as *waswahili*.

I suggest, then, that the thrust of the *mswahili* accusation is antagonistic to the suffusion of Haya everyday experience with such threatening forces as: money and markets, urban restlessness and fast-paced mobility, the deceptive individualism of contemporary sociality, and the oppressive banality of the state. This antagonism, though, arises not because Bahaya do not desire to participate in the social processes that promote these forces, but rather because they *must* participate in them. The *mswahili*, that is, is rebuked because he embraces these activities in a way that allows them to dominate and define his existence, rather than defining the significance of these contemporary practices for himself. I would further compare the characteristics of the *wachuluzi* with those of the *mswahili* so that the significance of this kind of contrast may be clarified. The *wachuluzi* pursued their trade through what were necessarily local ties. Haya farmers, strapped for cash, with even a small volume of coffee, could benefit from advances made available by *wachuluzi*. Their Asian patrons were legally excluded from residing anywhere in Buhaya but designated urban marketing centers, and so, in spatial terms, the systematic relations of the coffee trade further objectified a distinction between rural producers and urban trading houses, *wachuluzi* and Asians (Curtis 1989: 124).

Over the course of this century, Asians were eventually barred from trade in the colony, and Bahaya traders rose to greater political prominence through state-run marketing boards. The emergence of coffee marketing boards and later cooperatives, many with branches throughout Buhaya, not only demonstrated the strength of the *wachuluzi*, they also facilitated the ever greater dispersal of the trading practices they participated in. Coffee did not need to be bulked and transported to an urban trading house to turn a profit—only a disparity in the loan advanced and the final selling price, even on very small volumes (e.g., a single "bowl" of coffee, the harvest of one tree) was required.

The practices of the coffee trade thus became both more widespread and more firmly grounded in rural communities.

In some ways, as I have indicated, the exploitative potential of these relations may have been resented, perhaps even more so now that neighbors with only slightly more disposable cash could enter into these activities. But in my discussions with Haya men and women in the late 1980s, these traders were less resented than lionized. The coffee trade organized in this fashion clearly established fundamental inequalities in the income that could be derived from coffee. In 1990, for example, I found that roughly 20 percent of the total number of "farmers" marketing coffee at local cooperative sold over 75 percent of the total volume of each cooperative. By controlling the harvests of their clients, these farmers—acting as *wachuluzi*—sold an inordinately disproportionate volume of each coffee harvest, a pattern that Reining also found to be the case in the early 1950s (Reining 1967).[6]

Yet, the very men I knew to be in control of these harvests were never challenged as robber barons—nor were they dismissed as *waswahili*. Such men had, on the whole, emphasized their attachments to the communities of which they were a part, not only by sponsoring *biashara ndogo ndogo*, informal economic enterprises, but also by literally grounding themselves in the localities from which they came. Successful traders made sure that even when their travels took them far from family farmlands, they had established a significant, locally valued presence in their home communities. In an earlier era, for example, the *wachuluzi* were among the leaders of a movement (described in chapter 5) challenging British efforts to impose coffee planting regulations during the 1930s, a challenge that clearly aligned these marketers with Haya farmers hoping to secure control over the productive character of their family farms (Curtis 1989: 210 ff). These traders, and those who hold similar positions today in Kagera, often built highly visible rural homes, not only for themselves but especially for their sons, a way of further confirming attachments to place *through* time (see Weiss 1996a).

This concern with attachments to place is especially significant as Bahaya generally associate commercial transactions—and money in particular—with rapid movement and intensified mobility. As I have shown elsewhere (Weiss 1996a), Haya men and women claim that money that is made quickly (*biashara kwa haraka*) is also quickly lost, or "eaten." Money itself embodies these potent yet threatening qualities, being associated especially with cars and mobility (indeed, Tanzanian notes and coins are often given the names of vehicles—e.g., "Scania," "Pajero," and "Double-Cabin"). This moralization of speed and motion not only recalls the White Fathers' anxieties about "civilization," it is also an anathema to specific Haya values of landholding, values that emphasize the stability of persons and their connections to family-held farmland as their *ekisibo*, their "foundation," or "origin." It is no surprise, then, to find that the sale of land is vilified as the most threatening kind of commercial practice, nor that money acquired from the sale of land is held to be the most rapidly "eaten."

Given these evaluations of commerce, it is most telling (and perhaps ironic) to note that by the 1980s the Kiswahili term *wachuluzi* was rarely used to describe the prosperous middlemen of the coffee trade. Now they are simply called *abalimi*, Oluhaya for "farmers," the rather quaint term—with unambiguous spatial and temporal implications—for all members of the coffee cooperatives. As one neighbor put it, "Some call them *wachuluzi*, but I call them *baraka* (blessing). Who else will help you when you have nothing!" Indeed, one extremely successful trader I knew well drove a huge truck for the coffee co-op (a more visible symbol of the mobility of the coffee trade it would be hard to imagine!), but he was widely praised for the large family he supported and the extensive family farmland he maintained. Even as he *purchased* land from his neighbors he was applauded, while those who sold land to him (often because of the crushing burdens of debt exacerbated by the demands for cash that fed this trade) were despised—many of them even dismissed as *waswahili!*

Here, then, was a praiseworthy quest for profit, one made possible by the intensively global entanglements of coffee trading, yet directed toward the improvement of apparently "local" orders of value—even while pursuing individual gains at the expense of one's fellows. Here, too, lies the full significance of the *mswahili* as the scourge of Haya sociality. For while the *mswahili* has allowed himself to be driven solely by alien purposes, coffee traders—farmers née "tricklers"—have gained some purchase on the wider world and subjected it to their purposes. In effect, the *mswahili* embodies anti-Haya modes of social existence, while successful coffee traders manifest the Haya way to conduct business.

COFFEE'S (AFTER)IMAGE: SOME CONCLUSIONS ABOUT A HISTORY OF IDENTITIES

What I have described in assessing this Haya politics of identity presents some striking parallels with the White Fathers' discourse described above. Like the Fathers' understanding of the "wangwana," the *mswahili* is also understood as a mode of existence that departs from some more fully human, and social condition. The "wangwana" and *mswahili* are both tangible evidence, for missionaries and Bahaya respectively, of the dangers of unruly social transformation, and particularly reckless materialism. In both cases as well, this type, less a specific group of people than a way of being, a spectral figure of emerging conditions, is also a reflexive vision. For both the White Fathers and the Bahaya fully recognize that they are active participants in the very social processes they abhor. The "wangwana" and *mswahili* present their respective fears of what a well-trained catechumen, or a proper Haya farmer may become, and so these also present a *limit* against which missionaries and Bahaya might *successfully* define themselves. This counter-image, this figure of contrast thus provides a means with which to negotiate the complexities of a world that one hopes to keep at bay, even as one feels compelled to inhabit it. In this politics/poetics, then, "Hayaness" is not simply defined in increasingly codified opposition to "Whiteness," "Frenchness," or some other colonial position (cf. Comaroff and Comaroff 1991). Rather, Bahaya and White Fathers *collaborated* in parallel and mutually reinforcing imaginative procedures designed to undermine the negative potentials and enhance the positive opportunities of an otherwise intractable set of circumstances.

This in itself would be an interesting story, but its complexities do not stop there. Nor is it correct to assert the apparent symmetry of what was, after all, a highly unequal set of relations. The parallels I have described do suggest a mutuality to this history; but just as the Haya were vilified for their idleness by the White Fathers, the White Fathers were not exempt from the judgments of the Haya. Indeed, there is evidence that indicates that right at the origins of the coffee trade, Haya understood that coffee markets were a means whereby Europeans were transforming *their* coffee into something more valuable by an act of obvious deception. "The coffee business," wrote one Father, "is very active. They pay up to one rupee for a small basket of coffee that holds about six liters. The gossipers claim that it is made into 'moka' on the European markets. Too bad for the amateurs" (Diare du Poste de Rubya [Ihangiro]: 19 August 1906). This exploitation, facilitated by (overseas) transport and the selling of appearances that belie underlying realities, sounds suspiciously like contemporary notions of *waswahili* practice. While I never heard a Catholic priest or cleric derided as an *mswahili* in Kagera, their dispositions *were* routinely described in ways that resonate with this identity. The local priests and nuns, themselves all Tanzanians, and the majority of them Bahaya, were viewed with great skepticism by most of the villagers I knew. They were suspect because of the conditions under which they lived—outside of families and in quarters that had no clear resemblance to a "house."[7] These arrangements seemed disorderly, and quintessentially "unknowable" as though designed to keep outsiders from understanding, not only particular whereabouts of anyone at any time, but the specific relationship between persons and place. "Where do they live?" my friends wondered; "*Huwezi kujua*" "You cannot know." This intrinsic lack of clarity was further linked to the potential deceptions of their position. Priests presented the appearance of absolute propriety; but beneath that exterior, and within their unknowable confines you could be certain that the "Fathers and Sisters help each other out." Aside from these commonplace anticlerical suspicions, local priests were also felt to have largely material motives. The tremendous educational opportunities they enjoyed, in a nation where secondary schooling is almost an unimaginable luxury, were seen to be put to the service of largely personal gain. Priests were known as snappy dressers who routinely wore glasses. Some even said that upon being admitted to the priesthood each Father was presented with his own motorcycle.

It would be a mistake, though, to see contemporary Tanzanian priests as direct substitutes for turn-of-the-century French missionaries. Bahaya, like other Tanzanians, clearly distinguish the motives and character of different clergy from different eras. Still, it is important to recognize that contemporary clerics—and the ways in which they are imagined—are the product of the historical encounters described. The standardized (or slanderous) reputations to which they are subject today can never tell us how Bahaya viewed, or might have viewed, the White Fathers. Rather, these current-day images reveal how both the missionaries' fears about their delinquent catechumens as easily diverted by the "pursuit of pleasure," and long-standing Haya concerns with the deceptiveness of radically self-interested commercial activity have been articulated in a process of grappling with the moral quandaries of materialism. Fancily dressed, and sexually suspect clergy correspond in many ways to conniving *waswahili* and recall as well the dangerous "wangwana" of earlier decades, which indicates that Bahaya and White Fathers participated *together* in a counterpoint enunciation of identities. At times, the themes of this process recall one another directly, as the excesses of desire, alienation, and dislocation are condemned. Alternatively, the claims of Bahaya and the missionaries hold one another up as examples of the very limit which the other cannot be permitted to partake of. I would go further and suggest that even when their interests appear to coincide, the motivations for their protests are actually antagonistic: The itinerant wangwana has failed to "persevere" in his authentic being for the White Fathers; while the *mswahili* has failed, not to maintain his real character, but rather, to see his *potential* as grounded in a regional world where persons are engaged—sometimes in conflict, sometimes in common cause—with others. Further, the Muhaya, in the missionary view, needed to be elevated from his intrinsic condition of idleness, while the European, in the Haya view, was prone to mislead and exploit local farmers and traders. Each of these visions understands the dangerous prospects of commercial enterprise, but they comprehend the place of power (i.e., who controls and who is controlled *by* this commerce) in rather different ways. This counterpoint does reveal, though, that both the White Fathers and the Bahaya were entangled in a creative elaboration of their alternative places—and often unwelcome places—in a rapidly transforming world. Each molded the other after its own image, and simultaneously used that other in a reflexive fashion, now to associate, now to disassociate itself from the often fearful image it beheld.

My contention in this chapter has been that the fitful resolution (or complication) of the quandaries raised by the growth of coffee marketing are not reducible either to a simple "Christian" opposition to worldliness, nor a "traditional" Haya preference for local mores and forms of wealth. Clearly, any number of Christian missionaries in other parts of the world have seen commerce as a path to conversion, and many Haya did embrace the coffee trade over the course of the last century. It may be suggested, to follow the Weberian line, that Catholic missionaries were less inclined to see material pursuits as means to promote the faith. In his study of the Holy Ghost fathers in Uluguru, Peter Pels shows how a Catholic education, akin to what I have described in Kagera, emphasized "discipline" above learning (Pels 1999). Even as late as the 1940s these missionaries "complained that [teachers] became more and more interested in money and had 'no idea about their duties' and 'little faith'" (Pels 1999: 223).

While the situation in Buhaya at the turn of the last century certainly embodies a more general Catholic attitude, I would add that the specificities of the White Fathers' misgivings emerges in the *encounter* between themselves and their Bahaya interlocutors. The Fathers did not simply reject "materialism" and monetary spoils, they worried about the ways that unbridled commerce created "wangwana," an unruly mixture of persons: Christians and "rouleurs," converted Bahaya clerks, and apostate Baganda traders. Nor did Bahaya simply fear the dangers of buying and selling, dependency and exploitation. Rather they decried the deceptive appearances and dislocation of productivity, embodied by the *mswahili*, that commercial enterprise seemed so often to entail. Each of these perspectives is undoubtedly part of a broader, indeed, global discourse about the risks of colonial capitalism. Yet, the content of these global jeremiads takes on its specific form—and so acquires its concrete meaning—in the contingencies of this ongoing dialogue between these missionaries and this African community. The conversation between White Fathers and Bahaya provided the terms in which these moral anxieties acquired their enduring social relevance.

NOTES

1. I take the position that the names I have affixed to these peoples (e.g., "Haya" and "Swahili") are, of course, historical constructions—the "Haya" are self-conscious of their identity as a "people" only as a consequence of the sociohistorical encounters at issue here, and there is a vast and burgeoning literature on the vexed question of "Swahili" identity, as it is understood in such very different places as Eastern Zaire, Central Tanzania, and Zanzibar (e.g., Fabian 1991; Middleton 1992; Geiger, n.d.). Nonetheless, I would insist that while these terms of community self-identification, and a consciousness of cultural identity as such, are emergent within the context of colonial enterprises, it is also the case that there were *culturally different* social relations, categories, and actions engaged in these processes. "Hayaness," that is, is certainly a relatively recent entity, but the meanings and values—the culture—embedded in the everyday practices, and embodied in social agents I am here calling "Haya" have greater coherence and real historical depth than the limited issue of "ethnicity" implies (Sahlins 1993).

2. This exemplifies a highly predictable attempt by Haya farmers to enclave food from commodification, an avoidance of marketing food—especially staple crops—that continues to define local efforts to avoid using market values to determine the wealth that is created by food (Weiss 1996a).

3. To this day in Kagera, smoking marijuana is felt to give one strength and especially endurance; it is expressly associated with hard work and porterage, movement and transport.

4. Indeed, Haya merchants frequently traded coffee cherries from Bukoba for Ganda bark cloth. In this way the links of clothing and coffee have long-standing ties.

5. In my research in Arusha I have found that Tanzanians typically describe the "the people" of the nation (in the sense of the general public) as *Waswahili.*

6. My data from 1988–1989 for an admittedly small number of cooperatives suggest that less than one-quarter of the overall number of subscribers sell over three-quarters of the total volume of coffee marketed in Kagera. In my sample, of 122,342 kgs of coffee marketed by cooperatives with a total of 481 members, the 97 members (20.1 percent of membership) marketing the highest volumes of coffee sold 91,823 kgs, or 75.1 percent of the total volume. This figure, moreover, is skewed by the fact that those who market the greater volumes of coffee are much more likely to be registered as members of several cooperatives. Therefore, the 97 memberships cited above represent many fewer *individuals,* each of whom has multiple memberships. This, in turn, means that an even smaller percentage of *individuals* controls this share of coffee volume (Weiss 1996c).

7. The "Swahili-style" house that became widespread during the late colonial era in urban Tanganyika (Geiger, n.d.) was a style that resembled the Catholic quarters. It was a style that many Haya disdained as "mlango mmoja" "one door," which they associated with a kind of confusion, an inability to distinguish who lived where in the interior of a house. "Mlango mmoja" was also the standard colloquial euphemism for prostitution.

4

Wood, Land, and Water: A Colonial Arboretum

> For ten or so trees that we had cut down, the king has accused us in Bukoba of having cut down all the forests of Kiziba.
>
> Diare du Poste, Mugana: 16 April 1902

The transformations in consciousness evident in Haya uses of money, their interest in facilitating trade, and their understandings of wealth more generally under German rule were facilitated by the appearance of novel currencies, the introduction of literacy, and new modes of transportation; each of these was only one part of a much wider set of practices concerned with evaluation, measurement, and objectification. It was not, however, sufficient to introduce rupees and coinage, nor to impose taxes on "heads" and "huts," nor to establish prices for goods, in order to generate these unprecedented and unexpected understandings of value among Haya peoples. A crucial dimension of the processes that contributed to changing Haya modes of evaluation, and to novel configurations of property and personhood, were the ongoing efforts to transform Haya agricultural practice.

The White Fathers, as I have made clear, were plainly implicated in the very economic practices they decried. This entanglement is even more complicated, and in some ways of even greater consequence, when taking into consideration the broader material projects in which the White Fathers figured in the early years of the twentieth century, projects that directly affected the multidimensional Haya landscape. With respect to the cultivation and husbandry of coffee trees, as I have already suggested, the shift from vegetative to generative propagation made possible new ways of realizing the potential of coffee trees, helped to reconfigure the relationship between origins and products, and further altered the ways in which the value of trees and their harvests could be apprehended. This change in propagation represents but one of many attempts at innovating the agrarian techniques of coffee culture in rural Buhaya. These projects have a long history, extending from quite early in Haya encounters with Europeans and continuing right through the colonial and postcolonial periods up until the present day. At times agricultural campaigns in Haya villages have been pursued intensively, on occasion even brutally, and been the focus of considerable social concern and action. Still, there is good reason to argue that colonial and postcolonial agrarian reform enterprises have been "successful" in rather limited, specific, perhaps even peculiar ways. The changing value of coffee has transformed the political economy and sociocultural order of Haya communities, but that transformation is not a simple reflex of changes in the nature of coffee cultivation in this region.

Colonial strategies of agrarian reform, it must be noted, were not limited to efforts aimed at improving and expanding coffee production. Agricultural extension policy makers have addressed themselves to a host of botanical diseases and infestations; attempted to ensure Haya food provisioning by mandating the planting of pest and drought resistant crops; experimented with chemical, green, and bovine fertilizers; and, most important from the perspective of Haya farmers and their households, proposed significant changes in techniques for tending to bananas, the staple of daily meals throughout Buhaya. Moreover, these agrarian interventions were themselves situated in broader endeavors to alter the physical landscape by a number of methods. Constructing buildings, establishing roads, and locating colonial outposts like missions and administrative centers were just a few of the procedures that remade place in Buhaya. Taken as a whole, the historical reconstruction of the agricultural and geographical contours of this inhabited terrain can shed light on the shifting significance of coffee as plant life, harvested product, and commodity. A rich understanding of this reconstruction further indicates that Haya communities have frequently made sense of and acted upon these innovations and interventions through their engagement with coffee. In this and the following chapter, I argue that in adopting certain new methods, openly and explicitly resisting others, Haya farmers were most commonly *practicing* a kind of sustained indifference. Bahaya hindered and delimited the reform of their landholding and agriculture without attacking these reforms outright.

Throughout the colonial and postcolonial eras Haya farmers rarely attempted to expand their coffee holdings vastly, or even to increase existing levels of coffee production dramatically. Resources that have been devoted to making profits from coffee have been invested in commercial activities other than intensifying coffee planting. This sustained indifference, though, is not without its own significance. Neither the natural inclination of the "lazy Bukoba native," nor a failure of the "peasantry" either to be "captured" (Hyden 1969) or of the colonial state to permit the capitalization of the means of production (Curtis 1989),[1] Haya farmers' less than wholehearted appropriation of "improved" coffee cultivation provided an important avenue through which to exert a measure of control over their encounters with the global forces of capital and colonialism. Through an exploration of the many dimensions of colonial and postcolonial agricultural transformation in Buhaya, and focusing in particular on the implications of these transformations as revealed in the changing practices of Haya coffee production, this chapter and the next consider what "successful" agrarian reform might mean and how the appearance of widespread "improvements" might conceal a more complex reality.

Let me say a word about my method of presentation in the chapter. I am attempting to describe Haya agricultural activity as a system of value production, for the purpose of establishing a cultural context in terms of which the introduction of coffee, and the reconfiguration of the Haya landscape more generally, would have been experienced and acted upon. Because my focus is on the ordinary techniques of cultivation, and not, for example, declining access to arable land, or the fluctuating markets for particular agricultural products, or the administrative efforts to redefine the nature of landholding itself, it may appear as though my account is normative or "ahistorical." I do not think that this is the case, in part because my contention is that certain fundamental practices, and the values they create, have endured over the course of much the past century. As I stated in my introduction, many such practices and values remain inarticulate; it hardly seems worth commenting on the best way to weed a banana grove, for example. At the same time, I would note that there is, in fact, evidence for the fact that Haya men and women have been engaged in precisely such ordinary practices for a very long time.

Rehse's (1910) descriptions of the attention given to bananas on farms in Kiziba at the turn of the twentieth century were strikingly similar to my own observations at the end of the century. I would not wish, though, to make the evidence presented here, drawn from materials collected over the course of several decades, conform to a model of what is "typical." In what follows I do attempt to locate particular practices at specific historical moments as carefully as is possible; yet my primary intention is to characterize certain modes of practice that resonate over time and so shape the character of historical encounters over agriculture in Buhaya.

HAYA FARMLAND: KINGS, CLANS, AND HOUSEHOLDS

To reiterate, then, my purpose in this chapter is to provide an overview of Haya farming practices and engagements with the land in order to provide some basic orientations that will allow me to trace the consequences of agrarian reform in this region over the last century. Haya villages (sing. *ekyaro*) have long been composed of a large group of spatially contiguous households, each of which occupies its own farmland. These family farms, *ekibanja* (*ebibanja*, pl.) in the vernacular, are held by the most senior household head of multigenerational families. A father, for example, could designate an area of his ekibanja for his married sons (and, after 1944, to a daughter) to reside in and to cultivate, while retaining possession of this farm (or it may be multiple farms) as a whole until his death. As this generational arrangement suggests, such family farms are ideally transmitted agnatically, from fathers to sons, or senior male agnates to junior men. The borders of farms held by neighbors—including agnatic relatives living in adjacent households descended from a single ekibanja—are always recognized, and are often marked by boundary plants. Individual farmland possessed and occupied in this way is considered "wealth" as I have previously discussed this term. It is held by a person in virtue of their generational connections to those who have provided it for them, which in turn allows them to possess the authority to pass it on to their agnatic successors.

There is, however, an array of processes that complicate this ideal pattern of devolution. In contemporary Kagera, landholding is *the* primary site for the contestation of commoditization, as land held as what is now known as "clan farmland" (ekibanja *ky'oluganda*) is quite frequently subject to purchase and sale (see Weiss 1996a: chapter 7 for extensive discussion of the issues surrounding these controversial practices). But the tensions surrounding the sale of this household farmland have important antecedents in colonial and precolonial practices that also mitigated against the reproduction of lineal relations through the transmission of these "estates." To begin with, households did not always successfully reproduce agnatic relations. It was not uncommon in Buhaya for a household head to die without producing a male heir, and without agnatic kin to inherit his farm (indeed, demographic evidence suggests that reproductive success, owing to regular epidemics of venereal disease in the 1930s and again in the 1950s, was problematic through the early independence period; see Reining and Richards 1954). Such a condition, known as *okuchweka*, "to leave off," allowed control of the deceased's farmland to revert to the mukama, who could then dispense with it as he chose. In contemporary genealogies many Haya landholders report that they are living on a farm that was "bestowed" upon one of their lineal ancestors by the king. Throughout the British colonial era, the policy of indirect rule granted (but also struggled with) administrative recognition of the rights of kings to redistribute land for which no heir could be determined (Reining 1967; Austen 1968; Curtis 1989). It was also common for kings to organize the administration of their kingdoms by placing administrative agents, usually royals themselves, on "left off" farms that were more remote from the royal capital (*ekikale*).

Another way in which kings controlled landholding in order to establish administrative estates proved immensely important to the entire history of

Buhaya in the twentieth century, and continues to influence contemporary concerns about the attachments of people to their lands. Kings could designate a series of family farms, usually contiguous households, as "large farms"—*nyarubanja*—whose occupants became the "tenants" (*mutwalwa*) of a "landlord" (*mutwazi*) appointed by the king. The positions of "tenant" and "landlord" then became heritable statuses with respect to these lands. The expansion of the nyarubanja system with the rise of coffee planting, and the contested nature of land claims, as land sales and the category of "ownership" became the focus of British land reform policies, indicate that nyarubanja was a critical focus of the colonial and early postcolonial history of Buhaya. I will discuss these concerns below; but for now it is important to demonstrate the connection of these estates to Haya kingship, and its role in creating connections between land and social persons. Nyarubanja estates in the precolonial period could apparently be designated by a number of different methods. After a king died, for example, his capital would not be occupied by his successor; but this capital would become a nyarubanja *ya gashani*—"Large farm of the blessed grave"—and the householders who lived and worked on this estate would become the tenants of the royal mediums who practiced at these sites (Curtis 1989: 100). Or if the king's son cut his first tooth on a particular *kibanja* it would become an estate of the king, and its present occupants would become tenants (Mutahaba 1969: 7; see also Weiss 1992 for the importance of teeth to Haya personhood and agency). Further, it was easiest for a king to designate nyarubanja from those *kibanja* that he had most recently bestowed upon others. That is, the longer a clan or family could trace their lineal connections to a farm the more difficult it became to displace them (Mutahaba 1969: 6–7). These nyarubanja holdings never accounted for more than 10 to 20 percent of all the farmland held in Buhaya (Reining 1962: 63), but they were nonetheless important sources of patronage, labor, and tribute for their noble estate holders. And they permitted a king both to cultivate relationships with his noble clients and simultaneously to disperse these potential competitors, thereby preventing them from consolidating power (Curtis 1989: 99–100).

The attachments of persons to place facilitated by the powers of kingship demonstrate that mobility and dispersal, as well as locatedness and fixity were intrinsic elements in the Haya order of landholding. Moreover, they seem to be have been dialectically related. Simply put, in order for land to be bestowed as an enduring form of wealth upon landless subjects of the king, that land had to have been alienated (by royal decree, failed reproduction, or any other discontinuity in landholding clan relations). Further, people made dependent on a king in their search for land must have found themselves displaced from the lands to which they once were connected. This displacement might have been the result of a number of processes. In addition to the crises of war and famine that Haya most often cite as the motives for people moving in search of new farmland (a claim that demonstrates the force of Haya ideologies of landholding that emphasize the importance of attachment to farms and of remaining in place. Movement, by this reckoning, is a kind of pathology that would only be resorted to in desperation), Reining reported in the 1950s that an ekibanja was supposed to devolve as a non-partible unit, and brothers who were not primary heirs and whose senior agnates all had heirs of their own would thus have been required to look elsewhere for access to land (Reining 1967). My informants in Ihangiro in the late 1980s reported that all sons—and after 1944 all daughters—had always been entitled to inherit some of the land held by their household head, which suggests that Reining's report may represent a regional variation. Nonetheless, even if ekibanja were partible into smaller parcels, there would have been additional reasons to seek access to other lands. Farms might easily become too small to sustain all of a man's heirs after a few generations of devolution within a clan. It is also crucial to point out that relations between agnates often became untenable, as, for example, marital conflicts between brothers' spouses frequently lead to a severance of relations between clan members.[2] "Clanship" as a structural principle, then, did not ensure the continuity of landholding; and land is not merely an "estate" whose recognized status is an expression of enduring lineal social relations. Rather, clan identities and stable, perduring family farms were realized in relation to royal prerogatives that both underlay and undermined these forms of attachment. Kings could originate the endowment process that makes land a form of lineal wealth, and they interrupted those identifications as well. While absorbing detached farms lost through weakened ties of descent (the product of both failed social and bodily reproduction) a power they exercized even well into the 1950s, Haya kings simultaneously regenerated the bonds of farm and family by using these same farms to initiate new chains of wealth bestowal.

WEALTH IN DEATH

It is crucial to recognize, however, that these dialectical articulations of rootedness in place and movement across the landscape, endowment from senior to junior and divisiveness between agnates, and clanship and kingship are not merely structural relations in a conceptual order. These potentials for attachment and separation were realized, sustained, and ultimately changed through concrete sociocultural practices that were themselves subject, as this discussion will make clear, to historical shifts and transformations. An example of the kind of practices through which lineal attachments to family farms was insured is instructive. In my earlier discussion of royal places I suggested that the Haya kings' capacity to remake place and connections to the land were exemplified by their ability to move away from the capital of their deceased predecessor (see chapter 1).

This nexus of concerns surrounding land and death are worth considering in greater detail. Elsewhere I have written at length about the importance of death and burial to securing familial attachments to the ekibanja (Weiss 1996a). As Reining observed in the early 1950s, "[T]he most convincing statement a man can make in justifying the validity of his [farm] ownership is to say that his father is buried in his *kibanja*." (Reining 1967: 235). In the context of the nyarubanja system burial practices became concrete sites of struggle. In 1928, for example, the British, "indirectly ruling" through the Bakama Council, established new nyarubanja rules designed to limit the powers of landlords to extract rent from their tenants. Tenants, however, objected to the provision, codified in these rules, that they were not permitted to bury their dead on the farms they occupied without permission of their landlord. If this were permitted the tenants might challenge their landlord's authority by citing these graves as a tangible claim to actually "owning" the land on which they resided (Mutahaba 1969: 7; Curtis 1989: 108). In contemporary Buhaya, my neighbors also insisted that nyarubanja failed to recognize the significance of burial, but remembered this disregard in different terms. "Your father worked his whole life on his farm, and you bury him there, and then somebody comes along and kicks you off of the land he's left you! It isn't right!" is how one of them put it (Weiss 1996a: 217). In these two formulations, the rules as they were written or as they are recalled, burial substantiates lineal attachments to a farm in both retrospective and prospective terms (see Schutz 1967; Hanks 1996: 128). One buries the dead on a farm both retrospectively, because burying the deceased in his farm demonstrates the ongoing habitation of this recognized place, and prospectively, in order to confirm future attachments of the deceased's descendants to that place.

Contrast the implications and potential of these practices on the ekibanja, then, to the consequences of royal burial at the *ekikale*. When kings died in the nineteenth and early twentieth centuries, their graves became sacred sites, attended to by spirit mediums, and—as I have shown—propitiated by successive bakama during New Moon ceremonies. And yet, the deceased king's successor *abandoned* the grave and the farm and the residence of the capital. Each successive Haya king severed the very spatial continuities between royal generations that were, and still are, absolutely crucial to the formulation of clan and household identities. But the mukama did so precisely in order to establish for *himself* his own capital. Moreover, kings not only distanced themselves from their predecessors and created their own capitals, they further avoided the obligations of *fixed* attachments to particular places by maintaining a group of dispersed capitals throughout their realms among which they circulated. I noted above the White Fathers' observation that it was tough to keep track of the bakama because with every new moon they would "rush to change residences." Beattie also notes that the kings of Bunyoro maintained a set of different residences and perpetually moved between them (Beattie 1970).

These capacities to secure for oneself new moorings in place and to move among different places, to establish recognized centers of power and authority and to dissociate oneself from such centers of the past demonstrate that Haya kings encompassed the potential limits of attachment and separation, fixity and mobility that characterized this sociocultural order. In encompassing these limits through their actual practices the bakama could also *embody* the generative origin, or foundation for these possibilities. The king was not bound by the obligations of previous generations, even previous kings, in his connections to the land for he is himself the very source of all such connections. By separating himself from the graves of his royal ancestors, the same sites that—as all Haya landholders continue to recognize—secure farmers' positions on their ebibanja, the Haya king was able to demonstrate his ability to create attachments to place that did not depend upon, or even recognize, the authority of others to determine these attachments for him. In effect, by removing himself from connections created by the power of his predecessors, each mukama assumes the power to assert his connection to his kingdom as a whole—surely *the* definitive feature of "sacred kingship" wherever it is found—and so he maintains royal capitals throughout the land. The ability to produce these powerful attachments in place is a portable attribute of the ever mobile king.

As the originary source of identification with all places, the mukama makes it possible for others to secure their ties to specific farms. Unrestrained by the demands of generational obligations, the king's bestowal of wealth imposes precisely such obligations on others as an aspect of his authority. Again, this is not an "ancient" truth, indirectly shaping contemporary relations; it is an ongoing condition that was directly invoked in innumerable claims made even in late twentieth-century Buhaya. Indeed, Haya household members conventionally articulated their firm attachments to recognized places as obligations that ensued from the original bestowal of family farms to these households' agnatic ancestors by the king himself. Even when royal bestowal played no part in land acquisition, as is the case for all land acquired by means other than inheritance after 1963, the obligation to "stay by the graves of your father" remains a compelling defense of land claims. In the case of both commoner and king, then, sociocultural practices attending to death formulate the character of connections to the land and the authorities that create, maintain, or transcend those connections.

WORKING THE LAND: CONTRASTING TOPOGRAPHIES

Burial practices in Haya communities are perhaps the most morally charged focus for demonstrating and characterizing human commitments to and identifications with place. Carrying out these activities, knowing the records of and memorials to their enactments on a recognized farm, and referring to them in moments of dispute and crisis contributes to the formation of the social identities that reside in these lands, but it also shapes and informs the qualities of the lands themselves. Haya farms have long had a presence in Haya social life. They attract and recall, move people to act, demonstrate the character of those who dwell on the land, and furnish inhabitants with a perspective from which to encounter neighbors, paths, clearings, and more distant villages. While the multiple practices attending to death provide some of the most self-conscious, even dramatic, modes of constituting place and its residence, the Haya habits of inhabiting rural landscapes are more continuously enacted in the quotidian tasks of cultivation and farming. I discuss these activities and their implications, and much of what follows in this section, in rather different terms elsewhere (Weiss 1996a, chapter 4). The material presented here synthesizes and builds on that discussion. It characterizes agricultural practice at the turn of the twentieth century in Buhaya, and is offered as the context necessary to an understanding of the history of agrarian reform in this region.

From the viewpoint of agrarian activities Haya, land—*ensi*—is assessed in terms of a set of different categories. The most important division recognized in types of cultivated land is the one drawn between residential farmland, ebibanja (the sites of household occupancy I have been considering), and the open grasslands, known as *orweya*, that border on and occasionally surround Haya villages. In my earlier discussion of trees as icons of enduring place (chapter 1) I noted that the distinction between family farms and grasslands was most frequently recognized by the presence of trees on the former, and that planting trees was a practice that could objectify efforts to convert grassland to farmland, thereby changing the character of control over the land. Trees, and coffee trees among them, *are* a crucially important feature of farmlands, but they are by no means the sole attribute that would have distinguished family farmland from grasslands. The overall topographies of these worked places, for example, were—and still are—notably different, as patterns of planting and crop spacing, borders and central zones, movements into and out of these lands, and the spatial coordination between different regions—from one family farm to the next, or one grassland field to another—are all organized in ways that generate striking contrasts between ebibanja and *orweya*. So, too, are the qualities of the labor necessary to work these lands.

Distinctions have long been recognized in the temporality of work in its annual, seasonal, and daily cycles, and in the relative endurance or impermanence of specific sites of cultivation. Perhaps most important, a broad distinction is recognized in the gendered dimensions of agricultural activities carried out in family farmlands and grasslands. Men are identified with, but not the exclusive farmers of, the ekibanja, while women are strongly identified with, and in fact virtually the exclusive farmers of, the *orweya*. Finally—although food certainly does not take last place in the view of Haya villagers—food crops are the primary product of agricultural practice in each area.[3] On both family farms and grassland fields farmers grow a diverse group of foods, and the types of food grown within each place is quite different. I want to consider each of these parameters—the contours of the landscapes, the activities that inform these landscapes, and the products of those activities—as a means of conveying both a rich sense of the contrasts between family farmlands and grasslands, and an appreciation of this contrast as an *evaluative* distinction recognized by Haya men and women. For it is the value of these different places and practices that is at issue in the colonial encounters that strove to rework agricultural activities in Buhaya.

Family farms, as I have already indicated, are spaces both of cultivation and residence. The situation of the house on the ekibanja serves as a point of orientation for agricultural activities in many respects. While tree crops, namely banana plants[4]—*engemu*—and coffee trees—*omumwani*, cover all of the arable land of the farm, there is clearly a spatial pattern to their planting. This pattern (which has been reported from the late nineteenth through the twentieth century, Rehse 1910; Reining 1967; Weiss 1996a), while continuous in both temporal terms (at all points in the year bananas and coffee are grown) and spatial terms (these trees are planted throughout the farm), is not uniform. Rather, a relative gradient with respect to the position of the family house determines the spacing of trees. Those plants considered best for eating at family meals (large plantains) are grown closest to the house, and as plants are less and less appropriate for eating in household meals (sweet bananas, *obunan*, for snacks through beer bananas, *embile*, grown to be brewed for beer) they are planted farther and farther from the house. Finally, coffee trees are planted on the fringes of the farm relative to the house, usually interspersed among beer bananas.

This concentric planting pattern demonstrates, for Haya farmers, significant qualities of the household itself, namely enclosure and interiority. Plants intended for household consumption are immediately adjacent to the house itself (meals are only taken within the enclosed house by household members), while the plants more distant from the house may be offered to, or even intended for, non-household members. The topography of the cultivated ekibanja thus strongly identifies the household with the farm, as both the spatial position of the house and the sustenance of the household are the center and focus of Haya agricultural practice. Moreover, this spatial configuration not only secures a household in its own land, it further serves to define the relationship *between* households and farms. Each Haya household is the discreet center of its practices (i.e., there is no uniform spatial plan that coordinates the relation between houses within a village, or between villages) and positions its connections to neighboring and distant households at a remove from that sociospatial center. Simply put, plants relatively central to the home most readily move into that household, relatively peripheral plants most readily move away from it, establishing a pattern of sociality that reflexively defines each household's centrality as simultaneously its separation from other similarly centered households.

In topographic terms, residential farmland has long been organized as a set of discretely centered units, units whose very relationships to one another serve to demonstrate the separate independence of each. This sociospatial pattern conforms to the qualities already described as characteristic of Haya forms of wealth, which also ground the detachability of discrete, independent yet composite forms (composite since the ekibanja grows an array of crops, both for household and extra-household consumption, and as I shall describe both perennial and annual plants, and men's and women's products) in the matrix of collective relations. It is not surprising, then, to find that household farms have long been the most highly valued form of material wealth in Haya communities, as they fully exemplify the spatial as well as temporal qualities characteristic of such objectifications. These qualities are markedly distinct from those that characterize the terrain of the grasslands that lie at a remove from residential villages. In the early years of this century the *orweya* was simply open, unowned savanna. It was, and continues to be, the site of food cultivation, made possible by turning this notably infertile land (Reining 1967; Rald and Rald 1975) into small fields (*omusili*). In contrast to the ekibanja, these fields are planted exclusively with annual crops, mostly legumes like peanuts and field peas (*enshoro*), and, more recently, tubers like sweet potatoes and cassava. In topographic terms, the fields tend to be discontinuous areas with large uncleared patches of land between the small fields that have been prepared for planting. Their arrangement with respect to one another does not seem to be coordinated by a common pattern; in my contemporary experience, fields could be tilled perpendicular to one another, spread far apart, or even bordering on one another in some cases.

The grasslands are often found in relatively mountainous terrain, and the visible pattern of plots generations old grown over with grasses indicates that the fields could be tilled both across and down slopes (Rald and Rald 1975). Within these fields there is also no routinely focused pattern of planting. While family farms are centered on the household as the guiding orientation of cultivation, grassland fields have a more homogeneous and uniform appearance, as parallel rows of crops are planted in rectilinear spaces.[5] The distance of these fields from residential farms, and the planting arrangements within them suggests that, unlike ekibanja farming, *orweya* cultivation has long been relatively less closely identified with the households that engage in these practices. Indeed, the social composition of *orweya* farming groups (which often consist of women drawn from multiple households) as well as the ultimate uses of the harvested crops (which routinely circulate between households, villages, and even different kingdoms) confirms this distancing from the singular, independent Haya household.[6]

DIVISIONS OF LAND AND LABOR

The mere physical arrangements of these fields, while suggestive of wider understandings of objectification and of sociality, are not sufficient to account for the kind and character of the social relationships literally at work in them, relationships that constitute important connections between these agricultural locales. Household farms have long been held neither as freehold property, nor as collectively owned estates, but as land that is tied through time to collective relations, principally agnatic clans; but these are also understood as wealth "owned" or "ruled" by a specific individual, and through the first half of the twentieth century, always a male individual. Each household head—*ninyeka*—has a recognized authority over specific, spatially delimited, often carefully bounded farms. Juniors who inherit a single farm from an ascendant generation may all occupy what was once a unified place, but they will be told and continue to recognize the borders of their own farms with respect to one another. When relations between a generation of heirs have become strained—often precisely over questions as to the boundaries of their residential farms—these borders may come to be marked with *omulumula*, a plant that has been recognized literally for centuries as the most certain index of a boundary (Seitel 1986). Being a household head, therefore, entails a capacity to claim individual entitlement to an individuated, known place.

Nyarubanja tenancy proved especially contentious, as the efforts of the British administration to reform its organization thorughout the colonial era attest, in part, because the ability to assert and contest distinct, recognizable borders—and thus the close identification between a single residential farmer and the family farm he occupied that is necessary to assert the status of a household head—was seriously undermined. One former landlord I spoke with in 1989 lamented the fact that relations between neighbors had "become" contentious owing to the numerous changes in the nyarubanja rules in both colonial and postcolonial eras. And he attributed this contention to the fact that nyarubanja tenants did not mark their boundaries with *omulumula* in the past; rather, the limits to a tenant's farm might be marked only by placing the felled stem of a banana plant along a path, or cleared area of farmland. Of course, what he did not state was the fact that the area of the nyarubanja as a whole would be bounded and planted with these border plants, thus assuring that the landlord retained his identification with a recognizable unit of land, while his tenants were not entitled to exercise such "rule." This contrast between a relatively permanent, rooted, growing boundary marker and a highly perishable, felled, and finished banana stem as signs of a border's certainty and strength will prove significant when considering the kinds of practices agricultural extension projects have attempted to implement in Buhaya throughout this century. For present purposes, this difference demonstrates the value Haya household heads have long attributed to borders for establishing individualized connections of family farms to discrete units of farmland.

If the authorities of clanship, masculinity, household autonomy, and bordered delimitations are all in place (or subject to contestation) in Haya family farms, the fields of the *orweya* were socially organized along very different lines. The grasslands themselves, in the early years of this century were said to be "empty," lands that were not associated with the enduring tenure of any clan and not owned by any particular person. The fields that were worked in the *orweya* were, as they are to this day, highly seasonal and temporary. These fields are turned in plots that are fallowed from one season to the next, and no permanent attachment to these places endures beyond that season. The apparently ephemeral qualities of these plots do not, however, mean that they are known and worked in an ad hoc fashion. Grassland fields may be relatively detached from the relationships between individuated units of family farms that constitute Haya residential villages, but they are no less socially significant. To begin with, it is notable that while family farms are owned by single male household heads, grassland fields may be cultivated by a particular woman, or collectively by a group of women from the same, or just as frequently, different households. Both Rald and Rald and Reining reported that it was not infrequent to find groups of matrikin—sisters, mothers' sisters, and daughters—coming together from different villages to work a given woman's fields (Reining 1967; Rald and Rald 1975). Today, women's mutual aid societies (their *vyama)* typically contribute their labor to one another's *orweya* fields. In sociospatial terms, then, the ekibanja is a spatial site worked (in general) by its residents, which strongly grounds agricultural practice and provision in fixed attachments to that place; while a given expanse of *orweya* may attract women—some related by affinity, proximity, or simple friendship—from distant villages to a single, but shifting site of farming.

It is also the case that fields may be "ruled" by individual Haya women yet worked collectively. Individual cultivators frequently cooperate in farming, as each agrees to work with groups of women who circulate among the separate fields of their cooperative group at moments when intensive labor is needed. Such intensive work projects involving cooperation among groups of male kin and neighbors is not unheard of within Haya villages in order, for example, to pasture livestock, or to brew beer, or—well into the twentieth century—to construct a new house. But to my knowledge Haya men have never *cultivated* together on the farms of their fellow household heads. Such acts would be tantamount to admitting that one was unable to provide for one's own household and had to rely on the work of outsiders to feed one's family.[7] Cooperation between women extends to other aspects of agrarian practice. In spatial terms, the discontinuous nature of *omusili* fields is countered by the fact that the grassland is generally open so that perceptual, bodily contact between neighboring women working separate fields is relatively unimpeded. These connections are often enacted by frequent conversation and laughter among women at work, by sharing related activities—especially child care—for women farming different fields, and even by singing and intermittent dancing while farming. Further, as I have suggested, the crops harvested from grassland fields may be shared among members of a work party, or perhaps more frequently, pooled as gifts to be provided for major ceremonies and celebrations (Weiss 1996a: 115). The dimensions of grassland cultivation suggest a number of important sociospatial contrast with family farms. For if ekibanja farms relate to one another as contiguous, but separate, centered and bounded units, with *relationships* among farms confirming the *distinction* between them, *orweya* fields may be discontiguously distributed, but the relationships among these fields asserts the close connections between them. The active bodies of farming Haya women, their planting patterns, and the use of the products of their labor generate a sense that occupancy is shared within these grasslands.

In broad terms, there is a contrast in the gendered work and occupancy of family farms and grassland fields, as men are understood in Haya communities to be the primary farmers of ekibanja, while women farm in the *orweya.* This long-standing understanding, though, is belied by the range of practices carried out in each locale. Men are, indeed, responsible for the perennial "tree crops" of the ekibanja, planting, pruning, and harvesting bananas and coffee.[8] But women are also active farmers on household lands. On an annual basis, in the light rainy season (late October), women plant beans that cover the floor of the ekibanja beneath the shelter of bananas and coffee. In the present, corn is planted along with beans, although this crop is a relatively recent introduction (Reining 1967). The bean crop is harvested and shelled, again by women and often young children, in January and February before the heavy rains of late February and March. Moreover, this work often transcends the boundaries of family farm and household, as groups of women, neighbors and kin among them, cooperatively plant and harvest beans on in one another's farms. These legumes are a prominent relish at almost all Haya meals, a female complement to the male staple of boiled plantain and bananas.

In addition to their intensive cultivation of beans, as well as a number of seasonal crops like tomatoes, spinach, and chili peppers—all of which are planted in small quantities, usually in the immediate vicinity of the house—women also work on a daily basis at the never ending task of weeding the ekibanja. Weeding is carried out by all members of the household, but Haya men I knew thought that women "had the bodies for it." That is, women, it was claimed, could squat more comfortably close to the ground for long periods of time, as weeding often demands. Far from simply a naturalization of gendered roles that serves the ideological purpose of keeping men from engaging in this tedious task, this assertion about women's bodily postures—an assertion with which Haya women I spoke with often concurred—is indicative of a broader pattern in cultivation as a set of gendered practices. Men's work on the ekibanja not only focuses on tending to trees and their products, their bodies are directed toward vertical and upright agricultural activity. The tools, for example, that men use to cultivate and harvest bananas are iron blades attached to notably elongated handles. A thin, double-sided knife formed in the shape of a sickle fastened to a pole of well over six feet in length, the *olhuabyo* has long been used by Haya men to harvest stalks of mature bananas and to prune the overgrowth and dead leaves of the banana plant. In present day Buhaya, the stem of the banana plant after harvest is hacked through and then reduced to shredded mulch with commercially produced machetes. But at the turn of the century, the tool of choice for this procedure was the *omuholo*, a heavy spade-shaped blade, three or four inches across at the base and sharply pointed. This blade point was attached to a substantial wooden shaft, thicker and heavier than that of the *olhuabyo* but not quite as long. The *omuholo* is still used today, as it has been throughout this century (Rehse 1910; Cesard 1938b) to propagate new banana plants according to a specific sociocultural design.

Bananas grow parthenogenetically, as young shoots or suckers are put forth by the mature plants. In Haya practice, all but one of the shoots that surround the banana plant are eliminated, which permits the remaining shoot fully to absorb all of the nutrients in the soil without competition from other growing plants in its vicinity. The sucker allowed to grow will normally be the one positioned with respect to the mature plant in such a way that it will be supported by its parent plant as it grows (e.g., it will not grow into the parent stem, but away from it for counterbalance). This method of propagation is carried out with the *omuholo*, as banana suckers are "speared" (*okuchumita* is the verb, replete with sexual connotation in vernacular Haya; see Weiss 1996a), uprooted, and mulched to provide green fertilizer for the remaining shoot. As I noted earlier (see chapter 1), each new banana plant becomes part of a cycle of three generations. In addition to the single shoot is the mature plant that bears fruit, and supporting this mature plant is the hacked-through stem of this plant's parent. This stem of a previously harvested plant is allowed to remain standing (at a height of two to three feet) and is not uprooted until the next generation bears fruit, because the hacked stem continues to feed (*okulisa*) and support the mature, fruiting bananas with the moisture they contain. Once the bananas are harvested, then, Haya farmers hold that the previous banana stem becomes a source of sustenance, and especially moisture, for successive generations, both through the mulch of the hacked and shredded stem and the fluids that persist in the standing roots and stump of this former plant. The remnants of this stump are finally uprooted with the *omuholo* (again, "spearing" the plant) once its successor plant has had its bananas harvested, and this new stem then takes the place of the previous generation.

The other major activity of ekibanja farming carried out by men is pruning the banana plant. Dead leaves and dried-out bast are regularly culled from growing banana plants, and this near daily activity is carried out by men. Today a machete is most frequently used, but the *omuholo* was the tool used earlier in the twentieth century. There is also a more formalized and systematic pruning of a household farm's entire inventory of banana plants—which may reach well over one hundred mature plants—that is performed once a year just prior to the season in which beans are planted. This pruning, which follows on the longest dry period of the year, removes as much of the dried-out layer of banana bast as possible, leaving a stand of lush green plants. Pruning in this fashion ensures, according to Haya farmers, that the growing bananas are able to draw, or "suckle" (*okuonka*), as much moisture from the earth as possible. All of the pruned matter is then recycled, both returned to the base of the banana plants and distributed across the terrain as a mulch. The timing of this practice is also designed to provide a ground cover that retains moisture and nutrients in the soil in order to prepare the ekibanja for the bean crop.

TIME AND GENDER IN THE FIELDS

The gendered contrast of weeding and bean planting with banana harvesting and pruning, prevalent in Buhaya for well over a century, conforms to the general Haya assertion "men work above and women work below." This division seems more nuanced when in consideration of the total range of practices of family farm cultivation, for men's actions like "spearing" and uprooting old banana stems are not strictly concerned with things on high. Yet, even these practices are concerned with vertical growth, with promoting the successful movement from below to above, as shoots grow to maturity, and felled stems feed successive crops. Further, the male farmer's tools of his trade emphasize—even more strongly in the past than today—his vertical orientation. These masculine spatial and bodily praxes contrast even more strikingly with those of women. Haya women in the early years of this century cultivated their *orweya* fields with the heart-shaped hoes discussed as crucial elements of bridewealth. Unlike men's iron tools, these hoes were hafted to very short handles, which permitted women to use them with only one hand. Rehse's description from Kiziba at the turn of the century gives a sense of what this work required:

> Indeed the position of the woman while she is tilling the land makes quite a lasting impression on the mind. One cannot understand why they do not make use of a longer handle for their otherwise very practical hoes. If they

> did so there would be no need to work in a bent position but, according to our ideas the attitude of the body would be much more comfortable. The women work the soil with a short hoe in one hand and with the other one she at the same time collects weeds.

It is also worth noting that women's most prized crops in their grassland fields either grew close to the ground, like beans and field peas, or underground, like tubers (cassava and potatoes, both colonial imports adapted by women) and peanuts. What is especially interesting about this pervasive contrast between men's and women's work is that it is not simply the case that a gendered distinction is applied to a spatial division of tasks—as though some work were on the ground and constructed as female, and some work were in the trees and constructed as male. Rather, gendered Haya bodies inhabit space differentially, and so men's and women's performance of specific practices creates the spatial form of that activity. So, for example, women till fields with intentionally short-handled hoes, while simultaneously weeding, which *makes* their practice spatially "below." Men, too, work the ground unearthing banana suckers and stumps, but do so with explicitly elongated tools, standing upright and above their tasks, a form of bodily comportment that *creates* the vertical qualities of these actions. The spatial character of Haya cultivation is therefore not a "natural" feature of the growth of legumes, tubers, and trees, but is actively generated by the moving, gendered bodies of Haya farmers. These performative dimensions to these cultivation techniques are important, for they indicate that Haya farming practice was informed by an understanding of how qualities and values are embedded (and embodied) in specific forms of action, the very actions (and hence values) that, as I shall show, were subject to colonial reformulation.

Work in grassland fields, unlike work in the family farm, would seem to be an exclusive site of women's agriculture. Men do not grow crops in the *orweya*, organize the work groups that labor in these fields, or exercise much control over the circulation of their annual harvests. There are, however, some vital interventions that men make in grassland cultivation. To begin with, the crops grown in the grassland are all seasonal, and the temporality of cultivation was coordinated, or punctuated by men in certain respects. The king, for example, was entitled to the "first fruits" (*omwaka*) of the harvest from each grassland field. There is little evidence describing the practices entailed in the presentation of this produce to the king—the reinvigoration of the king's realm was rather focused on the New Moon ceremonies, as I have already indicated. It does not seem to be the case that a single period was designated for a ceremonial complex, as is characteristic of much of Southern Africa. Still, royal prerogatives to the first fruits of the *orweya* (alluded to, but not described by Rehse 1910) did seem to demonstrate the pervasive control over land that kings held and embodied.

While grasslands might appear to be unoccupied and unowned, even such "empty" land had a value in potential for the king who might transform *orweya* into ekibanja by decree. These seasonal prestations confirmed the capacity of the king to "make place" in this way and acknowledged that women working in the grasslands had converted that royal potential into a distinct form of value for themselves. Indeed, in the present day, when such royal prerogatives no longer exist, women working grassland fields often make offerings of first fruits to men who now own grassland regions as unconverted family farms. As I shall discuss, *orweya* may now be held as ekibanja that is owned by a particular clan and household, but that has not been transformed into land on which bananas can be planted and houses can be constructed. In such instances, the offerings made to the household heads who hold this land, like royal "first fruits" of the past, are equally an acknowledgment by the women who cultivate these grasslands that they are transforming the value of what is potentially family farmland into products imbued with a very different set of values.

In the early years of the twentieth century, the male kin and neighbors of the women who cultivated in the *orweya* also made important contributions to this work. If kings reaped the first harvest from these fields, Haya male farmers actually initiated the entire process of grassland cultivation by preparing these lands for tilling. Women could not turn the soil into fields until men had cleared the land of trees, roots, and scrub and cut the thick grasses of the savanna. Men then gathered all of these materials together and burned them as green fertilizers. Note, then, that men were again responsible for uprooting trees, cutting, and "slashing" (*okutema*, the term used for harvesting bananas) the growth of the *orweya* as they are for the ekibanja. Indeed, the *omuholo* blade was the primary tool men used for these procedures (Cesard 1938b: 500). Here, however, the uprooting and pruning procedures serve very different purposes. Each is a means of preparing the land for better cultivation, but the reduction of these acts to these functional ends ignores the specific qualities created through them. For example, on family farmland Haya men "spear" plant life in order to secure the continuous flow of moisture. Uprooting new shoots and old stumps is designed to ensure that mature, fruiting, and growing banana plants are supplied with sufficient fluid nutrients from both the soil and from other vegetative source (i.e., from the roots systems of plants past and present). In the grasslands, however, plant life is unearthed and slashed precisely in order to eliminate it altogether. Indeed, the plants themselves are burned and destroyed, which prepares the grasslands, *not* for successive generations of the same type of growth (which *is* the case for household farming, as culling banana plants permits the continuous growth of bananas), but for the introduction of entirely new varieties of plants.

The male manipulation of the *omuholo* on both family farms and unturned grassland does contribute to agrarian production. Yet in temporal terms the former practice is characterized by a concern with the continuous growth and reproduction of generations of perennial crops, while the latter facilitates an entirely discontinuous process of elimination and replacement. These contrasting temporal qualities of continuity and discontinuity at the level of agricultural processes further confirms a similar contrast in the lands themselves. For if Haya agnates struggle to ensure the permanent possession of family farms, grassland fields must be fallowed from one season to the next, and the same sites may be occupied in successive cultivation cycles by completely different groups of working Haya women.

LOCATING GROWTH AND DECAY

From a certain point of view it could be argued that Haya male agricultural activities across these fields of practice always entails destruction. In the grassland's preparation this kind of rupture seems quite evident, as undesirable plant life is culled to make way for distinctively different crops. On family farms, too, the work of banana propagation by men seems oriented to the final phases of growth and process. As banana leaves and bast wither and desiccate men cut them off. Banana stalks weighted with mature fruit are slashed through and their tall stems hacked to shreds. Even nurturing the growth of a new banana shoot is only achieved by carefully eliminating all other competing new shoots. These practices, which are virtually all that are required to maintain a viable banana crop, finish off productive growth. What is crucial to recognize, then, is that in the temporal ordering of productive sequencing characteristic of men's practice, completion is frequently tied to renewal as endpoints become points of origin.

The periodicity of banana propagation is a clear case of this connection between closure and renewal, as harvested and felled banana stems become the foundations (literally, the *ekisibo*, meaning both "origin" and "stump") for future growth. As I have described elsewhere, Haya sociocultural practices, and especially masculine practices, across a range of fields—from food provisioning, to clan formation and mobility, to house construction—work to articulate the acts and events of completion with those of origination so as to establish continuously renewable processes (Weiss 1996a).[9] I described a similar pattern of origin and completion in the vegetative propagation of coffee trees in chapter 1. The intentional elimination of concluded cycles often provides the necessary grounds on which new cycles may be initiated. This is not to say that all masculine destruction is necessarily creative, but rather to assert that Haya formulations of continuous, regenerative, and renewable productivity do entail a concern with completion and finality. And the integration of these elements is often achieved in masculine practice, as when uprooting becomes a form of nurturance. Outside of the sphere of activities oriented toward these regenerative processes, as in the case of *orweya* cultivation, such acts may have a less productive outcome and lead only to elimination and destruction. There is, then, an inherent tension in the potential of specifically masculine agricultural practice, as the links of completion and origination in a given context may prove tenuous, or renewal may fail, thereby rendering men's activities simply dangerous. As I will demonstrate, it is precisely this careful coordination of endpoints and origins, destruction and creation, and the risk of their decoupling that have been continuously threatened over the twentieth century's agricultural innovation.

Before moving on to consider the history of these agricultural innovations and their encounters with Haya farming, it is worth examining in greater detail the significance of a particular element in this cultivation complex that proved to be a regular point of contention. I have already indicated that much of the daily and seasonal agrarian activity on the ekibanja is focused on procuring and preserving moisture in the soils and plant life of the farm. This moisture, or simply "water"—*amaizi*—to most Haya cultivators, is a highly charged and complex material and symbolic dimension of agriculture, an icon of productivity itself. Haya farmers' concerted efforts to ensure the continual presence of moisture in the banana farms is important for a number of reasons, the least of which may be the necessity of water to sustain plant life. Indeed, from an environmental perspective, there would seem to be little imperative to make such efforts. Levels of rainfall in the most densely inhabited regions of Buhaya are among the highest in all of Africa, reaching upwards of eighty inches in some areas, and averaging around sixty inches per year for the region as a whole. Moreover, the grasslands tend on the whole to be considerably drier than residential farms, yet Haya women and men make little effort to secure water for fields in the *orweya*, but rely instead on what is usually sufficient rainfall.

The significance of moisture, then, lies in its connections to the ekibanja as a site of continuous residential occupation. Recall, for example, that men leave a significant stem standing after a banana's fruit has been harvested in order to "feed" the successor banana plant. This maturing plant "suckles" moisture that remains in this stem and root system. In this way, moisture serves as a direct conduit between generations, and agricultural practice *makes it* a tangible connection between the destruction of the harvested banana "parent" and the successful growth of the maturing banana "child." The process of renewal as a generative recycling of endpoints into origins is directly manifest in the moisture that marks the completion of one life and the initiation of its successor. Recall, further, that the life force—*amagala*—was often understood through the image of banana bast, still vibrant and sturdy, replete with fluid. I would add that this basic agricultural principle is further embodied in the royal person (see also Taylor 1991). Saliva from royalty, for example, was carefully attended to, even saved for future consultation.

The White Fathers note with amusement that one prince had among his retinue a "'grand crachon' [great spittoon] a dignitary unknown in Europe"

(Diare du Poste, Kashozi 16 August 1901). Moisture—both human and botanical—is a Haya *value*, as this practical knowledge of agriculture and concrete image of the dynamic vitality intrinsic to life itself suggests, a concrete embodiment of development and decline and thus an icon of self-sustaining growth. In effect, Haya farmers hold that the moisture contained in each banana plant ensures that the crop will maintain itself, and so this element is powerful objectification of self-sufficiency and independence. As cultivators often remarked to me in the late 1980s, the hacked-up stem of a harvested banana plant is "(S.) *mbolea tayari*"—"ready-made fertilizer!" Each plant, that is, is the source of its own renewal. Agrarian practice concerned with carefully preserving moisture in an already fecund locale is, thus, ultimately concerned with preserving this generative power.

It is worth noting, then, that the focus of male interventions on the ekibanja is the continuous flow of moisture—a healthy banana stem when slashed through at harvest will "put out a lot of water." In contrast, male actions in the *orweya* do not attempt to secure this potent value, rather their uprooting and burning leads to the accumulation of "salt" (S. *chumvi*) as the nutrient extracted from organic materials in the grasslands is colloquially understood. Salt is a figurative reversal of the qualities of water; indeed, in Haya understandings salt is explicitly hot and desiccating. Salt is, then, the appropriate product of actions designed to produce a discontinuous and nonsustainable agricultural practice, like that found in the grasslands. Again, men's practices and the salt they create may be productive. But the nature of that productivity, while crucial to the success of grassland cultivation, does not have the generative dimensions of agricultural production on enduring family farms.

The objective of producing self-sustaining crops is further relevant to the contrasting spatial forms of agricultural work and patterns of planting already described. Men's vertical, erect practice makes of each banana plant a discrete central position, whose products move out from that center (in the form of shoots, and succession) and ultimately return to that central point of origin (in the form of mulched banana stems and pruned materials) in order to ensure the perpetuation of agricultural production. The recycling of "moist" materials in this way is continuously focused on a central point of growth, a centrality emphasized by the vertical acts of masculine pruning and culling. On the other hand, feminine forms of practice—and, indeed, men's contributions to *orweya* cultivation—recognize no such singular centers. Instead women's work forges lateral connections across a more uniform terrain. Women's tilling and weeding are not just low to the ground; the performance of women's mobile bodies creates spaces that move outward and across a landscape that does not recognize fixed and enduring centers.

I should point out that while the agricultural work of men in the *orweya* may not lead to regenerative processes, the work of women can produce generative values. The source of this generativity for women, though, is less their agricultural work, per se, than the sociality that is established through the circulation of the foods produced in the grassland. Typically, women's crops are offered in affinal exchanges, or as return gifts from married daughters to natal homes on the occasion of marriage, birth, and death. Thus, the transaction of these products contributes to the ongoing reproduction of the groups of women—characteristically women who come to share virilocal residence through affinal ties, thus moving laterally and transcending "centered" places for a different purpose—that enable grassland cultivation to persist.

For both men and women, then, there are generative values at stake in agricultural practice, but for men this value lies more immediately in the qualities of the land and its occupants (human and plant) itself, while for women this value is secured when the products of these discontinuous locales are converted into enduring social ties. Again, these pervasive contrasts in the production of value, and in these practical understandings of agriculture as value producing, have proven to be critical to the encounters between rural Haya communities and the forces of colonial and neocolonial agrarian policies.

The main feature of agricultural practice scarcely touched on thus far, yet absolutely critical to this discussion, is coffee. I have previously detailed the characteristics and significance of vegetative propagation that flourished in Buhaya through the earliest years of the twentieth century. The present account of the generative dimensions of ekibanja cultivation confirm what I argued were fundamental parallels between bananas and coffee trees as concretizations of Haya notions of growth, process, and continuity as these are realized through masculine activities. Like bananas, coffee planted by vegetative propagation depended upon substantial points of connection between successive generations of the plant. Further, the standard practice of pegging branches to produce new plants nicely captures the dialectical relation between endpoints and origins, as the final forms of the mature tree becomes the foundation of a subsequent generation. The movement from above to below, high branches planted directly into the ground immediately beneath them, also demonstrates the verticality of growth, a spatial correlate to men's banana cultivation. These material connections between trees, especially obvious when newer trees remained physically attached to older trees in a latticework of bowed branches and blossoming growth, further emphasized the ways in which men's cultivation techniques were focused on centralized positions out from which growth proceeded.

While coffee parallels bananas in respect to these generational continuities, there are also important difference in the temporal dimensions of their cultivation. Coffee, for example, is a perennial tree, but it has a crop that is harvested on an annual basis. In most respects this means that coffee was given much less attention in the ongoing activities of ekibanja life. Most households at the turn of the century had very few, if any trees, and historical evidence suggests very little effort was made to maintain the quality of the crop or tree in most cases. The coffee harvest of April to May was a period of intensive activity, although even this may have been carried out primarily by agents of the king who made certain that he received the requisite tribute from the coffee stocks that he had originally supplied. In 1938, several decades after the introduction of a number of programs designed to promote proper coffee husbandry, the district's director of agriculture complained that Haya farmers saw coffee as a "wild orchard crop" (Director of Agriculture to Chief Secretary: 1938, cited in Curtis 1989: 95), a resource that needed no attention, which would seem an apt description of local actions with respect to these trees. Coffee trees were never cut back as they grew, and so often reached heights to four or five meters, and never achieved the fullness and density characteristic of coffee plants as they are grown in most other regions of the world. In addition to this difference in the daily and routine involvement in banana as opposed to coffee growth, coffee trees have a very different life span than bananas. For Haya farmers, processes of generational decline and renewal were an ongoing experience in banana planting and pruning, but coffee trees have a much longer life span, take longer to produce their crop, and the tree is not eliminated upon the harvest of its produce. The generative force of bananas, best embodied by their moisture, was thus continuously attended to by Haya men, while the "life force" possessed by coffee trees seems much less dependent on human intervention. Bananas sustained the lives of the families that tended to them, but coffee seemed truly capable of sustaining itself. At the same time, the death of coffee trees was not as routinized a procedure, nor as easily coordinated with the rebirth of their successors as was the case for bananas. Thus, the risk of destruction without renewal may have been part of the threat to its owner that the death of a coffee tree portended. It is not surprising, then, to find that coffee trees, as independent, long-living trees, were among the most powerful—and dangerous—cultivated incarnations of *amagala*.

REWORKING THE WOODS: MISSIONARY EFFORTS, 1900–1912

The critical value of Haya agricultural practice as I have described it is generativity. This is a capacity, or power that is both the outcome of productive actions that motivates those actions, and a grounding, or condition that enables productive actions to be undertaken. The staple foods grown on a family farm, the acts of rooting that forge ties between coffee trees, and most important, the moisture that "feeds" successive generations of bananas are all objectified forms of generative value that are produced on and through the household ekibanja. Generativity is formulated very differently, and is in many ways more attenuated, in grassland production. Still, the fundamental relationship between these places and their products is critical if we are to appreciate the full implications of cultivation as a value-producing activity. The contrasting values of these regions and the distinctive ways in which generative potentials are embedded in family farms as opposed to grasslands, banana plants as opposed to annual legumes as opposed to perennial coffee, have clearly informed Haya rural communities' encounters with transformations of agricultural practice in the region over the last hundred years or so, transformations that have been founded on very different understandings of growth, development, and value. Some of these transformations have been the result of explicit efforts to revise and improve Haya cultivation, while some agricultural change has been an unintended consequence of less specifically focused practices. Let me address some instances of the latter that were brought about by some of the earliest experiences of European colonials with the men and women of Buhaya.

As the epigraph to this chapter from the Mugana post indicates, the White Fathers had a significant impact on the physical terrain of Buhaya, at least from the perspective of the Haya people. These Fathers sought to cut down a number of large forest trees, primarily for the purpose of constructing the buildings of the mission stations and seminaries built in the early years of the twentieth century. Forest trees as useful resources also became part of wider projects that characterized missionizing interactions in the region. The White Fathers not only sought to harvest trees for their buildings, but in so doing they also extended the effects of colonial moneys that were used to pay for trees and the labor that cut them. Further, these missionaries saw the use of wood as in some ways tied to their larger purposes, for in addition to seminaries they also developed schools of carpentry on the grounds of their missions. And in connection with all of these undertakings the White Fathers also introduced new species of trees to Buhaya, including new varieties of *arabica*, as opposed to the indigenous *robusta*, coffee.

None of these novelties directly attempted to alter Haya practices of cultivations; even the arabica coffee was grown on mission farms and was not widely disseminated, or promoted for production on household farms by the White Fathers. Nonetheless, I will argue that these missionaries did have a profound effect on agricultural practice in Buhaya as they contributed to a reconfiguration of the area's landscape, with a concomitant shift in the gendered dimensions of cultivation, and reinforced distinct notions of property and place. At the root of these changes were challenges to Haya understandings of value, especially the links of value to growth and renewal, and at this level the agricultural innovations of the White Fathers ultimately laid the ground, so to speak, for innovative understandings of coffee.

It should be clear that the very interest of the White Fathers in cutting down trees would have evoked suspicion on the part of their intended Haya converts. The forests from which these larger trees were culled were especially prominent locations of the type of named and sanctified tree shrines (*ekiga-*

bilo, discussed in chapter 1). Oral testimonies from the 1980s indicate that, in some cases, entire forests were associated with powerful dynastic Bacwezi spirits, and the Bakama often maintained careful control over access to these regions. Yet much of the first decade of missionization by the White Fathers in Buhaya was spent attempting to gain access to such trees. There are countless reports of conflicts, even official trials for misconduct, brought about because trees were cut without permission, or from the wrong forest, or in too great a number. Given the importance of tree shrines as sites of sacrifice and propitiation for the sake of reproduction and healing, it is perhaps not accidental that the White Fathers were thought by many Haya to have brought the smallpox epidemic of 1912, a time when Haya parents were reluctant to bring their children to the mission for treatment for fear that the children would be eaten (Diare du Poste, Rubya: 12 October 1912). In any case, the missionaries' practices with respect to these trees clearly marked a departure for Haya communities who understood the significance of trees in very different terms.

In order to acquire and transport forest trees, especially those large enough for the substantial construction projects they had undertaken, the White Fathers employed Haya laborers. The payments to woodsmen and porters in the first decade of this century paralleled and in many cases drew directly on the system of taxation imposed by the German Administration. As I have already shown to be characteristic of this period, payments were made in both cowries and rupees, as well as hellers in the latter years of the decade. In addition to paying fees to Haya workers, the White Fathers came to rely on the corvée labor that could be conscripted as a part of the taxation process. This labor force put the White Fathers in a yet more entangled relationship with the Bakama, who regularly conscripted labor, both as a requirement of tribute and a right granted to them by the colonial Administration. The White Fathers, then, had both to get the permission of the royals to cut down wood and often had to pay them a fee in order to conscript corvée work parties. Figuring out payments to those who were not conscripted but cut and carried wood in return for cash often proved problematic. How was the value of this work to be determined? One example from 1908, again, relatively late in the decade, and a full decade after the introduction of colonial currencies, spells out some of the complications.

> Yesterday the wood porters of Ijumbi came to get paid. Each tree had been evaluated at a fair price for its transport: 1 rupee, 1 1/2, 800, 600 [cowries] according to its size and the number of men necessary to transport it. But this system did not appeal to the porters. They preferred that each received his own simbis [cowries], for example 600 for each. Well there are at times 40 men for a single tree, when 10 or 12 would suffice; that would give us quite an expense. They cannot comprehend this new system and refuse the "tinplate" [*fer-blanc*, i.e., the coins]. We have carefully explained how we

> are going to distribute this to them, [but] with much shouting they took off and left the *byome* [Haya for iron ore, i.e., coins] at the mission. Too bad for them. (Diare du Poste, Rubya: 28 May 1908)

Just what the porters from Ijumbi did and did not understand is not entirely clear from this passage. It's quite possible that they were insisting on what they felt were fair wages based on their own labor; after all, whether forty or twelve men "would suffice" for the job, none of these men were White Fathers. There is, though, another element in this "new system" that may have provoked what seemed to be the uniform and very vocal dissatisfaction of these Haya men, and that is the way that trees were now to be evaluated. It may be that these porters preferred that all men be paid equally and did not trust the missionaries to determine the work required for the task at hand; but it is also the case that the White Fathers specified the value of these tasks in terms of what became standardized differences between trees. Each tree was differentiated according to its *size* which then became an appropriate measure of the work entailed in transporting it. For Haya men of this period it seems plausible that this form of evaluation was objected to because it erroneously imposed a distinction in the value of what were incommensurably valuable trees (i.e., the White Fathers did not recognize that each tree—especially those growing in contested forest sites—was a unique entity), and then used that irrelevant distinction to measure differences between the porters' work.

In effect, the White Fathers' interests in the forests were to transform trees into lumber, which requires a value transformation and not just an axe. By making "grandeur" the measure of these trees' value the White Fathers transposed to the forests a similar process to that carried out with respect to coffee trees, now evaluated in terms of a volume of harvested cherries as opposed to the potential of particular trees as complete wholes. Both of these canonically modernist operations were to be facilitated by money—or *would have* been had money not been revalued (as the present case of refusal indicates) in Haya practice. It is, moreover, this "new system" of valuing objects that ultimately led to the differential evaluation of persons in terms of their ability to engage these forms of measurement by means of accumulation.

The development of schools of carpentry further facilitated the transformation of wood as a resource. The White Fathers did not elaborate in their writings of this period on their reasons for promoting this, in some ways, most Christian of occupations. There does not appear to have been much of an effort made to transform Haya architecture, or critiques of the inadequacies of local housing—although as early as 1907 the Mukama Luhinda of Ihangiro did order two houses to be built in a field just behind the mission at Rubya in the style of the colonists (Diare du Poste, Rubya: January 1907). Missionary carpentry seems, rather, to have been designed to raise revenue for the missions and to facilitate housing construction on the grounds of the mission.

This latter purpose proved to be a recurrent necessity in the first years of the twentieth century, for mission churches, barracks, and the houses of Haya Catholic catechists and neophytes were often subject to attack, burned to the ground by local communities whose motives—other than outright animosity—remain obscure to the White Fathers. It would be reductionist in the extreme to say that the White Fathers' treatment of trees was at the root of this protest, but the mission's response to these conflicts would have lasting implications in Buhaya. Given the difficulties they encountered, one of the White Fathers' strategic responses to these threats was to grow trees for themselves. In the first decade of this century the missionaries both planted seedlings, and also introduced new varieties of trees to the region, especially eucalyptus, which in the Kagera region today is ubiquitous, and known as *Mkalytus*. The place of tree planting endeavors in mission practice and the appropriation by Haya communities of new varieties like eucalyptus not only furthered colonialism's innovative regime of value, it had profound significance for all of Haya agricultural practice.

To assess this significance it is first necessary to address the ways in which the White Fathers came to occupy the land. Throughout Buhaya, these largely French Catholic missionaries had to cultivate relations with both the Bakama and the German Administration. The Germans tolerated and even promoted Catholic interests in the region as a counter to Anglican missionaries working in British-ruled Uganda to the immediate north of Buhaya. The Bakama engagements with German administrators were realized in different ways at different times. Some of the Bakama saw the European presence as a powerful resource that might be used to challenge the territorial claims of their fellow kings, and so attempted to cultivate good relations with the Germans. Other kings attempted to seek the support of the Baganda, powerful patrons whose imperial presence had been expanding prior to the appearance of Europeans.

Within this context of competing alliances and acts of accommodation the White Fathers came to occupy a position that was never transparently predictable. Kahigi of Kianja, for example, rapidly became a rising star in the eyes of the German Administration, as he regularly diverted tribute and deferred to their authority in the administrative *boma* at Bukoba on matters of succession and inter-kingdom relations. At the same time, he proved a consistent adversary of the White Fathers, unwilling to permit his subjects to seek the services of the missionaries long after other kings had done so, and routinely capricious (at least according to mission station reports) in his agreements with the Fathers to provide them with labor and supplies. The only land on which Kahigi agreed to permit the Fathers to construct their mission was open *orweya* near Kagondo, which became the site of Immaculée Conception (Diare du Poste, Kagondo: 3 February 1903). Other kings, however, ceded banana farms, and in some cases entire villages, to the missionaries. In some of these cases these land holdings created nyarubanja—to this day, for example, the farms that are part of the mission and seminary at Rubya are called "the nyarubanja"—a status that reflected the prestige that the missionaries were accorded, as well as the potential threat to the mukama they were perceived to present. The landholdings of the White Fathers in all of these cases, whether their presence was despised or privileged, placed them at a relative distance from the king, a position from which they were able to generate new modes of interacting with the landscape, and new social relations through which the products of the land were to be organized and controlled.

By the end of the first decade of the twentieth century at all five mission stations—(Bukoba (La Sainte-Famille), Marienberg (Notre-Dame des Sept Doleurs), Bwanja (Notre-Dame de la Paix), Kagondo (Immaculée Conception), and Rubya in Buhaya—the construction demands and fiscal needs of the White Fathers were being met to a significant degree by the cultivation projects they had undertaken. Coffee was planted on the lands granted to the missions at all of these stations. The coffee cultivated, however, was not an intensification of locally available varieties, as new varieties—known by the Fathers as "Guatémala"—were imported from Central America. On some of the larger farms controlled by the missions a few thousand coffee trees were planted; even Immaculée Conception, situated in the midst of undesirable grasslands reported that it had managed to plant "250 caféiers" in 1907 (Rapports Annuels—Kagondo, 1906–1907: 131).

These trees, however, do not appear to have been widely accepted by Haya farmers as appropriate new crops for their family farms. In spite of this intensive coffee planting at mission stations, as well as the mandatory planting campaign begun in 1905 under Mutahangarwa of Kiziba, coffee exports from the entire region of Buhaya never exceeded 300 tons (Curtis 1989: 712) during the decade, and a significant percentage of that volume was grown on the farms of the White Fathers themselves. This initial reluctance to embrace coffee planting, I will contend, has proven to be a hallmark of Haya coffee production throughout the twentieth century. Even after more determined efforts increased coffee exports to their highest levels of close to eleven thousand tons during the depression, coffee maintained a relatively marginal status in Haya cultivation.

The history of this reluctance, evidence for which will be explored in greater detail below, should be approached in terms of the values of Haya cultivation and landholding already described. New varieties of coffee acquire a specific character in relationship to these practices, transforming the values of Haya agrarian activity as they become transformed by these values. The White Fathers' early attempts to cultivate "Guatemalan" coffee may not have had a direct and immediate radical impact on Haya production of these trees; but understood as simply one dimension of a wider set of transformations in the husbanded terrain of Buhaya promoted by these missionaries, the place of coffee in relationship to the values of Haya agriculture can be seen to have been shaped in significant, if entirely unintended, ways by the White Fathers. So, for example, while a good number of coffee trees were planted by the White Fathers, their numbers pale in comparison to the number of trees they planted for timber. In 1907 Kagondo had planted two hundred fifty coffee trees, but over two thousand eucalyptus, and twenty-five thousand trees for carpentry; Rubya had but a "few hundred" coffee trees (on a large and fertile holding of ekibanja land), but upwards of five thousand eucalyptus, and twelve thousand *nshambya*, a tree indigenous to the region used primarily for firewood (Rapports Annuels 1906–1907: 131–2).

The introduction of the eucalyptus, still widely grown in Kagera, would seem to have been tremendously successful. Eucalyptus was favored as a promising transplant in part because it grows very quickly even under conditions, unlike Buhaya, of relatively little rainfall. Haya villagers today also recognize as an added benefit of eucalyptus the fact that it can be cut when still relatively "green" and does not require curing before it can be used as firewood. Eucalyptus is one of the most prevalent sources of firewood in Kagera today, but it is not without its problems. According to the Haya who spoke with me these trees are so strong that they "drain" the moisture from family farms, and this strength is demonstrated by the thick, red, bloodlike sap (*amajuta*—fat, or oil) the eucalyptus exudes. These qualities made eucalyptus a *cultivated* tree that, nonetheless, was inappropriate for growing on ekibanja land. Instead, stands of eucalyptus were grown in separate plots in the grasslands bordering residential villages, not in shifting fallowed fields like most *orweya* produce, but as permanent "tree crops." Note, then, that the introduction of these trees created what was, in effect, a hybrid form of cultivation that challenged Haya forms of value in a host of ways. The eucalyptus is a tree that provides for household consumption in the form of firewood, that nonetheless saps the soil of moisture, the quintessential element in household agricultural productivity. It thus becomes a grassland plant that acquires permanence in an otherwise discontinuously tended domain.

Beyond these symbolic, if no less material, dimensions of the eucalyptus tree itself, Haya farmers' apparently rapid appropriation of this plant had a significant effect on the relationship between grassland fields and family farms. And it is at this systemic and relational level of agrarian practice that the White Fathers' woodland interests would prove to have a major impact on Haya coffee cultivation.

As I have already shown, the continuities of family farmland, on which trees were cultivated, as a social form were highly fluid. Both the obligations and tensions of agnatic succession, in concert with the land-endowing capacities of kingship made family farms the ideological focus of stability in place, but actual residence and clanship itself equally depended on the dispersal and rupture of social relations. To complicate this pattern further, it is important to recognize that the contrast between family farms and grasslands—a contrast that, as I have described it, objectifies and evaluates spatiotemporal differences in continuity and generational endurance—is itself a *fluid* division realized, not as two intrinsically different types of land, but through different practical modes of inhabiting the land. *Orweya*, that is, could be converted into ekibanja under the proper conditions. In agricultural terms, such a conversion has long been recognized to be a terribly difficult process, as the quantity of inputs in manure and mulch required to prepare the grassland soils for banana cultivation were unavailable to most Haya farmers. In administrative terms, however, Haya polities at the turn of the century and into the colonial period did permit this conversion. In order to transform *orweya* into ekibanja a farmer had to pay a nominal fee to the mukama that permitted the farmer to plant the *orweya* with a plot of trees, an icon of the newly permanent tenure of the land. These small wood plots, or *ekishambu*, were in effect an expression of the farmer's intention to ultimately convert the grassland area into a residential farm.

Given the difficulties of this land conversion task, the actual creation of residential farmland out of grassland plots has never been very common. However, the introduction of new varieties of trees like the eucalyptus, trees that were cultivated, highly desirable as sources of firewood, and readily marketable for use in the new enterprises of carpentry and woodworking, made possible the increased conversion of grassland into extensions of family farmland.[10] Plots of land on which trees were farmed as permanent resources on land held under enduring tenure by particular households proliferated in Buhaya during the twentieth century. The relationship between grassland and family farmland was, thus, remade by this historical process, as previously open land became held as clan-based farmland. What was always a possibility in this system, now became a more eminently practical venture given the kinds of trees introduced by the White Fathers that could readily be cultivated and consumed.

But note, again, that this new plant life not only changes the relationship between *orweya* and ekibanja by expanding the holdings of household heads—thereby further marginalizing and diminishing the possibilities of women's grassland agriculture—it also transforms the character of family farmland in significant ways. Trees grown under these new conditions are now necessarily peripheral to the household itself. Eucalyptus is seen to actively threaten the banana crop, and so is kept out of the residential space created by banana cultivation. Further, the use of eucalyptus stands, or other woodlots as a defining feature of clan-held farmland, challenges the links between residence and permanent tenure in crucial ways. Grassland fully converted to family farmland would generally become a site of household occupation. Even if the converted land was not adjacent to the farm to which it became appended, as was always the case for farmers whose farms were not at the edges of a village near open grassland, a house would be built on this farm. The new occupant might be the son who would move into this farm expansion upon his own marriage, or a household head with a larger farm might marry another wife to reside on and work this additional land.[11] Land planted with eucalyptus, though, is necessarily separated from productive banana farmland, and it can therefore never become inhabited.

In some respects, this new form of permanent tenure exemplifies the characteristic contrast in the topography of ekibanja cultivation, as plants grown for relatively external relations (notably beer bananas and coffee) are planted at the periphery of a household farm. Stands of eucalyptus are equally removed from household enclosure, and the product is always intended for wider consumption than the household that grows them. Yet the growth of these new stands of trees, not as a means of initiating a connection to, or expansion of residential land, but as separate site of cultivation, becomes peripheral in a distinctly different fashion. Unlike the distal plants of the ekibanja, new tree plots do not take their orientation from a localized center toward which, or away from which their growth is directed. These trees are not incorporated into a continuous pattern, they are altogether detached from it, usually in fields remote from the household itself. Without a house to focus the spacing of cultivation, or the movement of agricultural products, the trees of these woodlots—like the produce of grassland fields—are less directly linked with the productivity of the household that maintains them.

The new woodlots are peripheral, owing both to their spatial distance from places of residence and the fact that their growth is not organized by the pragmatic spatial and temporal patterns that embed effective agriculture in viable households. Plots of cultivated trees may be held as clan-based lands under enduring tenure, but their perennial growth does not serve to strengthen the links of generative clan relations to particular places. In effect, the peripheral zones of household farms, always directed toward places and persons beyond the house, now became both distant and distinct from the household. The household, in this new method of enclosing and planting clan-held land, is no longer the topographic and social *center* of domestic productivity. This shift in spatial orientations consequently alters the links between external relations and internal relations as dimensions of Haya sociality. The dialectic between these socio-spatial relations are coordinated in ways that make each Haya household an independent and central point in inter-household dynamics; but the innovative distancing and separation of particular households' peripheries calls into question the primacy of the household as a focused grounds for controlling this dynamic. The certainty of these independent centers in this way becomes increasingly tenuous as their peripheral holdings become ever more remote.

As I will show, the alteration of these spatial relationships, the emerging detachment of the households' spatial limits, and the consequent potential decentering of households in Haya sociality all had profound implications for coffee, a crop that would increasingly come to occupy these productive margins as never before. Indeed, early German administrators encouraged the planting of coffee trees in *orweya* plots (Curtis 1989: 94). This experiment clearly "failed" if one measures success in volumes of harvested coffee, but—and this is a point to which I shall return—it may well have succeeded in demonstrating the new place of coffee in Haya experience. The White Fathers' interests in building for themselves, and hence their introduction of new trees, situated as these projects were with respect to the social and spatial fields of Haya practical understandings of the land, thus contributed to a fundamental transformation of these landscapes. New ways of engaging the land through novel agricultural practices generated new ways of recognizing the attachments among persons and places.

In this chapter I have examined Haya agriculture over the course of the twentieth century by focusing on certain core values of generativity as these were produced by, and embedded in Haya farming practices. The persistence of certain techniques, the spatial distribution of plants in both household farmland and grasslands, and especially the gendered organization of cultivation demonstrate that these values have endured over a long period of time and played a crucial part in Haya efforts to grapple with colonial efforts to reform landholding and agriculture. The implications of these values for the revolution in coffee planting and marketing ushered in under British colonial will be addressed more directly in chapter 5. But it should also be noted that the White Fathers, whose reluctance to support coffee marketing has already been described, played an important part in refashioning both landholding and agricultural practice. I have shown, for example, that the White Fathers introduced new possibilities for inhabiting the land, and new modes of evaluating place with their intensive efforts to plant and harvest trees for timber. These efforts reconfigured the Haya landscape, enabling a significant shift in the bonds of households to their land. Both the enduring values of Haya agriculture, and the landscape remade by the White Fathers under German colonial rule, provide the social, cultural and material context for addressing the intensification of coffee cultivation in Bukoba in the coming decades.

NOTES

1. Curtis's argument is more complicated than this, but it does offer a normative framework, as his title "Capitalism Fettered" suggests. My interest is less in what Haya sociocultural practices inhibited than in what they made possible.

2. I have described some of the tensions that led to the dispersal of agnatic relations and the subsequent initiation of new clan "origins" in Weiss 1996a, see "The Legacy of

Tomas." The structural significance of affinity and agnation for landholding includes: conflicts between women's rights to land as daughters, and these same women's husbands' expectations of their wives attachments to virilocal residence; links between marriage as a husband and access to land as a son which often promote rivalries between brothers; and sisters' conflicts with brothers over residence and land access upon divorce, quite common in Buhaya precisely because of the tensions that emerge around landholding. All of these issues are crucial to an understanding of Haya landholding as a sociocultural practice; but they are too complex for this discussion which is only concerned with landholding as a context in which to appreciate agricultural practice on the land.

3. Many plants are recognized for their medicinal value, but such plants are not actively cultivated to my knowledge. Indeed, a vernacular term for medicinal plants in Haya is "weeds," a word that suggests that such plants are not intentionally grown. This understanding of medicines as weeds may also contribute to their potency, as it suggests that they have powers that are spontaneous and intrinsic, and therefore independent of human attempts to produce them.

4. From a botanical perspective, bananas and plantains are not trees but grasses. But in Haya understandings of plants they are understood to be and are treated like trees.

5. While it's difficult to determine the historical depth of these practices, the current terrain in Buhaya does bear clear traces of overgrown grassland fields, all arranged in long, parallel rectangular patches.

6. This is not to say that produce from the *orweya* is not meant to provide for household consumption, or that the women who work these fields do not contribute to their own families. Rather, I would argue that the potential to circulate the crops grown here—to offer them as gifts, for example, to members of a woman's natal household, to sell them in weekly markets, or to contribute the proceeds from this sale to collective non-household based associations—is far greater for such crops than it is for the products of the *ekibanja*.

7. "Feeding" and "eating" in Buhaya are value-laden practices, and hierarchical political processes as well. Those who are "fed" by another person (and by implication cannot feed themselves) are dependent on and owe their allegiance to that person (Weiss 1996a: Chapter 5). "He who feeds you is he who rules you," according to the Haya aphorism (Seitel 1977: 202).

8. Women may engage in these activities, although in my experience women that did so claimed that they would not if there were men in the household capable of performing these actions. Further, men may be responsible for these practices as those who *authorize* others—men and women—who ultimately carry them out.

9. I would further suggest that this characteristically Haya focus on the importance of properly controlling finality and destruction in ways that direct these conclusions toward new origins and growth illuminates the Haya concern with death as the ultimate foundation, and frequent justification, for continuous ongoing activities.

10. Woodworking was practiced in Buhaya prior to this century, but the nature of carpentry changed significantly. Haya housing did not make extensive use of wood, with the notable exception of the house posts, hewn from long sturdy branches, that supported the structure. The materials that overlay a house frame were largely woven out of reeds, grasses, and other fibrous materials. Wooden implements, like gardening tools, weapons, or kitchen utensils, were shaped out of limbs and branches. Individual trees were culled for the sake of particular woodworking projects. For example, a beer canoe would be carved out of an entire tree, or a specific tree might be selected to become the source of a royal drum. Firewood was often gleaned from the branches of dead trees. Rehse reported that

fires were lit on long branches, which could be continuously fed into the hearth in a single piece. This suggests that forest trees were not cut down and chopped into piles of fuel, as is generally the case today. In none of these instances, then, were trees seen as sources of lumber that served as the raw material out of which wooden furnishings were fashioned.

11. Haya men in the present day often claim that having a large farm to tend is a common motive for a man to marry more than one woman.

5

"A Wild Orchard Crop": Contentions in Agricultural Innovation

The White Fathers' tree-planting efforts would have a significant effect on the character of coffee cultivation in Buhaya over the course of the twentieth century. These effects were realized to a degree through the intentional propagation of new coffee varieties on mission land; but perhaps even more consequential were the unintended and indirect effects on farming topography—which in turn had an impact on coffee—brought about through the truly intensive, and highly successful propagation of trees grown for lumber and firewood. Agricultural reforms of coffee production under colonialism, though, were clearly not limited to such roundabout methods. Throughout the twentieth century there were repeated and sustained attempts to get Haya farmers to grow more, and eventually better, coffee. As early as 1905, as I have already stated, the mukama of Kiziba, Mutahangarwa, attempted to promote the widespread planting of coffee. Mutahangarwa used both the coercive force of his *ruga ruga* military troops to enforce this production, but also converted some of his own extensive landholdings into coffee plantations worked by the tributary labor (*ensika*) of his subjects.

The German Administration strongly supported precisely this method of enforced production, and in 1911 even undertook their own administered propagation scheme, requiring each Haya farmer to plant fifty coffee trees (a level that was actually never attained under German authorities). The *rezident* at Bukoba in this period, Major Willibald van Steumer, in defending these policies argued for the necessity of

> the harsh monarchical constitution and the power of the sultans and the sub-chiefs to educate their subjects, by compulsion if necessary, for economic undertakings so long as the natives have not attained a cultural development appropriate to the needs of the colonizing power. (cited in Austen 1968: 94)

This policy offers a rather early statement of a persistent vision in this region, and a commonplace in colonial encounters around the world. This vision directly links economic endeavors—here in the form of agricultural innovations—to a process of education necessary for the promotion of "cultural development." The terms of this equation in Buhaya would remain remarkably constant over the course of this century, even as the specific content of the categories were much debated. Officials of successive agricultural extension campaigns may have described the inadequacies of their unsuccessful predecessors as overly harsh, or generally indifferent to local concerns. But in all cases Haya farmers, especially with respect to coffee husbandry, are seen as shackled by the weights of "tradition" and "superstition" or, less generously (in terms that recall the White Fathers' earliest assessment of Bahaya), "indolence" and "ignorance"—all of which conditions require educational interventions. The notion of education as an instrument of development was, in fact, a centerpiece of indirect rule as it was articulated by Donald Cameron. Cameron was appointed governor of Tanganyika in 1925, after serving as chief secretary to Lord Lugard—the principle exponent of the policy of indirect rule—in Northern Nigeria. In his view, education was not just a method to be made use of, it provided the very justification for a program of indirect rule, or, as he preferred, "Native Administration." In the memoir of his service in Tanganyika he emphasized this very point. "Why," he wrote,

> must we have Administrative Officers in a country like Tanganyika or Nigeria? it may well be asked. They are not to be found in the United Kingdom or in the Dominions; the county of Surrey has no District Officers. The reason is, naturally, that in the United kingdom and in the Dominions the people are literate and educated and have through the course of many generations imbibed the percepts of law and order which must regulate the conduct of a civilized people; they can readily learn, through the newspapers and otherwise, the day to day acts and regulations of the Government which affect their lives. This is not so in Tanganyika, or in the Protectorate of Nigeria save in a very minor degree. Other means must therefore be found for communicating with primitive and ignorant people. (Cameron 1939: 77)

The nature of the colonial instruction as it was implemented in Buhaya (if not envisioned by Cameron) as well as its postcolonial legacy, its implied vision of Haya culture and society, and its understanding of how education is most effective as a transformative project are all crucial to the history of coffee production in the region. Indeed, lessons about coffee growing were among the most explicit methods used to inculcate the "percepts of law and order" in Bukoba in the 1920s and 1930s. Equally entailed in this history are the range of Haya farmers' responses to these educational efforts, responses that often addressed the implicit form as much as the explicit content of these lessons in cultivation and culture.

My exploration of agricultural reform projects of the 1920s and 1930s is one dimension of my broader concern in this chapter, which is to address the changing ways in which coffee came to inhabit and reconfigure the Haya landscape in this era. Just as the White Fathers' introduction of tree stocks and massive sources of timber rendered the ties of households to their lands more tenuous, so too the reforms in coffee cultivation advocated by British (and, in the independence era, Tanzanian) officials were understood to threaten household farmland as a source of productive value. In the face of sustained and substantial globalizing and modernist forces, as coffee planting and coffee marketing proceeded apace through the 1920s and 1930s, as profits and harvests rose and fell, what part did Haya farmers' concern for the value of their own activities play in defining the place of coffee in their worlds? How did their desire to enhance the self-perpetuating character of agricultural "wealth" as previously detailed articulate with the demands of intensified cash cropping?

TEN MILLION TREES: EARLY BRITISH COFFEE CAMPAIGNS, 1917–1924

The propagation campaigns of both Baziba and German officials were only moderately successful. The large plantations Mutahangarwa attempted to develop never accounted for a significant percentage of the total volume of coffee harvested in Kiziba, as coffee production remained focused all but exclusively on small family farms. As I have already noted, coffee production from 1900 to 1910 remained low; even after compulsory planting was initiated by the German Administration, levels of production rose at a very slow rate (see Curtis 1989: 712 ff. for levels of coffee exports in Bukoba from 1905 to 1961). These fits and starts under German colonial rule gave way to much more intensive coffee propagation efforts once the British Administration was established after World War I. In 1919, a massive planting campaign was begun under the new district officer, D.L. Baines. Baines instituted a policy that, in its first years, required that each Haya farmer plant hundred coffee trees. Between 1919 and 1924 it was estimated that ten *million* seedlings were planted (Mukurasi 1970: 7). In a fashion reminiscent of the Germans before him, Baines promoted his intensification of coffee production through the elite administrative structures of the Haya polities. Frances Lwamgira, a member of the Bito royal clan of Kiziba who had already established himself as a crucial intermediary under the German Administration, was called upon to tour Buhaya along with Baines encouraging the distribution of coffee seedlings (Curtis 1989: 92). And the Bakama themselves—soon to be organized into the Bakama Council as "Native Authorities" able to govern within the colonial administrative order of "Indirect Rule"—were ordered to develop coffee nurseries at their capitals from which they would distribute seedlings to their subjects.

This undertaking was but one part of an ongoing process that fundamentally transformed Haya kingship. Quite aside from the unmistakable subordination of the Bakama to the British Administration and the reduction of kings to salaried bureaucrats—with salaries drawn from taxes on coffee proceeds—the values of kingship were reimagined by these endeavors. The shift from vegetative to generative production maintained the central role of kings in distributing coffee plants, now in the form of seedlings and not cuttings. But the character of that distribution was thereby altered. Coffee no longer bore the substantive links to royal stocks in the ways once possible. This redefined, in effect, the *place* of Haya kings in Haya culture and society, producing a new configuration of the landscape. The portability of coffee cuttings, I have argued, iconically conveyed the portability of the king himself, which sustained, in turn, the identification of the king with the entirety of his realm.

Now, Haya kings became increasingly immobilized in a number of respects. They were no longer able to maintain capitals throughout their kingdoms or to abandon the *ekikale* of their fathers, but instead built permanent residences that were passed from generation to generation, a permanence that was further enforced by British interests in sites of cash crop production that were not to be abandoned. Further, the strategic character of these dispersed capitals was undermined, as the borders to each of the eight Haya kingdoms were fixed under British rule (this in contrast to the Germans, who had rewarded allies and punished adversaries by changing the territorial divisions of the kingdoms; Curtis 1989: 75–76) and internecine politics were administratively discouraged. Lastly, the production of nurseries at the *ebikale* made them singular central locations out from which these seedlings moved; kings no longer moved across the landscape to rule, they now administered stable sites that motivated the movements of others.

This last shift is crucial, for it concretizes the changed potential of the mukama. Whereas the king's capacity to provide land for his subjects—in the form of both family farms and grassland fields, in recognition of which he received tribute from those productive lands—had been a *generalized* capacity, a potential for conversion immanent in all of the land in his kingdom, the planting of coffee nurseries would come to convey the sense that power emanates from a fixed *particular* locale to which the king is tied. Royal power, in sum, no longer pervades the landscape, but is fixed in newly bounded sites. In this way, kings were really much more than glorified civil servants, for they became exemplars of a new order of space—and value—namely, private property. The king's capacity to generate wealth would now derive from his administrative responsibility for quantitative increases in the number of coffee trees and volume of coffee harvests. This transformed relation to coffee, an object always iconic of wider royal spatial potentials, was further implicated in the Bakama's new authorities over landholding itself. Nyarubanja, as I suggested, had been oriented toward placating and relocating royal allies and adversaries, and assuring royal connectedness to all corners of a kingdom.

As coffee planting campaigns proceeded under German rule, sprung as it were from the farms of the kings' capitals, the royal organization of place became less concerned with the distribution of royal allies across strategic positions, and more concerned with providing them with sizable income-generating estates. Commoner households became increasingly incorporated into more and bigger nyarubanja holdings by royal fiat, yielding ever larger volumes of coffee to be paid by newly created tenants to their newly created landlords. The British Administration quickly recognized the exploitative potential that nayrubanja gave the bakama, and further recognized that coffee planting itself had exacerbated this exploitation. However, in spite of regular efforts to restrict the rights of the bakama to seize family farmland, to register farms to prevent their ready conversion to nyarubanja, and to limit the obligations of tenants to their royal landlords, the nyarubanja system itself was maintained and defended under Baines and Cameron. In effect, the abuses of native administrators were regrettable, but they were also necessary if agricultural reforms intended to improve coffee cultivation were to be successfully implemented (Austen 1968: 175). In any event, the tensions surrounding nyarubnaja in this period indicate that a regime of value concretized and disseminated by the intensive agricultural extension of new forms of coffee husbandry clearly entailed novel practical understandings of wealth. Wealth that had been materialized as individuated attachment to forms derived from collective bestowals was now to be achieved through accumulation facilitated by massification.

It would be a mistake, though, to suppose that this intensive colonial production of the mechanisms and practices of "development" that made accumulation possible were uniformly and enthusiastically absorbed by Haya communities. It is clear, for example, that even in present-day Kagera many forms of material wealth, notably land and food, are not unambiguously subject to the calculus of market values promoted by British coffee campaigns. Indeed, Haya men and women have explicitly rejected the notion that land and food are readily convertible for cash—in spite of the fact that such conversions routinely took place throughout the twentieth century. The Bakama did have their potency diminish over the years of British colonial rule; coffee was no longer understood as a materialization of "life forces" or royal presences by the end of the 1920s. But coffee was still widely used for sacrifice throughout the colonial period, and to this day *akamwani* is a recognized rubric for offerings. The royal clans of Buhaya no longer have the capacity to bestow wealth in the form of farmland. Nonetheless, many Haya farmers continue to this day to trace their attachments to their family lands to the acts of a king's bestowal in the past. And land itself is still described and acted upon in contemporary Haya communities as a form of "wealth," an objectification of values whose conversion into priced "property" is possible, but always highly problematic (Weiss 1996a).

What I want to do at this juncture is focus this contestation in values, a kind of "double-voicing" in material practice attuned at once to local concerns and global imperatives, on coffee specifically. While it was the case that coffee seedlings were planted in numbers heretofore unknown in Buhaya during the 1920s, and levels of coffee exports from the region soared during the twenties and thirties, the ways in which these rates of planting and production were practically achieved bespeak a certain uneasiness on the part of rural farmers. As important, that is, as the sheer number of seedlings and volumes of coffee generated by this colonial agricultural campaign undoubtedly were, an adequate appreciation of the value this new coffee had for Haya households requires a consideration of the specific forms through which farmers appropriated these trees.

It has generally been argued that the successes of Baines's planting program can be attributed, in part, to the participation of Lwamgira and his abilities to "persuade" Haya farmers to comply with British agricultural policy (the crucial "educational" dimension of agrarian reform is thereby acknowledged). Of even more importance, however, was the steadily rising price of coffee through the mid-1920s (Austen 1968: 161; Mukurasi 1970: 8; Curtis 1989: 93ff). The global demand for coffee was booming from 1923 to 1927, and the price per kilo of harvested coffee during this period was two to three times the price of earlier decades (Curtis 1989: 92). Still, I would suggest that the incorporation or expansion of coffee trees into ekibanja agriculture entailed certain risks from the perspective of Haya households, risks that, as the subsequent history of coffee husbandry reveals, turned on the potentially ambiguous juxtaposition of values embodied by a cash crop now extensively rooted in a generative domain. Coffee harvests brought a good price through the 1920s, but they might also exact a price on household viability, and most explicitly the generativity of the land itself. Strategic modes of reconciling these distinct possibilities would characterize Haya coffee cultivation over the coming decades.

These differential potentials are reflected in scholarly accounts of coffee's prominence in Haya social life of this period. Jervis, writing in at the end of the 1930s, a tumultuous period (to be described shortly) said that

> owners of banana plots were each compelled to plant 100 trees among their banana trees. Resentment of the crop was born in the initial compulsory

> order to plant. . . . Coffee trees became debilitated, and the quality of the crop deteriorated steadily. (Jervis cited in Mukurasi 1970: 7)

Curtis, though, in his review of this historical era, holds that "there is no question that in the 1920's coffee became a sort of madness in Bukoba," and claims that

> The immediate benefits of growing coffee overshadowed the long term dangers: the Bahaya had become fully committed to participation in an exchange economy subject to changes in the terms of trade over which they had no control. . . . The other factor which facilitated peasant enthusiasm for coffee was the ease with which it could be integrated into the existing crop cycle. Simply put, the Bahaya had much to gain and little to lose by planting coffee. (Curtis 1989: 93)

My contention in considering the implications of the massive agricultural innovation projects of the twenties and thirties is that these two perspectives are not mutually exclusive. Coffee could readily become "integrated into the existing crop cycle" of household farms, even as the "trees became debilitated" and the coffee "crop deteriorated steadily." Haya coffee husbandry offered neither an enthusiastic embrace of the huge profits to be reaped by intensive cultivation, nor a simple resistance in the form of neglect and abandonment to the coercive force used to promote this crop. Rather, rural farmers' incorporation of coffee trees into their farms became, and continues to be a way of articulating Haya agency with respect to the forces of colonialism, globalization, and market pressures. A form of control over these controlling forces could be realized in Haya efforts both to adopt and reject the cultivation of these trees.

CHANGING PRICES, CHANGING VALUES: COFFEE PRODUCTION IN THE 1920s AND 1930s

How did Haya farmers respond to Baines's coffee campaign? The number of seedlings planted in this period is unquestionably impressive, but precisely how were all of these new trees planted? It is difficult to reconstruct in textured detail the particulars of innovative agricultural practices in the absence of relevant documentation, written or oral. Certain aspects of this early campaign, however, are recorded, precisely because they posed difficulties for successive officers of the colonial regime, whose policies were often designed to overcome the shortcomings of this initial effort. It is clear, for example, that new coffee trees were consistently interplanted with bananas, but were always planted on the peripheries of the ekibanja. This pattern certainly conforms to the topographic organization of cultivation already described, but it posed certain

Photo 5.1. Flourishing banana plants, grown adjacent to the house, are closely identified with the power of a household head.

challenges under these new conditions. From the perspective of both Haya farmers and colonial agricultural officers, the peripheries of the family farms were less fertile and less productive regions than those more central to the house. For farmers, these central regions were necessary to the well-being of the household and further demonstrated that well-being in the lush growth of bananas meant for family meals. (Rald and Rald 1975: 111). These staple plants were continuously harvested and mulched, thereby enhancing the fertility of these focal places and ensuring access to food supplies.

Peripheral zones in the ekibanja had a very different temporal cycle, as these beer and snacking bananas were harvested, not for daily household provision but for more punctuated collective practices of exchange, or marketing, or brewing, or donation. In turn, this meant that these areas of the farm were mulched with the recyclable products of the agricultural cycle less frequently, and so its trees did not thrive in the ways that trees adjacent to the house did. The crops of this periphery, meant for "outsiders" from the perspective of those "inside" the household, were less crucial to household sustenance and were not permitted to consume as many of its productive resources. Thus, the high price Haya farmers received for coffee in the early years of British colonial rule may well have contributed to the intensive planting of coffee on ekibanja lands. But though ever higher cash incomes would seem the incentive for increasing coffee production, they cannot account for Haya planting patterns that intentionally kept new coffee trees out of the most fertile zones of family farms, thereby effectively reducing coffee's productive potential. Planting in these fertile zones was motivated by a different set of values, those of generativity and renewal, whose significance came increasingly to be defined in relation to the values of coffee and cash.

From the point of view of colonial coffee husbandry, the peripheralization of these new trees in otherwise fertile lands would come to create a number of difficulties that depleted coffee production overall. Coffee received less "green" fertilizer in the form of stems, leaves, and other compost, since they were planted among less frequently harvested bananas. Further, since they were always kept out of the central, highly productive zone adjacent to the house, coffee trees were rather densely spaced in those areas in which they were planted, a situation that diminished both coffee and banana yields. As I have already shown, Haya farmers not only planted coffee trees in their farms' peripheries, they were further uninterested in expending the energy required to cut back and trim these trees as colonial policies of proper crop management dictated (but never enforced—Rald and Rald 1975: 55ff). This is not to say, however, that coffee trees were never attended to, or only worked during harvest. Rather, it seems that Haya farmers treated the life cycle of coffee trees in ways not dissimilar to their bananas. Just as banana cultivation required the routine pruning of desiccated and withered leaves and bast, coffee cultivation permitted Haya householders to pare dead branches from the growing trees; indeed, dead coffee limbs remain a source of firewood in many rural Haya homes. Further, just as old banana matter was immediately recycled as the mulch for subsequent banana crops—a technique aimed at ensuring a supply of moisture for growing plants—coffee material in the form of fallen leaves and blossoms, as well as overripe cherries, remained on the floor of the ekibanja as a source for generational continuity, and the transformation of finished into renewed growth. These newly planted coffee trees, then, embody an emerging tension. At once removable cash crops and the living products of a viable household, planted in peripheral zones while still tended to in keeping with the dynamics of generative growth, coffee trees conjoined Haya concerns with acquiring new forms of material wealth while maintaining productivity. Household heads, thus, welcomed coffee while simultaneously keeping it at arm's length.

In the throes of what must have seemed a wildly successful reform project, the British Administration took little interest in these cultivation techniques. Coffee production soared through the 1920s and well into the 1930s, and the colonial interest in both increasing exports and creating a market for imported European goods was well satisfied.[1] By the end of the 1920s, though, colonial officers worried that the decade's global coffee boom would bust and destroy the market for Bukoba's *robusta* product, and so began to take notice of the poor quality of the Haya crop. The creative response of Haya householders to the simultaneous demands of global markets and local wealth, embedded in their agricultural practice, was scarcely relevant to the district officer who, in 1926, bemoaned the "inferior wild coffee" (Bukoba District Annual Report: 1926) produced by these methods—a harbinger of the director of agriculture's 1938 description of Haya coffee as a "wild orchard crop." From 1928 through 1937 a series of reforms were proposed, and occasionally implemented, all of which were designed to improve coffee quality. In 1928 the first coffee rules were forced through the Bakama Council, over the objections of the kings themselves, who were loathe to interfere with ekibanja cultivation practices. The sticking point of these rules was the requirement that farmers sweep up the detritus from beneath their coffee trees and burn it (Mukurasi 1970: 10). This rule was designed to eliminate the coffee berry borer (*Stephenoderes*) by removing infected berries and eliminating the breeding material of this pest. For Haya farmers, though, the proposed methods of elimination posed a direct challenge to their control over their own farmlands. The process of recycling, connecting past productivity with future developments thereby ensuring the fundamental components of agricultural value, was replaced by a discontinuous process of elimination.

Haya concerns with maintaining the moisture of the ekibanja, iconic of generative growth and essential to coffee as well as banana cultivation, were confronted by the potential loss of ground cover provided by these organic mulches. Further, it is quite possible that the prospect of burning materials grown on the family farm would have posed similar risks. Fires, as we have seen, were essential to grassland cultivation, but in that site were directed toward a clearly discontinuous form of production. Burning the grasses initiated new fields, but these fields are necessarily fallowed and abandoned once their harvest is complete. To introduce open fires on family farms, or even—if it seems unlikely that fires would have been lit on family farmland—to burn its dead products, would be to concretize a discontinuous process of land management, and so to threaten a household's attachment to its farm. Moreover, Haya communities were already familiar with publicly organized campaigns to openly burn the contents of a family farm (witness their treatment of the White Fathers' buildings), as this was their own preferred method of evicting a person who had been determined to be a witch from their home and village.

The initial rules designed to improve coffee quality, lacking the support of both kings and commoners, were never pursued very vigorously. A set of revised rules established in 1930, which eliminated the requirement that ekibanja land be swept free of fallen coffee cherries, was implemented with somewhat greater success, but even these rules did not bring colonial officers into the family farms of Haya household heads (Curtis 1989: 160–162). What did bring about a more rigorous set of rules and a greater determination to see them enforced was the rather sudden collapse of the world coffee market in the mid–1930s. The onset of the depression saw the average price of Bukoba coffee fall from £58.4 in 1929 to £26.3 per ton in the following year. Coffee prices did manage to rebound through the middle of the decade. In 1934 the price reached £37.1 per ton, and in that year and the following, coffee production in Buhaya reached the highest levels of the entire colonial period, with close to eleven thousand tons marketed. The same year—1935—in which production peaked, however, prices dropped to a level as low as they had been since the early years of Baines's coffee planting campaign, £22.9 per ton. The very next year, with production just having reached an all-time high, the volume of coffee marketed plummeted 40 percent, from 10,882 tons in 1935 to 6,463 tons in 1936. In fact, coffee production for the next twenty-five years of colonial rule remained closer to the latter level than the former.

Two immediate observations can be made based on these mere statistical indices. First, the British concern with these falling coffee prices, long anticipated but only intermittently acted upon, clearly brought about a more serious and concerted effort to improve the quality of coffee grown in Buhaya so as to attempt to receive the highest possible price for their crop. Second, it is crucial to recognize that the response of Haya farmers to declining prices was *not* to pursue the expansion of coffee production. If high cash returns seem to have provided some incentive to grow more coffee, lower prices clearly did not stimulate greater production in an attempt to recover lost income. It would be simplistic to seek a causal relationship between depressed prices and falling production. Some have observed that the declining yields of coffee trees in the late 1930s may have reflected the aging plants grown from seedlings in the early 1920s (Curtis 1989; Mukurasi 1970). While this factor is not insignificant, it must be noted that—even with the ongoing planting of new seedlings—coffee production, having risen steadily and dramatically under British colonial rule through the mid-1930s, *remained* relatively low throughout the pre-independence period. This empirical evidence of continuous indifference to coffee production needs to be accounted for, not merely in terms of the calculus of risks and benefits, but with reference to an emerging historical process.

Haya farmers' engagements with coffee were a means of demonstrating their willingness to engage in the order of commercial relations that attempted to direct agricultural practice. Falling prices might have been experienced in these terms as the failure of a system of prices to adequately evaluate the productivity of household activities, as much as they were a straightforward loss of cash income. Coffee became, in virtue of Baines's intensive planting campaign, a privileged medium for regulating local and global entanglements. By the Second World War it was already occupying the land in ways that reshaped its productive potential, and was providing an income now unambiguously necessary for everyday household provisioning. Still the effects of these conditions created by coffee could be *acted upon* by Haya farming practices that continued, in both colonial and postcolonial eras, to look warily on intensification of coffee production in favor of the growth of valued bananas, beans, and other foods. If cash crops had, and still have, a value in Haya communities, the forms of value they embody can still be displaced.

COFFEE RULES, "FAILED REBELLION": HAYA RESISTANCE IN THE 1930s

It is further important to realize that these farmers' responses to rising and falling prices, their embrace and rejection of coffee itself, were part of a dialectic informed by the specific form of *British* attempts to promote better coffee husbandry, as much as they reflected characteristic Haya notions of productivity and value. In this regard, the New Coffee Rules of 1937, a direct response to the precipitous decline in coffee harvest of 1936, are a central dimension of this encounter. These "Instructions for Coffee Growers" were forced through the Bakama Council, still reluctant to intervene on household agricultural land, and this time the colonial Agricultural Department, as opposed to the Native Authorities, took it upon themselves to ensure their enforcement. These rules reintroduced the measures opposed in 1928, requiring the sweeping up and elimination of diseased coffee berries, and added yet further regulations.

At this point, the British administration was most concerned with the quality of coffee produced in the region, and the rules did focus primarily on coffee husbandry. They required, for example: the proper spacing of coffee trees; approval of current crop husbandry by the agricultural officer before new coffee trees could be planted; a host of measures to ensure the proper drying and winnowing of coffee cherries before their sale; and a number of regulations designed to curb coffee disease, including the reporting of all disease to the Agriculture Department, and the requirement that all diseased coffee trees be destroyed (Curtis 1989: 210). In response to these directives many Haya farmers simply uprooted all of their coffee trees to avoid the intrusion of agricultural inspectors (Mukurasi 1970: 11).

But uprooting coffee trees was, in many ways, a mild reaction relative to the wider response to the Agricultural Department's initiatives. What seems most to have provoked Haya farmers, though, were a few provisions in the "Instructions for Coffee Growers" that directly affected banana cultivation. Agricultural extension officers were now permitted to order the removal of banana plants in a "coffee plot" (a term that demonstrates a gross unfamiliarity with Haya agriculture, Curtis 1989: 210) if these were determined to interfere with the spacing of coffee trees. Further, the Agricultural Department was also concerned with the spread of the banana weevil as a threat to Haya "subsistence," and the new rules required that farmers remove the entire banana stem upon the harvest of the fruit in order to eliminate this pest (Austen 1968: 224–226; Mukurasi 1970: 11; Curtis 1989: 209).

These measures provoked an unparalleled Haya response, and one of their very few demonstrations of open resistance during colonial rule. In the early months of 1937, Haya farmers met agricultural extension officers at the borders of their farms with shouts of *"Twaiyanga!"* "We refuse!" To underscore this refusal, these farmers brandished spears. The rules themselves promulgated techniques that were relatively simple, that could be—and were expected to be—carried out by any Haya farmer. Moreover, there does not appear to be evidence of the coercive force, or even brutality that was occasionally associated with the massive planting campaigns of earlier decades. Yet, these past colonial enterprises did not generate an explicitly resistant movement like *Twaiyanga*, as it came to be known. It is not, then, merely the intrusion of colonial officers onto households (an intrusion that would seem greater in the twenties than it was in the thirties), nor the conservatism of a peasantry fighting to preserve their "right to live as peasants" (Curtis 1989: 211) that elicited this armed refusal. Rather, it must be recognized that the simplicity of the 1937 "Instructions for Coffee Growers" and relatively "hands-off" approach of the administration belie the fact that these efforts were felt by Haya farmers to pose a direct threat to household heads' capacities to ensure their control over the very sources of household viability.

Uprooting the moisture-laden stems of harvested banana plants—to say nothing of the outright elimination of some banana trees—was a measure that, as I hope is clear by now, undermined the generative links between agricultural cycles, an absolutely fundamental component of a household's attachments to the land it occupied. Not surprisingly, the new coffee rules, primarily motivated by the British concerns with coffee quality, were understood by Haya villagers as an attack on their ability to grow food. Mukurasi notes that during *Twaiyanga*, local farmers

> suspected the colonial rulers of having introduced the banana weevil in Bukoba so that the subsequent shortage of food would make the Bahaya work for a wage to buy "ugali" [maize meal]. Now the idea of uprooting banana stumps was seen as a colonial plot to hasten the destruction of the banana plot. (1970: 11)

Curtis also found that

> The Agricultural Officer reported that he had been accused of *personally* introducing coffee disease into Buhaya so that the peasants would be ruined and forced to work for the white settlers who planned to come and take their land. (1989: 211)

In effect, these two perceived dangers, famine and land alienation, were part of the very same process. Residence in ekibanja land, for Haya households, is a means of ensuring their ability to feed themselves (and thereby not be fed by—hence, be dependent on—others); and feeding a household—thus enhancing its reproductive abilities, assuring the continuity of its plant life in the recycling process (plants thrive when a house eats well) and more generally promoting its well-being—is explicitly understood as a way of assuring continuous attachment to the land. Indeed, the links between eating well and effectively holding the land have deep and enduring historical resonances (dare I say "roots"?) for Haya communities. For example, similar reports of devastation to those threatened in 1937 were to circulate surrounding the *bikonya* ("banana stem") legislation of 1953, legislation introduced to curb the spread of the banana weevil through the same uprooting techniques.

At this point, Haya farmers again saw these requirements as a means of driving villagers off their farms, farms that would be taken over by European and Asian landholders for whom Haya men and women would be forced to work as wage laborers. And at a much earlier period, Rehse (1910: section 7, p. 14) reported that Baziba elders recalled the nineteenth-century raids by Baganda forces into Kiziba as catastrophic episodes in which villagers whose farms had been pillaged were reduced to digging up banana roots and eating them for sustenance. Such a dire practice vividly portrays the debilitating conjunction of displacement by a foreign power, abject hunger, and uprooted trees. And precisely this deadly conjunction was portended for Haya farmers by ongoing British attempts to improve coffee quality.

The tall, vertical presence of growing banana plants, the scrupulously maintained continuities between elements taken from above contributing to growth moving up from below, the recycling of finished products into productive potentials, all of these material processes are critical to the Haya householder's efforts to establish *his* presence on a centered, viable domain. Such techniques were clearly not of interest to British administrators; indeed, these very methods were directly challenged. Moreover, it was not only the force of these generative processes that was threatened by these new rules, it was the emergent *relationship* between the growth of foods and the production of coffee as a cash crop, a relationship carefully crafted in Haya agricultural experience, that was at stake. The reference to *ugali* cited by Mukurasi's informants provides a revealing commentary on exactly this relationship. *Ugali*, a porridge made from flour—generally maize meal—is something of a national dish in Tanzania, but it is despised as a meal of hardship by most Haya men and women, who much prefer the bananas they grow for themselves.[2]

To be forced to "work for a wage to buy 'ugali,' " as Haya farmers in the 1930s feared colonial policy would require of them, is not simply to be deprived of a preferred food, it is to alter the place of food itself in social life. Purchasing *ugali* for food shifts the balance between household food provisioning and the cash cropping of coffee, as it renders *both* of these products subject to the same means of evaluation. Food, like coffee, can now be bought and sold. While British agricultural policy never attempted to promote the marketing of bananas in Buhaya on a significant scale, the department's coffee rules showed that they conceived of agrarian activity and agricultural land within the family farm as uniformly subject to the same principles. Bananas were to be treated as crops that contributed to or led to the deterioration of coffee production, as the entire ekibanja became a homogenous zone of improvement.

What were the consequences of the *Twaiyanga* movement, a movement that lasted all of two months? The few analysts and observers of Haya history and culture who have considered these events have tended either to lament their limited effects, or noted the relatively minor, and ultimately repressive changes in the "realpolitik" of indirect rule that they inspired. British administrators, for example, deposed some of the bakama they found to be ineffectual in dealing with these "riots," and they focused their ensuing agricultural extension activities on education as opposed to intervention. More pessimistically, Iliffe sees this movement as a simple failure owing to its lack of a leadership that could orchestrate protests at village and district wide levels. The *Twaiyanga* actions were "demonstrations rather than serious contests of power" (Iliffe 1979: 286) in his view. The "seriousness" of these actions is, of course, a matter of perspective and goes to the very heart of these matters. For beyond asking about the "extent" of the "success" of *Twaiyanga* we might, instead, insist that the forms of consciousness through which Haya farmers demonstrated their protests ably captured the values they felt were at issue, and did realize the vision of farming they were defending. Coffee trees were uprooted, coffee production did not accelerate, and banana cultivation continued unabated.

Indeed, the very premises of agricultural practice, with respect to both coffee and bananas, remain the same in Kagera today as they were at the end of *Twaiyanga*; as Mukurasi put it in 1970, "The farmer of the 1930's is basically the same as the one of the 1960's" (Mukurasi 1970: 9). Inspection officers were effectively refused entry into household farms, kept out, as Haya men recall, by the *omuholo*, the same "spear" that is emblematic of masculine production and intervention. Haya farmers seem to have made clear just who would be uprooting what. Moreover, the "failure" to collectively organize may be seen less as a weakness of *Twaiyanga* than as one of its very goals. Agricultural practice on ekibanja land in Haya communities was a means of asserting household autonomy and self-sufficiency. It was, and remains, a man's mode of demonstrating that he "feeds himself" and does not defer to others in his own home. Collectively coordinating a resistance project concerned with removing the intrusive policing of such places and activities might itself have constituted exactly the kind of intrusion to which Haya farmers were opposed.

THE DEMONSTRATION EFFECT: A POSTCOLONIAL EXAMPLE

The *Twaiyanga* protests, in my view, were neither an atavistic defense of tradition nor a feeble attempt at politics. Rather, they captured, in terms both subtle and forceful, Haya farmers' pragmatic efforts to engage with ascendant conditions of modernity, and to refashion and concretize those conditions in modes of being and doing suited to a specific local world. Coffee was the principle focus around which these processes of engagement were formulated. This crop was not simply the most potent vehicle of European overrule and global capital, for its full significance emerges through the array of articulations it made possible. As trees that had both a rather long history in Buhaya and a profoundly transformed recent past in the colonial period; as plants interspersed among the most vital and valued of familial foods, yet clearly removed from the most productive zones of household cultivation; and as crops whose harvests provided an increasingly necessary cash income, yet whose production was intentionally curtailed, coffee facilitated the creation of new modes of Haya agency relevant to the new world it ushered in. *Twaiyanga* was an apt embodiment of these innovative, if fragile, agencies as well as an expression of the tensions and contradictions entailed in their establishment.

Many of these contradictions have been experienced by Haya men and women through the particular forms taken by different agricultural extension campaigns. Colonial attempts at "educating" the "lazy Bukoba native stick[ing] his plants in the ground" (Bukoba District Annual Report for 1926, quoted in Curtis 1989: 157) ranged from the use of military force, to the establishment of royal exemplars, to attempts at scientifically motivated systematic surveillance. I want to shift my historical focus forward at this point, to consider yet another technique of instruction, one that demonstrates the enduring character of many of the contradictions that envelop coffee production in Buhaya as well as the resilience of Haya agency in these matters. The Annual Report for 1959/1961 of the Bukoba Cooperative Union (BCU), a cooperative agency authorized to oversee the coffee industry in Buhaya in 1950, said that

> Apart from the ten million older coffee trees already existing, the Coffee Board and the Union's nurseries have supplied more than six and a half million seedlings to growers. In addition to these, the farmers produce their own seedlings. It is therefore amazing to find that coffee production in Bukoba and Karagwe has not really increased for something like twenty years. Certainly there is something wrong. The cause will have to be found and tackled at source. (Mukurasi 1970: 22)

In order to address this "something wrong" with stagnating coffee production, the BCU provided a budgetary allotment to treat coffee pest control, a long-standing concern of agricultural extension policy in Buhaya generally seen as the greatest strain on coffee yields. The agricultural section of the union used its funds to provide an insecticide spraying program. This program was hindered by a number of factors. While the spraying service was free, farmers did have to pay for the insecticide, and this clearly limited the campaign's success. Further, coffee trees were still largely unpruned throughout the region, and spraying sprawling trees proved to be of limited effectiveness. Thus, in the second spraying season the union instituted a pruning campaign to facilitate pest control. Both of these measures, spraying and pruning, were looked on skeptically by the vast majority of Haya farmers, who feared that these measures would cause coffee trees and ekibanja growth more generally to dry up. Indeed, to this day, chemical fertilizers are seen as especially toxic because of their desiccating effects. Green and sometimes bovine manure are always preferred, if a farmer is able (as most are not) to make any inputs at all.

Haya concerns with moisture and desiccation are, was we have seen, a recurring theme in agricultural practice and innovation. Activities that might be said to "intrude" onto farmland cultivation, using materials like pesticides and chemical fertilizers in order to supplement the products of the farm itself seem to be experienced or anticipated as potential threats to moisture, that is, to the plant lives' source of its *own* renewal. The prices for these services were reasonable, but certainly the fee for any service already understood to be dangerous prohibited the widespread adaptation of the spraying and pruning programs. Ultimately, less than 20 percent of trees in the region were treated during these campaigns, and their effectiveness is even further diminished since it is evident that a few trees sprayed with insecticide in a village filled with unsprayed trees will not be well protected (Mukurasi 1970: 22–30).

What is especially intriguing about the union's programs is less the nature of the resistance they faced than the reflexivity they demonstrated in their own conception of their mission. The "target of the campaign," according to Mukurasi, "was not just the coffee pests; an attempt would be made to fight superstitions" (Mukurasi 1970: 23). The union clearly recognized that farmers would be reluctant to accept their methods, and so conceived of pest control as a project in education as much as eradication. It was understood that funds for pesticides and pruning would be limited, but it was hoped that poorer farmers would see the benefits of these techniques in the coffee trees of the wealthier farmers who could make use of them. Thus, new agricultural extension policies in the early independence era in Kagera, often under the auspices of Haya administrators, had a firmer grasp of the concerns that confronted Haya farmers, but continued to see their role as one of "fighting superstition," educating local peoples toward higher levels of cultural development.

These intentions achieved an apotheosis of sorts with the development of "demonstration plots," farms developed in accordance with the methods of *Ukulima wa Kisasa*, "modern farming." Establishing these plots, explicitly conceived of as teaching tools (BCU Report 1964/65–1967/68 cited in Mukurasi 1978: 23ff), was itself a daunting undertaking. Farmers whose lands were determined to be in need of improvement were approached and offered the services of the union. Staff from the BCU would do all of the labor, uprooting all of the plants on the plots of land, and replanting them following the new methods to be promoted. Plots of one acre were sought, and the land was to be divided into three regions: a half-acre plot interplanted with coffee and bananas as was standard practice in the region, and two quarter acres, one with monoculture of coffee, the other with monoculture of bananas. Monoculture was promoted as the most efficient method of cultivation, and the quarter-acre plots were to be heavily mulched and sprayed to prevent pest infestation. Farmers who agreed to turn over one-acre units to the union received all of the produce of coffee and bananas from these plots, but had to keep records of the size of their harvests and the prices they received for them. In all seventy-four such plots were developed throughout Kagera by 1968. Rald and Rald's survey, done in the midst of the process of demonstration, indicate that these programs had limited, but not negligible success. What seems most successful from their reports was the promotion of the use of grasses as mulch in ekibanja land. All other inputs remain difficult to acquire (and are not uniformly desired); the methods of monoculture, however, have very rarely been implemented.

It is important to note, when assessing this process of "demonstration," that the very forms these programs took, their conception of the education project, and the specific techniques they employed to "demonstrate" the methods promoted, reinstatiated many of the contradictions that characterized coffee production in the region. To begin with, the BCU tried to situate the demonstration plots themselves "close to the main roads" (BCU Report 1964/65–1967/68, cited in Mukurasi 1970: 37), which would make them highly visible and expose them to a higher density of traffic. If demonstration is your aim this would seem a reasonable strategy. It must be recalled, though, that precisely this sort of exposure and visibility has intrinsic risks. Haya perceptual fields are highly attuned to the dynamics of vision and display, and recognize that those who make themselves visible to others also render themselves subject to their authority (see earlier discussion of visibility and power, chapter 1). The BCU may, then, not only have demonstrated new agricultural methods, but the fact of *demonstration* itself as the primary means of promotion conveyed a message of power and control. By using farmers to create an appearance for others, one highly exposed and open—situated directly on main roads whose presence in Kagera today poses a serious challenge to the continuities of spatial grounding (see Weiss 1996a)—the Union displayed its invasive control over subordinate farmers. The techniques of surveillance, including the "simple" procedures of recording harvests and the prices received for them, incorporated into this regime of demonstration further instantiated the ways in which the *availability* of these ekibanja lands as visible and enumerable zones made them subject to external controls.

There was an additional dimension to these "demonstration plots" that had a somewhat greater impact on Haya agriculture, and that was the development of monocultural plots. On the whole, Haya farmers have not attempted to replant their ebibanja, segregating bananas from coffee, respacing their trees, and spraying with chemical pesticides. The BCU, however, also made extensive use of the *ekishambu* plots, those areas of grassland planted with trees and converted to land that becomes held as clan-held farmland. As I have indicated, the White Fathers' introduction of woodland trees expanded these holdings considerably. Now, the development plot scheme found that land planted as *ekishambu* could be converted to monocultured coffee plots much more readily, with far fewer inputs, than open *orweya*. These clan-held but inhabited sites thus lent themselves to the techniques of "modern farming," and one still finds a few small fields devoted strictly to coffee cultivation in Kagera today.

However, it is crucial to recognize that "modern farming," where it has been applied on such plots, has been limited almost exclusively to *coffee* cultivation; bananas are still never monocultured whether on long-standing ebibanja or recently converted *ekishambu*. This conversion process objectifies, in effect, the culmination of the transformations begun under the White Fathers, transformations that subject land and its products to new forms of evaluation, and decentered that productivity from the dynamic of interhousehold relations. Coffee can now stand alone—but only in some instances, for those farmers able to provide the inputs still needed to make such a shift, and on land whose status remains marginal to the overall system of landholding in Kagera. On the whole, Haya farmers continue to intersperse coffee with bananas, households rarely attempt to hold land that they will not also seek to reside in, and this interplay of forces, local and global, centered and dispersing, remains anchored—if continuously contested—in the lands that provide for their own renewal.

The history of agricultural innovation in Buhaya, and especially the trajectory of intensification in coffee husbandry and production, would certainly have been registered as a significant success story in the annals of Tanganyikan colonial rule. A region at the peripheries of the German and British colonies, far from the coast and the centers of trade and development in East Africa, could nonetheless account for 10 percent of the income from the colony as a whole at the time of independence (Mukurasi 1970: 22). Coffee trees that had once been judiciously planted under royal and cosmological scrutiny were distributed by a network of cooperative nurseries by the end of British rule—literally millions of trees were planted during a forty-five year period.

Many Haya peoples themselves benefited beyond question as a result of these processes. The educated elites of Kagera, risen to prominence through rising coffee incomes, have established a legacy that remains prominent to this day in Tanzania. As Priscilla Reining notes (1973: 215), "In the early fifties, the Haya were considered and, indeed, regarded themselves to be among the wealthiest of peoples in what was then Tanganyika." This panegyric to a cash crop, and its palpable effects on local self-consciousness, though, diverts attention from the experiences, practices, and values of many in the Haya communities that tended these trees. A consideration of these features of this history, as I have offered here, details a more complicated picture. Coffee was a prominent concern for Haya farmers, but the nature of that concern was ambiguous and fraught with uneasiness. At each moment that coffee extension proceeded, Haya peoples struggled to define for themselves the place of this product, and the meaning of its "benefits," for themselves. This struggle led them to situate coffee itself at a remove from those things that mattered most, to harvest when harvest was due but otherwise largely neglect this crop. The importance of coffee may, indeed, have much to do with the successes of Haya peoples under the British colonial administration. Yet the value that Haya men and women have ascribed to coffee also reveals that nothing succeeds like indifference.

NOTES

1. According to the Bukoba District Annual Report for 1926 (cited in Curtis 1989: 92), "The gross value of Bukoba exports rose from £76,539 in 1921 to £147,838 in 1923, and £341,231 in 1926. In the same years, the value of imports rose from £52,759, to £123,037, and £191,904."

2. See Weiss 1996a, chapter 4, for a more detailed discussion of the significance of *ugali*, and the problematic values of a food that is also extensively commoditized food in Haya communities.

6

Extraordinary Measures: The Techniques of Modernity

> Weights and measures are practically unknown. Banana beer is sold by the bottle, but then the size of the bottle varies. Coffee and grain are sold by the load, but the weight of a load varies considerably. The price of bark cloth varies with the size of individual pieces. Elephant tusks are valued according to their marks. Hollow measure and weights are non-existent in Kiziba. They do not know how to measure surface or distance. . . . [T]hey do not even measure the plot for building a house.
>
> Herman Rehse (1910: chapter 9, p. 6)

The revaluation of coffee in Haya communities has been a complicated cultural process, one that has required the promotion of innovative techniques and practices as well as the inculcation of new forms and media of value itself. As we have seen, British, German, and French colonial efforts at engendering these novel uses of coffee, in activities ranging from planting trees to paying taxes, would be taken up by Haya subjects—but in ways that neither embraced nor rejected these transformations in anything like a straightforward fashion. The emerging relations and practices of the colonial coffee economy in Buhaya, and the modes of consciousness that informed them, were, I have suggested, characterized by what many analysts of colonial contact have termed "hybridization," and what I would describe as a form of "double-voicing," or (if the extra-linguistic dimensions of this practice are to be emphasized) a "double-praxis." That is, a single set of sociocultural actions in a colonial, or postcolonial, world may be attuned simultaneously to the motivations and meanings of both local and global orders of relations and categories. Haya agency was—and is—expressed through an ongoing concern with asserting the importance of the generative values grounded in specific modes of inhabiting place, or of securing control over valued objects. And coffee has become a critical medium in the Haya sociocultural order for making such assertions.

Yet coffee is not simply an oppositional form, one whose presence permits the delineation of a categorical *contrast* between the local and the global, or tradition and modernity. Rather, as their agricultural concerns and uses of money indicate, coffee affords Haya subjects a means of articulating their engagements *in* the modern world of which they—and all of us—are a part. Increasingly dependent on the income derived from this cash crop, yet continuously withholding some of their harvests from the market; tending to trees within the purview of generative household lands, yet assiduously peripheralizing these plants from the most productive soils, the residents of rural Haya communities have powerfully made known their place in the colonial and postcolonial order of things through coffee.

The persistent ambivalence surrounding the social position of coffee in Buhaya must not, however, lead us to conclude that Haya communities are blithely indifferent bricoleurs at the fringes of the global coffee economy. The Haya sociocultural order—to say nothing of the actual social experience of Haya persons—has not merely perpetuated itself as a discrete totality or maintained a judicious distance from the often brutal machinations of international commerce. While Haya farmers did and do attempt to exert control over the values of agricultural production through their coffee cultivation, it seems those values were also strongly influenced, in a relatively short period of time, by the persuasive powers of cash cropping and the "religion of the rupee." To argue, as I have, that Haya coffee cultivators strove to act on the world in terms that mattered to them, should not be taken to mean that these terms have been entirely unconstrained. The revaluation of coffee in the region has profoundly and irrevocably altered relations of power both within Kagera—and perhaps especially between Bahaya coffee producers—and those of us who are coffee consumers.

All the parties to this remaking of coffee were subjects whose actions were motivated by meaningful expectations and intentions, but surely not all parties exercised the same *capacity* for action through their efforts. Transforming the value of coffee in Buhaya entailed the generation of new structural forms of inequality that continue to be of real consequence in Kagera until today. Further, it must be made clear that the different ways of valuing coffee, and the range of meanings embedded in this substance in Buhaya, were never simply shared *uniformly* by all Haya persons. I would insist that there are identifiable systems of orientation, mutually understood forms, signs, and practices—in short a Haya sociocultural order—whose *coherence* is necessary to sustain the routine interactions and communicative activities of collective existence. Yet, this coherence does not preclude the possibility of contention and conflict in social life, and such struggles certainly surround the social life of Haya coffee.

The range of responses and array of meanings made possible by the transformation of Haya coffee has been, in short, highly differentiated and fraught with inequities. Colonial enterprises, as many observers have noted, are (at a minimum) difference-making procedures, and a detailed exposition of the trajectory of coffee over the course of the twentieth century in Buhaya makes this clear. The critical and more complicated questions that we must ask of these enterprises are: what are the differences wrought under these conditions that actually *make* a difference; and which procedures are those that most *effectively* bring these differences about? How, for example, could rupees be described as the "dominant religion" of the Haya as early as the end of the first decade of the twentieth century? How could coffee exports from Buhaya account for 10 percent of the total income from Tanganyika in 1960, while the total volume of coffee production in the region had remained essentially unchanged for more than thirty years? In Kagera the continuously developing techniques and methods that constituted coffee marketing relations were clearly central to the wider reformulation of Haya social worlds. As other analysts of colonial policy in the Lakes Region have held (Curtis 1992; Austen 1968; Bunker 1987), marketing was the social process that mattered most in generating new orders of meaning and power. Marketing in coffee in both colonial and postcolonial eras has been crucial to the Haya sociocultural order at a host of different levels, from making and breaking the fortunes of celebrated local marketers, to organizing the rhythms of agricultural activity throughout the region, to shaping and entrenching relations of social class.

In this chapter I consider the ways in which commercial interactions involving coffee not only contributed to the institutionalization of such significant social inequalities, but further became exemplary features of an emerging Haya consciousness of their entanglements in the world at large. Coffee trading, that is, came to provide Haya men, and a few women, with an apt illustration of the alluring and invidious nature of colonialism, globalization, and modernity. In particular, I examine how the nature of these entanglements has been assessed in Haya communities through the development of certain concrete techniques and practices of measurement and enumeration that became characteristic of the coffee trade. These techniques are at once material forms, like weighing, timing, and transport, and social relations of patronage and exploitation. These emerging techniques did not simply "represent" the effects of colonialism on the Haya, rather these were the very forms that constituted modernity as sociocultural reality. What will also be clear is that these techniques have their own social and cultural complexities. They must be grasped both as a set of restraints, promoted by the interests of coffee's colonial administrators, and as a series of strategies that presented Haya farmers with possibilities for asserting their place in—or distancing themselves from—the global relations embedded in coffee transactions.

OF CARAVANS AND KINGS: TRADE TECHNIQUES IN EARLY COLONIAL BUHAYA

It is worth pausing to consider what I have already shown to be a dense welter of projects introduced and implemented in just the first decade of colonial overrule in Bukoba. In the span of a very few years, rupees were circulating as the sanctioned currency of the German Administration and soon after enforced by the imposition of taxes. Coffee trees acquired a distinct commercial potential, and in 1905 coffee planting became compulsory by royal edict in some realms of the region. Further, these measures clearly impressed themselves upon Haya practice and consciousness quite rapidly, although not always in ways that might be anticipated. Haya subjects of the German colonial administration recognized colonial currency, even as they measured it in the incompatible terms of cowries; kings mandated the production of cash crops, even as they continued to make offerings of coffee sacrifices during New Moon ceremonies. Part and parcel of these diverse transformations were the techniques and activities of coffee marketing. Marketing coffee in Bukoba as it developed in the earliest decade of the twentieth century was defined in terms that continue to be relevant down to the present day.

The articulation of commercial practices with diverse cultural identities did not, of course begin with the coffee trade in the twentieth century. As I have noted above, the kingdom of Karagwe was implicated in the caravan trades of the nineteenth century as a strategic position that permitted traders from both the Coast and the interior to get an overland route around Lake Victoria, thereby gaining access to the powerful Baganda. Objects and persons from Karagwe also moved along these routes, as the travelers' narratives reveal. While Karagwe was active in this trade to some degree, it is difficult to assess the impact of these activities on the other Haya kingdoms along the lake. These polities did not have the direct contact with the Swahili caravans that Karagwe did, but they would seem to have felt the effects of this trade indirectly, both through the goods that could be acquired in their trade with the peoples of what is now Uganda (including Toro, Ankole, and Nyoro, as well as Ganda polities) in return for Haya coffee, in addition to bark cloth and occasionally ivories, and through the political instability fomented by the caravans that caught up the entire interlacustrine world. Whatever the impact of the caravan trade on Haya peoples through the nineteenth century, marketing under European colonial rule would be significantly more extensive and intensive. Still, the caravan trade, and the cultural differences it instantiated and produced, can be seen to provide an important context for the subsequent commercial activities administered by successive colonial regimes.

Coffee, for example, was initially traded in the colonial era along the same routes that had been established by the caravans, and often in tandem with the same objects that had been the staples of that trade. Reports from Kiziba in 1906 note how the Baziba are constantly

> on the road trading in mbugos [bark cloth], hoes, goats. . . . All the time, the Baziba are on the go: they have mbugos, they forge iron . . . but they have no goats, no salt, etc.; there you have it, a long-distance trip for petty trade. Another time they go all the way to Toro to buy ivory. . . . [T]hey find them (i.e., rupees) working in Entebbe or Kampala; they put themselves to work for the Indians, trading for their accounts. Among them, with their crafts, their mbugos, their hoes, their coffee, many can find the four rupee tax. (Rapports Annuels—Bwanja, 1906–1907:127)

Here we have an apt summary of the early years of European rule in Kagera, and some of the issues at stake in its cultural politics of value. The imposition of taxes creates a requirement that is satisfied by an intensification of trading practices and routes already well established in the region. Trading in goods, as prestigious as ivory, as banal as salt, is facilitated by an early—and brief—accommodation between the German and British administrations that have divided these East African territories. But this is not a simple reproduction of an enduring cultural pattern. By 1906, coffee was being planted in this very kingdom, Kiziba, under a royal edict—a mandate intended to generate an income for the mukama, and imposed under threat of martial retribution.

It seems, then, that coffee is being treated in this period in complex ways. It has been established as a cash crop, grown to be marketed, to enable new colonial subjects to comply with new colonial taxes. In turn, these subjects of a new regime should have met their obligations to the old—if newly fashioned—regime through this same medium. Coffee, that is, is meant to generate royal tribute, now in the form of a cash income. Yet, the intensification of the trading opportunities created by a colonial administration here permits these Baziba to pursue an alternative means to generating value, one that seems to depend upon royal patronage, even as it denies it its due. Moreover, it seems quite probable that the coffee being traded in this way at this period also included *amwani* intended for consumption by Baganda and others. The multiple commodity potentials of coffee in this period, in other words, generated modes of diversion (Munn 1983; Appadurai 1986) which, like all such diversions, strengthened the importance of the overall process of evaluation (here, the monetary payments for the coffee crop), while they also delimited the extent and uniformity of that evaluation. This ready availability of diversion proved, as we shall see, to be a prominent feature of coffee marketing over the course of the twentieth century.

Equally important in the development of these market potentials are the forms of identity and the making of subjects implied in these practices. Earlier I described the ways in which the establishment of nurseries on the grounds of royal capitals effected a significant transformation in the project of modernity. Land could be evaluated as private property just as the fruits of its productivity could be measured as an accumulated volume. This conversion of the royal *ebikale* did not occur until some fifteen years after Mutahangarwa's coerced planting campaign, although this king did transform at least some of his land into a plantation designed to yield a cash income. This transformation was promoted by German and Haya authorities as a means of both complying with colonial rule and retaining the prerogatives of royal domination. It seems, though, to have altered the character of kingship itself, and to have revealed the emerging contradictions between European administration and royal authority. Promoting coffee meant expanding the market potential of this crop in ways that enabled Haya subjects to circumvent their obligations to the bakama in this period. This much is implied by a host of early sources that describe a "frightening depopulation" of the region—indeed, there are accounts of entire villages being deserted—as Haya commoners fled the demands of royalty (Rapports Annuels—Rapport Général de Mgr. Hirth 1906–1907: 121).

The paradox of the earliest attempts to exploit the profit-making possibilities of coffee production is that the very possibility of profit—and royalty's own dependence on the market as a source of value—seems to have made royal control over their subjects more tenuous. As we have seen, the coercive, military force of the mukama of Kiziba had to be extended over his own kingdom, and not only in warfare with competing claimants to power, in order to enforce coffee-planting requirements. More interesting is the fact that the intensification of coffee production for—still largely royal—profit was conjoined throughout Bukoba (and not only in Kiziba) with a massive exercise of constraint not seen before. All of the bakama's demands for corvée labor, not only for coffee planting but for building projects and land clearing, steadily increased in the first decade of colonial rule.[1]

The suggestion of the German *rezident* that the "harsh monarchical constitution" of Haya "sultans" was necessary to promote cultivation and "economic undertakings" more generally may well have mistaken an end for a means. Royal powers of compulsion were powerfully shaped by colonial instruments of overrule—the coffee market among them—but also rendered all the more severe because of the ways in which such colonial mechanisms simultaneously promoted and subverted kingship. The emerging coffee market bound kings and subjects in a cycle of brutality, as Haya men and women could flee the demands of the bakama's dominion, now sanctioned by colonial rule, in pursuit of the very commercial activities that made the extension of that same royal control ever more necessary and desirable.

We have also seen that the production of subjectivities was both embedded in coffee-related practices—agricultural and commercial, ritual and routine, local and global—and was further subject to intensive discursive attention. The White Fathers' ruminations on the nefarious implications of the material enterprises they both denounced and engendered demonstrate not only that new modes of identification and new possibilities for expressing desire were made available by the transregional—indeed, global—coffee trade, even from its very earliest days in Kagera; they also disclose the complex ways that colonizer and colonized formulated the moral dimensions of subjectivity by mutually articulating a concern for a set of important differences. These differences were reflexively exemplified in the immediate example that both "Africans" and "Europeans" provided for one another—and so deracinated Africans typify the anxieties the White Fathers have about their own mission, while mobile, powerful, and wealthy priests are the Haya standardized nightmare of commercial success gone astray. Here we see, as numerous observers have noted before (Sartre 2001; Fanon 1967; Comaroff and Comaroff 1997: 22), that colonialism's efficacy in producing colonial subjects has to be grasped in dialectical relation to its transformation of the values and practices of the colonizer. The fact that these morally charged conflicts over identity and action were—and continue to be—especially pronounced with respect to the changing possibilities of coffee commerce is indicative of the ways that coffee in Kagera has provided a medium for both alterations of the objective landscape and changes in the constitution of colonial subjectivity.

MEASURES FOR MEASURES

In my earlier discussion of colonial currencies, I argued that commensuration and contrast (or complimentarity), which are often understood as forms of objectification that distinguish "commodity" and "gift" exchanges, have to be understood in relation to one another in the course of social practice if we are to comprehend how currencies—like cowry bundles, iron hoes, and rupees—mediate the generation of wealth. I recall this discussion in order to point out that the problem of currency standards (which are never quite standardized) leaves an important dimension of transaction open to further examination. "Commodities" are literally commodious because they can be measured against one another (Renfrew 1999); a thousand cowries, a rupee, a shilling may all become standardized as units of such measurement, but then the question remains: what is that standard being measured against? How much gold measures what length of cloth? What wage stands against a finished pair of shoes? Or, in the case at hand, how is coffee to be reckoned such that some unit of its measure can find an equivalent in money? The resolution to this question is by no means self-evident. It cannot be reduced to the simple matter of adopting a uniform volume, weight, or quantity. Indeed, just as currency standards are themselves derived, not from abstract rules that regulate exchanges, but through the use—or avoidance—of particular currencies in specific contexts, so, too, the units by which coffee would become subject to commensuration were subject to the practical purposes of Haya farmers and traders.

This issue may seem overly arcane, but my contention in this chapter is that the different strategic possibilities of measurement and quantification upon which the coffee trade depends are central matters in colonial history, and not only in Bukoba. Struggles to control this trade were often manifest in struggles over the forms this trade took—over the timing of payments, over transport, over the very kinds of units that could—and could not—be equated and transacted. Such conflicts are not the parochial concern of a few rural farmers and traders; rather, their significance lies in the fact that they pose a challenge to the terms in which "modernity" was conceived and institutionalized. For insofar as modernist practice understands time and space, and thus knowledge and value, to be subject to uniform and universal scales, struggles like those found in Buhaya demonstrate the extent to which modernity is always partial and plural. Putatively objective measures often conceal the social projects through which they are implemented, and (post)colonial subjects have challenged the contention that they could ever be universal, unmoored from their relative value in social contexts. In what follows, then, I assess the ways that transformations in the commonplace measures of the coffee trade might be understood as struggles for the signs of modernity.

A simple, but devastating, procedure underlies all colonial measuring techniques—counting. The evaluation of coffee trees and their volumes as well as houses for hut taxes, acreage for development schemes, and persons for a census all require some kind of enumeration. Again, the apparent simplicity of this procedure is belied by the complexity of social experience, "The time for taxes has returned," wrote the White Fathers in 1905, "The 'bahandiki' [Haya for "writers"] begin by counting houses, women children, cows, goats. The people are afraid" (Diare du Poste, Mugana: May 1905). This fear cannot be dismissed as an atavistic ignorance of rational mathematics. To this day, throughout Africa, and no doubt much of the modern world, counting—perhaps especially counting people—is an intrinsically suspicious act. Every neophyte field worker knows that asking someone to tell them how many children they have is unlikely to produce a quantitatively useful datum. And this not only because parents are likely to include stillborn and deceased offspring, or even anticipated pregnancies in their modes of reckoning, but because the question itself is provocative.

Counting people is akin to witchcraft for many. The explicit enumeration of kin can be a form of foolhardy boasting of precisely the sort that is likely to arouse dangerous jealousies. Drawing unnecessary attention to one's good fortune inspires those who, in the standardized motivation of Haya sorcerers, "don't like to see you advance." To count, moreover, is by definition to *delimit*, and so counting even a number of children, cows, goats, acres, etc., so meager that it is unlikely to incite even the most envious sorcerer, is to risk curtailing the future possibilities that these forms of wealth might possess. Therefore, in the 1980s, it was an ominous gesture to count the number of bananas available to a household, or even to count out the number of bananas that were prepared for or consumed at a meal (Weiss 1996a: 149 ff.). The delimitation that counting depends upon threatens to diminish the *generative* potential of value, perhaps especially the value of persons and food (each both the source and the outcome of one another), which, as I argued in chapter 2, Haya men and women seek to objectify and augment in their social interactions.

While the specificity of precise counting was—and remains—problematic, there are, as I have already indicated, ways of reckoning the value of coffee. Coffee that can be transported to Baganda and beyond and transacted for bark cloth, royal patronage, and even currency is surely subject to some mechanism that establishes an equivalence—that is, to some form of measurement. What determines the suitability of some forms of measurement, while others—like the simplest forms of counting—are met with antagonism? In an important essay on the semiotics of measurement among Sri Lanka's tea-estate Tamils, Daniels notes that the workers on Sinhalese plantations deploy alternative terminologies of measurement. The language of the estates, according to Daniels, is appropriate to the managerial productive regime of a plantation economy. It includes terminologies that belong to "a rationalized system which favored precision over approximation, universal standards, units of measurement, over contextualized ones" (Daniel 1993: 572).

In contrast to this language of exacting precision are the terminologies—and artifacts—of approximation, terminologies derived from the measurement of family gardens, and, more commonly today, from practices of provisioning a household by purchasing and preparing foodstuffs. Such measures include the *cuntu*, "ideally a cigarette tin, not unusually a condensed milk tin, and sometimes a half a coconut shell," as well as such commercial practices as filling a customer's sack with grain, sugar, dahl, etc., and throwing in "a little extra" (Daniels 1993: 574–575). The former language of precision and universality Daniels calls "agronomic terminology," and the latter language of approximation, flexibility, and relativity he dubs "(folk) agricultural terminology" (Daniels 1993: *passim*).

In what follows we will also find a distinction drawn between precision and approximation as well as worries expressed about maintaining the distinction between the two. Even more important than this parallel in divergent terminologies of standardization (and isn't "modernity" in all of its instantiations always concerned with the relationship—and boundaries—between such divergent forms?) is Daniels's recognition of the fact that even the "objective" language of agronomy is itself a semiotic form, and so provides a pragmatic poetics in the lives of Tamil tea-estate workers. The kilos of harvested tea leaves, or feet and inches of irrigation trenches, can effectively articulate a structure of feeling, standing metonymically as they do for an entire regime and history of oppressive labor and displacement. Furthermore, beyond these metonymic possibilities, agronomic terminology is always embedded within embodied practice. The agronomic grading of tea (from tender leaf to mature leaf to coarse leaf) thus becomes an apt expression for a woman's marriageability (from young virgin, to mature woman, to old maid), and the instruments of plantation production (the measuring stick laid flat across a pruned bush) are taken as derisive terms for a passive masculine posture (and thus, impotence). My analysis of the development of measurement in Bukoba's coffee trade is equally interested in the ways that "objective measures" are integrated into a lived world of meanings and values. What we find is that measures of volume and weight, and the material implements that make them possible, are both units of standardization (which nonetheless never become standardized), as well as forms of *experience* that come to constitute the qualities and characteristics of social relations.

STANDARDS AND PRACTICES; OR CANS AND BASKETS IN THE TWENTIETH CENTURY

We have already seen that coffee trees as discrete, enumerable entities have been subject to transformation since the earliest years of this century. A coffee tree grown from a seedling differs in important ways from trees grown from cuttings. This new propagation technique was also an economic and social form, the bonds of shared cuttings replaced by a quantifiable volume of seeds. Yet it is important to point out that alongside this "agronomic" innovation alternative measures of coffee persisted. While the quality and quantity of coffee cherries harvested has been the sole concern of the succession of colonial and post-colonial administrations, individual coffee trees have continued to be important items of Haya social transaction. Throughout the course of this century, for example, Haya landholders have explicitly recognized coffee trees as heritable objects (Rehse 1910; Cory and Hartnoll 1945). It is especially common for nonresidential kin, such as affines, maternal relations, and married daughters, to be awarded coffee trees in recognition of their contribution to the life of the deceased. These trees become, in effect, icons of the indivisibility of the family farmland in which they are found. Such coffee trees are necessarily relative units of measure, as their yield will vary from year to year, so its value cannot be equated with a simple monetary sum. Like the ekibanja on which they grow, the value of such inherited trees is, therefore, never simply reducible to a volume, or quantity of uniformly divisible units. Further, since those who inherit coffee trees almost always reside at some distance from the land they grow on, the trees they inherit must be cultivated by those who continue to reside on the family farmland. In this way, coffee trees, even when they are transacted, remain embedded in a social collectivity. In all of these different respects, the heritability of coffee trees constitutes the integrity of both the social relations that cultivate inherited trees and the non-partibility of the wealth that mediates these relations. Coffee trees, that is, can remain both units of measure, and icons of an indivisible totality even under contemporary conditions of cash-crop farming.[2]

Not only have coffee trees continued to exemplify an integrated totality under these conditions of inheritance, volumes of coffee cherries destined for a global market have also been subject to a host of "irregular" measures. Again, we find that even as standardization in measurement is imposed, these standards are never strictly uniform. The White Fathers' observations about the "one rupee for a small basket of coffee that holds about six liters" (Diare du Poste de Rubya [Ihangiro]: 19 August 1906) suggests that a volume of coffee cherries was subject to a standardized measure quite early in the colonial era. Still, Rehse's claims, highlighted above, that coffee was sold by "the load" even as the weight of a load "varied considerably" (Rehse 1910: chapter 9, p. 6) suggest a certain flexibility to the size of this "small basket." While we have documentation that attests to the rising volume of coffee exported from Bukoba in the early years of the twentieth century, it is difficult to reconstruct with any precision exactly how concrete parcels of coffee were measured, exchanged, and transported as the coffee trade expanded. There is evidence, though, that the question of measurement was contentious. As late as the 1940s, well after the booming coffee trade that saw the ascendancy of the *wachuluzi* traders, and even after some of the most extensive British efforts to regulate coffee trade and production had taken place (see Curtis 1989: 210, and chapter 5 above), Cory and Hartnoll noted the ambiguities of coffee measurement in Buhaya. According to these authors' *Customary Law of the Haya Tribe*, the amount of coffee purchased by coffee brokers, the *wachuluzi* described above (chapter 3), "is usually stated in terms of debis [more commonly, *debe*, an empty metal canister, often used for importing kerosene, or petroleum, or tinned foodstuffs like margarine] or baskets full" (Cory and Hartnoll 1945: 204), neither of which is a uniform measure, either in terms of its divisibility into composite units (cf. grams, centigrams, kilograms) or its comparability with other measures (how many "baskets" are there to a kilo?). Moreover, Cory and Hartnoll point out that these measures were, themselves, subject to dispute. "NOTE: Most growers prefer the basket measure because of the danger that the buyer may enlarge a debi by soldering on a false piece" (Cory and Hartnoll 1945: 204; see Burke 1996: 75–77) for a similar discussion of paraffin tins used as standard measures in colonial Zimbabwe). The logistics of the "basket full" measure are then detailed:

> The measure basket (kiibo) full: In every village there are one or more baskets, belonging to individuals, each of whom is known to all the villagers as the kiibo of so-and-so. The amount which each basket holds is well-known. Every villager, at the time of the coffee harvest, measures his crop in one of these baskets before taking it for sale to the coffee buyer. Though he may not understand the weights kilo and frasila and cannot read the scales, everyone knows that so many baskets-full should bring him so much money and can argue with a buyer, who, trading on his inability to read, tries to give him less than his due.
>
> These baskets are also used in many transactions between the inhabitants of a village; the fact that they are owned by a third person forms a check on the amount transferred in case of future questions. (Cory and Hartnoll 1945: 204)

This brief, seemingly trivial observation, provides a wealth of information about measurements, and—more important—their place in forging a local consciousness of globalization, exemplified in the coffee trade. To begin with, these practices clearly demonstrate an understanding of coffee trading as a business highly susceptible to corruption, the soldered canister being the surest sign of that danger. This is an especially telling point given the fact that Cory and Hartnoll were writing in the 1940s. The way in which the potential corruption of devious measures, exemplified by the *debe*, is countered is also revealing. Note, to begin with, that the *debe* as a standard is a measure of approximation (like the Tamil *cuntu*) because of its variable size, with a volume relative to both its original content and its (improper) transformation. Moreover, the *debe* is a concrete as opposed to an abstract measure—that is, the *debe* is a measure of a *particular* substance (kerosene, cooking oil, etc.), and so enters into local social practice as a ready-made object. In effect, it is as though the very act of measurement itself is intrinsically bound up with the flow of new and global commodities. To counter the deceptive potential of this material means of measurement, Haya coffee growers chose a deliberate strategy. Rather than agreeing to adopt an abstract, universal, and homogenizing *system* of measure, like kilograms or frasila, farmers chose an alternative but no less approximate and relative measure, the basket. Cory and Hartnoll make the offhand suggestion that such a measure compensates for the Haya farmers' inability to "understand" the technological apparatus of uniform weights and scales, but there is nothing intrinsically more complicated about scales than baskets—or tin cans. What differs is both the control that farmers could (and could not) exercise over these techniques of measurement and the concrete form that such measurements took. As an object, the basket is validated, or authenticated as a *standard* by completely different procedures than pounds or kilos. The basket is not only a standard relative to a specific social context that is within the community that agrees to its use; the basket is also legitimated as a standard by the social actors "known to all the villagers" that possess these measures.

The basket, then, is not a volume that instantiates a specific abstract measure, it is a concrete measure that expresses the character of social relations. And so it is the validity of the reliable relations embedded in these measures that counters the risks associated with reading scales and tinkering with tin cans. Yet in this regard, these baskets are really no different from other measures, abstract or concrete, precise or approximate. Like kilos and frasila authorized by colonial administrators, and metal canisters emptied of their commodified contents, baskets are *social forms* whose significance derives from the ways that they circulate, the purposes to which they are put, and, thus, the social worlds they constitute. The coffee trade that embeds these social worlds in such global forms as international commodities markets and "agronomic" measurement were thus actively engaged with by Haya farmers through practices that reasserted the legitimacy of local (although by no means "traditional") modes of knowing and doing. Baskets, that is, become standards that authorize and are authorized by the tractability of the social relations that employ them, even as they facilitate the globalization of those relations.

These techniques for measuring in the coffee trade have an important legacy in contemporary Kagera as well. The use of commercial containers, emptied of their original contents, as standard measures is pervasive throughout Africa—and is probably commonplace in all parts of the world. In Buhaya in the 1980s, brown half-liter Safari Lager beer bottles, distributed by Tanzanian Breweries, were widely used as both containers and units of measure for everything from kerosene and cooking oil to locally brewed beer and gin. And this in spite of the fact that Safari Lager was virtually unavailable in rural Kagera at the time—and was certainly far too expensive for any but a very few villagers. As many people remarked to me, "The bottle the beer comes in is a lot more valuable than the beer!" The use of such bottles highlights the ways that the creation of standard measurements continues to be linked in social experience to the circulation of concrete commodities (see also Weiss 1996a: 177–178). It further suggests that the circulation—and especially the scarcity—of these commodities, destined to become receptacles for quotidian exchanges, can powerfully shape a consciousness of one's position in wider pattern of interconnections.

Especially interesting is the place of the basket, the *ekiibo*, in its current relation to coffee. Baskets are no longer the standard unit of measure in transactions between coffee growers and traders, a relationship to be discussed in greater detail below. And *ekiibo* is not, to my knowledge, the ordinary term used for basket in Buhaya. More frequently heard are the terms *kikapu*, in Swahili, or *entukulu*, which is a basket most frequently used for interhousehold exchanges among matrilateral kin (see Weiss 1996a: 114 ff.). An *ekiibo*, though, in contemporary everyday parlance, refers to a small plate, woven from spliced reeds. This plate is used in Haya households for presenting cooked coffee cherries to guests, whether neighbors visiting in the ordinary course of events, or distant relatives, past and prospective affines gathered for more elaborate ceremonies in which *akamwani* is offered. These few coffee cherries, offered as a demonstrations of a houses viability and generosity, are served on an *ekiibo*, often with a short strands of twisted papyrus—*ekishisha*—with which guests will stroke their fingers, in order to "wash" or *okunaba* prior to picking up coffee cherries.

Elsewhere I have described this set of material forms and gestures as a kind of simulation of a meal, in which coffee cherries and washing with papyrus appear as the minimal elements of "food" and "washing" that constitute Haya meals (Weiss 1996c). But the replication serves explicitly to *contrast* a filling meal with a mere bit of *akamwani*, a food that "can never fill you up," because "feeding" others is also a means of asserting dominance over them. The gesture of coffee hospitality permits guests to partake in (and hosts to display) the productivity of a household, while retaining their independence from it. The appearance of a few coffee cherries on an *ekiibo* tangibly captures the "visibility" of host's offering, a visibility iconically confirmed by the crisp, white *ekishisha*, an object prized for its visual and tactile qualities. Such commonplace and ceremonial presentations thus attest to the importance of coffee as a medium for "making things visible" which I have suggested is equally central to its place in Haya sacrificial ritual (see chapter 1). Coffee offered in this way provides a means of constituting the transparent, unsullied, open, and incorruptible (all qualities connoted by "visibility" more generally) values of a household as the foundation for hospitable interhousehold relations.

From this perspective, the fact that coffee is today served on an *ekiibo*, whose genealogy entails a collective, locally standardized means of transaction, suggests that the history of the coffee trade has been routinized in commonplace Haya social interactions. The *ekiibo* becomes an emblem of a reliable standard, and this reliability and legitimacy in turn infuses the "measure" of coffee presented in these (no longer concave) baskets. What is noteworthy, then, is that an instrument of standardization (albeit informal and approximate) that facilitates legitimate commercial exchange—and as a direct challenge to potential fraud—comes to embody the virtues of coffee transactions that are specifically *withheld* from market relations. A dialectic clearly emerges between precision and approximation, uniform and relative measures, as the values generated through globalized relations—including Asian merchants, German and British colonial officials, Swahili as well as Haya traders—are used to articulate the character of local connections. The doubled-praxis of contemporary coffee offerings indexes both of these relations, and their entanglements in Bahaya history and society. And the *ekiibo*, for its part, continues to function as a means of measuring values, no longer as an instrument for establishing equivalencies, but now as a medium for expressing a *supplement* in a vital social order. The *ekiibo* measures that "little extra" (Daniel 1993: 574–575), only a "mere bit of coffee," an absolutely unfilling food, the smallest of gestures that (as with the token offering to all-powerful sacred kings, living and dead) elicits ever greater blessings.

PAYING FOR TIME: CROPS, CASH, AND MORTGAGING

Before describing the instruments of measure relevant in today's coffee trade, I want to make note of a critical dimension of coffee production and sale that has also been subject to measurement in ways that reveal the dynamics of the dialectics just described. That dimension of social practice is time. The temporality of coffee production, and especially of the coffee trade, has come to be measured in ways that have profoundly shaped the Haya cultural order. The system of crop mortgaging that began in the 1920s was known as *obutura*, a term that refers to the unripened coffee cherry. It is this not-yet-ready for harvest coffee that is the object of *wachuluzi* speculation; a trader offers money to a grower on the promise that the eventual yield of the coffee harvest will provide him with a tidy profit in return for the advance. *Wachuluzi*, as I have indicated (chapter 3), were able to make substantial profits on these advances, and independent traders were a powerful political and social force in colonial Tanganyika (Curtis 1989; Smith and Stevens 1988; Hyden 1969). In 1950, the Bukoba Native Co-operative Union (BNCU) was founded, in principle to "Africanize" the coffee trade and to facilitate the centralized processes of agricultural extension and quality control (Mukurasi 1970: 18ff). The cooperative was intended to promote "cooperation" between the government and the farmers (i.e., to manage production more directly), not to promote cooperation among those whose livelihoods rose and fell with the coffee trade. In actual practice, the co-operatives aimed to undermine the power of the *wachuluzi* traders. Within a few years of its founding, the BNCU had eliminated the rights of individuals to renew their trading licenses, and the individual societies that, together, composed the union, took all responsibility for the acquisition, transport, and sale of Bukoba's coffee crop. It became illegal for a farmer to sell his coffee anywhere but his local cooperative society, a legal monopoly that persisted through decolonization into the era of *Ujamaa* and after (Curtis 1989; Rald and Rald 1975).

While the BNCU was the sole institution for the sale of Haya coffee through independence, in practice farmers have continued to sell coffee on a black market, to traders—some still known as *wachuluzi*—who can advance money in times of need. The terms of these moneylending relations, have, if anything, become more onerous in the post colonial era. In part, as noted in chapter 3, this is due to the devastating effects of currency devaluations, which, in 1986 for example, permitted advances in shillings valued at ten to the dollar to turn into coffee sold to a cooperative for a price inflated to reflect a shilling valued at forty to the dollar. The *obutura* system has also become more onerous because of a "rationalizing" practice adopted by the BNCU designed to stabilize the income farmers received for a cash crop that is notorious for its price fluctuations. Each year, prior to the harvest the union would estimate the proceeds of the anticipated sales. Then—after deducting its own operating expenses—the union would pay out 75 percent of that projected income to its registered farmers. Once the entire crop had been harvested and sold, the full value of the farmers' crops was then paid. This method, with a "first" and "second" payment system that came to be known as *bakiza*, (Swahili for "leftovers"), while intended to provide farmers with an income even in the worst of years, exacerbated the exploitative potential of crop mortgaging and moneylending all the more. Now, *wachuluzi* with sufficient funds could estimate (or more frequently, underestimate) a farmer's yield, and provide him with an advance equal to, or a bit more than the estimated "first" payment, and simply pocket the balance of the "second" payment when that payment was made.

Again, in consideration of currency changes the total price a broker could receive was substantially higher than the advance originally made. Nonetheless, and in spite of explicit efforts to curtail—indeed, to illegalize—independent coffee traders, there is little doubt that black markets in coffee have been extremely active since independence. In part, this trade has been facilitated by the proximity of Kagera to both Rwanda and Uganda, where coffee prices have been much better.[3] But the two-payment system is especially important to the renaissance of the *wachuluzi*. A great many Haya farmers are suspicious of this system. "They say that second payment is coming, but when you ask for it, it's always 'Tomorrow! Tomorrow! Tomorrow!'" one young man told me. The second payment is ever in doubt, rarely comes up to the expectations of the anticipated proceeds for the year, or, as often as not is "eaten" (i.e., absconded with) by the staff of the cooperatives. And so, for a great many farmers, the *wachuluzi* are a source of certain income, even if it comes at exploitative rates. Better to take what you can get when there is no guarantee that the full price for your coffee crop will ever become available.

Which brings us to the significance of time. The second payment has become the very essence of unreliability and unpredictability. It is typically described as a form of corruption and evinces the corruption of the state, of the elites that control the cooperatives—even of money itself whose worthlessness is most tangibly demonstrated by the declining income, especially in the late 1980s (Roseberry 1996), Haya farmers received from coffee. The second payment in these contexts embodies unfulfilled promises. At the same time, the second price, when it does come through, can be taken as an astonishing boon. When I told one man that the second payment had just been paid that day he remarked, "Today, the farmer's job is just eating and drinking!" That is, the second payment is a source of pure pleasure. Similarly, Rald and Rald noted that in 1971, at the height of anxiety over *ujamaa* in a certain ward in Ihangiro, the second payment "turned out to be higher than for many years. People in that ward now praise the wise leadership of President Nyerere and want the M. P. for that area to be their representative forever," (Rald and Rald 1975: 48). In effect, the second payment is experienced as uncertainty with respect to a *forecasted* future—which is the foundation of the two-payment payment. It is precisely such temporal uncertainty that lies at the heart of the Haya proverb *Ebyo mbwenu ti bya nyenkya, n'ekibi kya mpya*, "The things of today are not those of tomorrow, that's the trouble with money" (Weiss 1996a: 188).

Beyond the uncertainty that Haya farmers experience, the two-payment system instantiates a more general transformation in temporality that relates to the broader transformations of measurement in its modernist forms. The presupposition of this quintessentially modern method of reckoning time is that the totality of temporal activity is a product that can divided up into, or recombined from a group of homogenous units—in this case prices. The two-payment system is a form of "rationalization" insofar as it conceives of value as the product of market relations, hoping to maximize gains and minimize losses. The value of coffee is thus determined by forecasting its future price yield. This indeterminate future is then homogenized, so that a quantifiable percentage of it can be determined (the first payment). The second payment is only paid (or, not paid at all) as a balance after the market price has been paid for the final yield. Note that by this method of measuring time, the future and the past are definitively separated from one another. This is not simply by duration or succession (i.e., because the future comes after the past), but because, in social practice, the future is calculated and acted upon in ways that are entirely different from the past. Rather than seeing past, present, and future as part of a continuum—much less a generative pattern (as we have seen to be the case for Haya agriculture, landholding, and inheritance)—the future is necessarily indeterminate, while the past is, *by definition* fixed and immutable. In fact, the past is not only the fulfillment, but the *completion* of the previously forecasted future. The past is a "leftover" as the Haya vernacular would have it; it fills in the indeterminacy of a forecasted future with "actual" events—here, total sales—actual, because past, and thus determinate.

DOMINANT AND AMBIGUOUS MEASURES

In looking at the means of measuring thus far considered, a persistent dialectic emerges. Coffee trees can be inherited, linking persons, places, and objects into a nexus of generative, integrative values—yet these same trees are annually harvested to supply their recipients with a regular income. The baskets used to facilitate a booming, highly speculative coffee trade also come to exemplify bonds of legitimacy, solidarity, and generosity—bonds that are important to coffee commerce *as well as* the refusal to participate in that commerce. Even when we turn our attention to those mechanisms of measure that, in present-day Bukoba, are relevant strictly to the coffee trade and never to relations of hospitality, or sacrifice—mechanisms like payment structures, regulatory authorities, and currency devaluations—we find that the themes of this dialectic continue to formulate both the social relations and meaningful experiences of Haya men and women, farmers and traders. The interplay of approximation and precision, totality and partibility, and intimacy and distance still shapes the commercial coffee terrain in Kagera. In this chapter I have described the ways that the *obutura* system of crop mortgaging begun in the 1920s and still active at the end of the twentieth century has proceeded by means of a number concrete measures. In the practices of modern day *wachuluzi* and their clients, baskets are no longer used as standard measures of coffee volume.

Today, the commonplace term that describes a volume of coffee transacted between a grower and a trader is a "bowl"—*bakuli*, in Swahili.[4] More important, this bowl measure, a relative and approximate measure like many of those already considered, has to be seen in relationship to an alternative measure that has an abiding significance in Bukoba in this—and previous—centuries, namely, the annual harvest of a single coffee tree. Growers can arrange transactions with coffee traders selling their future harvest and receiving an advance either for so many bowls of fresh or processed coffee[5] to be delivered upon harvest; or for the total yield of a given number of trees, which traders and those who work on their behalf will harvest and process themselves. The different consequences of these forms of sale—and of measure—tell us a great deal about class relations in Kagera as they have developed in relation to the coffee trade.

As I indicated in my earlier discussion of the way that materialism and commerce have come to shape local identities in Bukoba, coffee traders (in their various forms throughout the twentieth century) occupy a paradoxical, even astonishing social position in rural Haya communities. There can be little doubt that the coffee trade, and the *obutura* system of crop mortgaging in particular, has contributed to the differentiation and entrenchment of social classes throughout the region. In 1990, for example, I found that roughly 20 percent of the total number of traders marketing coffee at local cooperative sold over 75 percent of the total volume of each cooperative—that is, by controlling the harvests of their clients, these traders sold an inordinately disproportionate volume of each coffee harvest. Reining's work from 1951 to 1953 (Reining 1967) indicates that a similar consolidation of coffee sales was already in place. This is especially significant, as her research was carried out at a time when the BNCU was actively discouraging traders by delicensing them; further, it was a time when coffee prices were booming, so that growers might expect to receive a good income even without the traders' advances.

In the best of times and the worst of times, the coffee trade since the early days of Baines's planting campaign has been funneled through a small group of entrepreneurs, those with capital to advance to cash-strapped coffee growers. Aside from this enduring class entrenchment, what is so remarkable about this degree of consolidation in the coffee trade is the fact that, in social and cultural terms, the brokers who so dominate the trade, and seem so directly to exploit the hardships of their friends and neighbors, are scarcely criticized for their actions. Just the opposite, in fact. The most successful traders in Kagera are routinely praised and lauded for their efforts. As Rald and Rald note with scarcely concealed contempt and dismay:

> Many smallholders pick their coffee themselves but sell the product directly (fresh or dried) to the coffee traders for the first payment. These people may be old farmers with no one to help them with the drying and processing and transport to the Society, or they may be people who merely want to satisfy an immediate demand for, e.g., beer. It may also be necessary to sell to a trader if there is an illness in the family at the time of the coffee harvest, Thus, the trader has innumerable opportunities to buy coffee and in certain cases a village may be completely dependent on one trader.
>
> What makes the whole exploitation through trading more difficult to combat is the lack of feeling of exploitation among the smallholders. They merely look upon the *obutura* buyer and the traders as benefactors, because they have no other way of obtaining money at any time of the year, when they are in need. (1975: 113)

In the mid-1980s, when the state implemented "The War of Economic Sabotage" under Sokoine and Nyerere, a campaign designed to hold entrepreneurs accountable for gouging customers and stockpiling inventories in order to wait for inflation to drive up prices, many businessmen had their possessions confiscated, and some were even incarcerated (see Pietilä n.d.; Tripp 1996: 60 ff.). In Kagera, where a good number of shopkeepers got their start—and continue to operate—as *wachuluzi*, the state's actions only served to enhance the reputations of traders who were seen to have overcome such formidable oppression (Weiss 1999).

The enthusiasm that Haya farmers continue to express for moneylenders and traders undoubtedly has many sources, some more prosaic than others. It is indeed the case that there are few sources of cash available to most rural households, especially in moments of crisis, or unpredictable setbacks. Coffee brokers have also served as culture brokers in a broader sense, making not only cash, but commodities of many varieties available to Haya villagers, early in the twentieth century through their ties to Asian merchants, more recently through access to black market goods from Rwanda, Uganda, and Kenya. The "multiplier effects" of success in the coffee trade are also important. As I have suggested, prominent coffee brokers have routinely become entrepreneurs, opening small shops, running private buses from villages to the regional capital in Bukoba and, especially, providing capital inputs that permit small businesses to operate everything from kiosks selling candies and cigarettes, to fishing canoes that bring in highly profitable tilapia and Nile perch from Lake Victoria, to clothing sellers who trade in used clothing, *kanga* and *kitenge*, at weekly markets. The desirability of these products and practices may well help us to account for the tremendous esteem that coffee traders enjoy, but it must not be forgotten that the investments such brokers make and the goods they can provide are also available at usurious costs. The dependency of growers and farmers on brokers—as well as their exploitation—is often amplified by the the "benefits" of commerce. How, then, do we account for the fact that exploitation is almost never a concern in these relations? Why are the interests of a powerful few so roundly praised by the vast majority who—to a degree—provide them with this power?

In part, the social dimensions of trader-grower relationship are crucial. Indeed, it is a misnomer to present this relationship in terms of a *difference* between grower and trader, farmer and broker. *All* Haya traders are also farmers, living and working in homes and farms very much like (if occasionally somewhat larger than) those of the neighbors (and even kin) from whom they purchase coffee. As I noted in chapter 3, the successful and astute *wachuluzi* have invested themselves in their rural communities, not only because they support local traders, fishermen, merchants, and the like, but also insofar as they assert their *presence* in a village as farmers and kinsmen. Coffee traders build houses and raise bananas, passing these forms of wealth on to their children. It must also be pointed out that while relations of exploitation may exist between traders and growers, traders are themselves dependent upon a wider set of constraints. I was friendly with a number of sons of wealthy entrepreneurs who worried that in spite of the resources available to them, they might never have the opportunity to pursue a secondary education or find reliable employment. There is clearly a "face to face" quality in the "trader-grower" relationship, so that even the wealthiest of entrepreneurs remains a human figure. Further, no trader attempts to "rationalize" his business by intensifying his *production* of coffee; a successful trader—like any successful farmer—seeks to cultivate more acreage that he hopes to plant with bananas, that his wife will plant with beans, and perhaps maize. In short, the successful trader does not allow the *place* of coffee to dominate his practice or his position among his neighbors.

It is also the case, I would argue, the particular form the coffee trade has taken over the years helps to ameliorate any antagonism that might develop between growers and brokers. These aspects of the trade return us to the dialectics of intimacy and distance, totality and partibility characteristic of coffee commerce more generally, and, once again, of measurement in particular. To appreciate this dialectic we need to recognize, as I alluded to above, that the bowl measure as opposed to the harvest of a single tree enables different *strategies* for participating in this trade, and these strategies illuminate class relations in Kagera. No longer a locally crafted woven basket, but now an enamel painted tin bowl (often produced in China) has become the measure of coffee traders' transactions.

While the bowl, like the basket before it, and like the sale of an entire coffee harvest, is an approximate measure, the implications of sales by the bowl are quite different. Such bowls, for example, are also used for marketing grain in weekly markets, especially millet used by Haya brewers as a fermenting agent in banana beer and gin. These bowls have, then, a clear place in the circulation of commodities; themselves an imported product they also facilitate commercial transfers. Nonetheless, it is not uncommon for bowls to be used as measures in coffee-brokering relations. The bowl enables certain kinds of transactions relative to the harvest of an entire tree. A bowl may used by a grower who has need of a limited amount of cash in advance, but wants to retain control over the balance of his crop. This presents certain risks, though, as a farmer may find that his entire yield does not meet a full bowl; the farmer, already cash poor, would then be expected to make a monetary return equal to the balance of his debt. Similarly, a broker with less capital may choose to advance money for bowls full of coffee because he is unable to provide an advance equal to the price and yield forecasted for an entire tree.

Again, when operating in such small volumes, the broker takes a risk that the price of coffee will decline precipitously between the advance and the final sale of the crop, which may actually make his business unprofitable. Although it is always an approximate measure, a bowl is not a *projected* amount (like a tree's total yield), it is a fixed sum, agreed upon ahead of time, and satisfied by payment in full after the crop is picked. What is clear, though, is that the use of a bowl as a measure provides greater flexibility for both the broker and the coffee farmer, as each can control smaller sums of capital and product. Yet, the price of this flexibility is significant. Not simply because of the increased risk entailed for both farmer and trader, but because the use of a bowl as a pricing measure makes it possible to evaluate coffee in *increments*. The bowl divides up the totality of a tree's crop and offers an alternative unit by which to calculate and forecast both the yield and price of a coffee tree.[6]

This incremental instrument has, in fact, become the source of some suspicion in Kagera. Both selling and buying coffee by the bowlful are acts that are met with derision. Bowls, like buckets of the past, are about the potential for corruption, a tainted possibility, the sundering into fragments of what is rightfully whole. In effect, they are taken as akin to land alienation; a likely candidate for selling off their family farm begins the process by selling off their coffee bowl by bowl. Unlike the sale of coffee trees that provides a more substantial amount of money and can contribute cash to the support of an entire family in dire circumstances, those who sell coffee by the bowlful will be accused—if only by gossiping neighbors—of using that lesser amount of money on some individual and capricious whim, usually the purchase of banana gin. Reciprocally, those who purchase coffee by the bowlful not only have less money to offer than *wachuluzi* who purchase the entire crop of a coffee tree, they also are characteristically described as people whose attachment to the land is more tenuous. Sons, for example, who find themselves dispossessed from a family estate often attempt to settle in the infertile lowlands—the *oluhita*—beneath the volcanic escarpments of Buhaya.

These lands are both unlikely to provide sufficient food to ensure the viability of a household and disconnected from the patrimony embodied by a clan farm. Thus, those who are so abject as to end up in the *oluhita* may well find themselves trying to make a bit of money by speculating on coffee, buying a few bowlfuls and hoping to turn a profit when the first and second payments come in. In effect, those who sell and purchase coffee by the bowlful are held to have no concern for the future inhabitants of "clan" lands; in the Haya imagination if not in actual practice, a wayward son who begins by selling off bowls of coffee may ultimately find himself selling farmland, moving to the *oluhita*, and becoming a coffee trader, buying coffee by the bowl to support himself.

Those traders who enjoy a place of real privilege in their community have the resources that permit them to purchase coffee by the tree, and stand to make enormous profits from the advances that they make. They also have the resources, as described earlier, to diversify their investments and thereby to generate significant incomes when the coffee market is in serious decline. But I do not think the social prestige that such traders enjoy is simply a reflection of the economic resources they control. Class, like all culturally mediated relationships, entails the effective deployment of the signs through which privilege gains social currency. Purchasing a coffee crop by the tree, and not the bowl, is one such sign of social distinction. *Wachuluzi* who make advances for a full tree crop permit the farmer to retain the integrity of his trees, to continue to engage with his trees as totalities, not quantities subject to an incremental logic. A broker who purchases a tree's crop can even be understood as a kind of inheritor of the coffee trees growing on clan land. Like heirs to coffee trees, such traders allow the family farm to remain a unified form of wealth. In fact, some of the most powerful traders do enjoy relations of "fictive" kinship among their neighbors, often becoming godparents to Christian clients, and occasionally known as "mjomba" (Swahili for mother's brother) around the village. The significance of buying coffee by the tree, then, goes far beyond an economic logic. Indeed, the flexibility that buying coffee by the bowl permits resembles the logic of forecasting and budgeting, saving and planning much more closely than does the less incremental mode of purchasing a tree's entire yield.

The value of purchasing coffee by the treeful, like the other measures we have seen, emerges in a dialectic. The totality of the coffee tree is a valued measure that provides a means of participating in the global coffee market without simultaneously subjecting the family farm to the absolute values of the market. The coffee tree thus becomes a hegemonic measure. By preserving the importance of the singular coffee tree, the dominant class of traders in Buhaya not only reap significant profits, they effectively reproduce themselves as a class, aligning themselves with the values of the community whose continuous clientage assures their ongoing subordination.

Introducing the symbolic dimensions of relations of domination embedded in the singular coffee tree returns us, in a sense, to where we began. Like Haya royalty in centuries past, powerful coffee traders so thoroughly control the sale of coffee to state cooperatives that they receive coffee from their clients as virtual sources of tribute. Coffee is still grown on family farmland, yet the meager amounts of coffee most farmers harvest is transacted to powerful agents in hopes of tremendous returns. The *wachuluzi* themselves have adapted certain royal forms of distinction. Like royalty, they move with regularity across the landscape, the most powerful of traders not only collecting coffee from clients and selling to coffee societies in far-flung locales, but also fixing *attachments* in these locales, buying land and providing patrilineal heirs with futures grounded in local points of origin. Like kings, these powerful traders exercise a *de facto* monopoly on a crop that is simultaneously a commonplace feature of daily life throughout the region. It seems quite likely that the model of royal power embedded in control of coffee has been influential in contemporary commercial practice. Although the foundation for profit and value today is utterly different, the mechanism by which coffee is measured in transaction—and so the way in which it enters into social arrangements—is modeled on abiding forms of prestige and power. Yet this continuity is certainly *not* the mere replication of a "traditional" Haya cultural pattern. The traders' appropriation of royal lifestyles derives quite clearly from the *changing* character of coffee in Buhaya. Powerful traders are able to deploy these approximate, flexible measures—even as a means of asserting and promoting a kind of solidarity with those they exploit—because they are engaging in a form of double practice. The trader confirms the enduring values of integrity, generativity, and intimacy while at the very same time he uses those values to enable him to make substantial profits in a highly speculative, commercial economy. It is only because incremental, economistic, and homogenized modes of reckoning value have become so very central to everyday life in Kagera, only because of the globalization of the coffee trade, the prospects for land sale, the utter banality of commerce that the *alternative* measures of totalization, approximation, and relativity enjoy the esteem that they do today.

In his magisterial study of Chicago, Cronon discusses a monumental yet mundane transformation in the marketing of grain during the 1850s (Cronon 1991: 97–147). Corn and wheat once stored and shipped from across the prairie in gunny sacks could be loaded onto railroad cars bound for Chicago by means of grain elevators. This simple procedure, as Cronon describes it, had extraordinary consequences to the development of agriculture and commerce in the Chicago, the United States, and the world. Opening up sacks and emptying them onto elevators meant that markets no longer sold farmers' physical crops, but rather sold abstract quanta that represented a percentage of a homogenous volume of grain. Where once an Iowa farmer's sack of corn could be valued according to the quality of its concrete content, after the advent of the railroads, farmers received a payment that was based on an abstraction, the price of the total harvest of corn—a homogenous volume to which his sack made only a small contribution—transported to and sold in Chicago. This system of marketing—and measuring—grain would "sever . . . physical grain from its ownership rights . . . [making] it abstract, homogenous, *liquid*" (Cronon 1991: 145). Here, then, is a shift in measurement that carried with it a revolution in commerce, the development of a mass market in agricultural produce, and the necessary conditions for the futures trade that would come to dominate Chicago's Board of Trade—as well as the two-payment system of the Bukoba Native Co-operative Union.

This shift from the concrete to the abstract, from the specific substance to the homogenous volume is at the heart of this discussion of coffee's measurement in Buhaya. In the case of Bukoba's coffee, as opposed to Illinois's grain, the relentless transition from the particular to the general is not quite as clear. In their compelling entanglements with a powerful, global coffee market, both Haya farmers and traders attempt to negotiate an uneasy tension between these alternatives. They hope, on the one hand, to secure access to the resources, not all of them monetary, that a transnational market can make available; yet they strive at the same time to assert control over the terms in which they participate in, or avoid, such regimes of value. I might note one last measure that neatly captures this intense ambiguity—the very same burlap gunny sack, *gunia* in both Swahili and Haya, "whose enclosure," says Cronon (1991: 145), "drew boundaries around crop and property alike." What may have been true on the nineteenth century American prairie, is much less certain in Kagera today. To process coffee for sale to the cooperative society it must be carefully cleaned, sorted through to remove twigs, unripened and rotted cherries, and then dried before it is stored in gunny sacks for transport. Those farmers who sell their own coffee directly to the society will painstakingly spread out their coffee crop on reed mats in the courtyards of their homes. This is a rare display of wealth for Haya households, whose spatial

Photo 6.1. Coffee prepared for sale to a cooperative society, drying in the courtyard on reed mats.

aesthetics emphasize the importance of enclosure and interiority as ways of controlling one's own viability (Weiss 1996a). At the same time, the exposure of coffee in this way suggests that this coffee is intended for the market, and not for the sustenance of the household. While Haya might be suspicious, in similar circumstances, that this kind of exposure poses a risk that jealous observers might bewitch such appealing coffee, many Haya told me that coffee laid out to dry in this almost public way is inviolate. Any attempt to bewitch it, or even steal it, would redound to afflict the incautious attacker. But, such coffee does pose a threat once it is loaded into gunny sacks for transport.

Gunny sacks that are not immediately taken to the society for sale are carefully sequestered in a farmer's back storage room, a kitchen, or a bedroom. To leave a sack of coffee in a sitting room where guests might enter would only invite trouble. This is not only because people are worried about theft; much more common are worries that an unknown visitor might sit on a coffee sack, or pass something in through the wide-weave of burlap, thereby polluting its contents and threatening the household. Even gunny sacks that are filled with materials other than coffee—dried cassava, beer bananas, or even garbage—are worrisome containers in many Haya homes. Similarly, the *gunia* is a topic of everyday rumors about the co-operatives. Farmers are suspected of filling the middle of their bags with stones and dirt to increase the volume of their coffee. Because the bags enclosure permits such deception, coffee inspectors may slash holes in the sides of the sacks to look for other substances, which cause farmers to complain that they are losing money when the coffee falls out of the holes in the bag and doesn't get weighed. The sacks are also cited as contributing to more systematic fraud. Workers at the cooperative societies are often suspected of weighing a sack of coffee, paying the farmer for his sale, and then taking the coffee around back of the society to friends who will transport it to another society to be sold again. In effect, the gunny sack is taken as an instrument of homogenization, each sack identical to all others on the surface, and so infinitely interchangeable with any other. Little wonder, then, that the *gunia* that takes crops from outside the house to be stored inside are fixed upon as sources of corruption, for by their homogenization and concealment they risk unraveling the substantive links to coffee that farmers—quite literally—cultivate. The gunny sack embodies that transition between a farm's concrete productivity and the abstraction of the market and, like so many objects at the juncture of ambiguous borders, are taken as vehicles of contamination and corruption.

THE PLACE OF AGENCY IN SOCIAL FIELDS

These ambiguous borders have been the defining parameters of Haya agency in the twentieth century. Much of contemporary writing about globalization has addressed itself to precisely such ambiguities, and the borders that objects like Haya coffee can make, subvert, and transcend (Hannerz 1996; Waters 1995; Miller 1995; Burke 1996). Borders, as these studies remind us, are at least as much about connection as they are about differentiation. From a certain perspective, such connections might be understood to make coffee a "hybrid" form, as a substance at once a ritual offering and cash crop, family farm legacy and "wild orchard" product, royal medium of power and colonial vehicle of "improvement." Hybridization, whether as a descriptive or analytical term (Comaroff and Comaroff 1997: 59; Friedman 2000; Sahlins 1999) has certainly been one of the watchwords of both (post)colonial interpretation and studies of globalization (Hannerz 1992; Appadurai 1996). A good deal of work suggests that drawing attention to hybridity provides a means of challenging prevailing assumptions about "culture," and "authenticity" that tend to reify practices and categories and, thus, to treat encounters like colonialism as a dualistic phenomena, the confrontation of "us" and "them" (Pels 1999; Bhabha 1994; Fabian 1991). By contrast, notions like hybridity describe the emergence of new forms of practice and value that demonstrate the inextricable connections generated at the sites of diverse, but interpenetrating social fields. Hybridity, therefore, also becomes a matter of performance, its meanings relative to the specificities of a context of action. Thus, frames of the action, registers of speech, modalities of expression, participation by an audience—all these performative features of practice are critical to the interpretation of hybrid forms of social action. Absent these contextual features, it is impossible, not only for the historian or anthropologst, but for participants in a social field, to understand how to trace the references and implications of the gestures and utterances of a performance. If we are to see the virtue in coffee offered in an *ekiibo*, or get the jokes about motorcycle-riding priests, or know where to plant a coffee seedling—to take examples already seen in some detail—we have to ground these practices in precisely these metapragmatics of social action. I have tried to capture a sense of such metapragmatics as they emerged and altered over the course of the twentieth century. The ambiguity of Haya coffee is, I have argued, implicit even prior to the advent of colonial coffee regimes. The "doubledness" of coffee, its iconic apprehension of relatedness via separation, is a potentiality available in every coffee transaction, whether those transactions are poured out in small woven baskets, loaded into cooperative transport, or bequeathed to outlying kin. In all these ways, the pragmatics of coffee exchange index coffee's hybridity, not only in its genealogy, but in its future potential.

Still, I use the term hybridity sparingly, and with some reservations, for reasons that relate to a more fundamental concern with the place of culture and history in social action. If, as recent writing indicates, performance is central to hybridity, the "now-ness" and "here-ness" of a frame of action being the site at which new meanings arise, this also points to what I take to be a serious limitation with the notion of hybridity. Scholars drawn to this notion often emphasize its diffuse and elusive character, thereby refusing to see social experience as strictly determined by an overarching entity like "class," "tradition," or "structure" more generally. There are good grounds for rejecting the mechanistic application of these interpretive strategies. But, if overdetermination is too reductive, is nothing any longer determinant (Comaroff and Comaroff 1997: 19)? How can we get a purchase on the *concrete* social worlds as they are *experienced* by those who inhabit them (Friedman 2000)? Is the creative mixture embedded in hybrid practice entirely unconstrained, subject to motives and intentions developed "on the spot"? This hardly seems a viable claim to make about processes like colonialism and globalization, especially with respect to so volatile a commodity as coffee (see Friedman 2000 for a trenchant critique of the current anthropological fascination with hybridity).

There are, it is true, many Haya farmers growing coffee today who welcome the ready cash they can receive from their local coffee brokers. I have not, and would not, dismiss their willingness to enter these relationships as a form of "false consciousness" that neatly serves the interests of a dominating class. Haya farmers have motives—they pursue values that matter to them—that are articulated in these forms of clientage. These farmers' actions are never simply the reflex of "objective" demands, they are expressions of socially and culturally constituted agency. This assertion, however, does not mean that all Haya farmers are capable of *controlling* the contexts or the terms in which they act. From a political economic perspective, it is clear that the agency of certain participants in Kagera's coffee trade is more *effective* than the agency of others. Declining soil fertilities accelerated by the introduction of exotic timber, the partition of patrilineal estates into ever smaller fragments, the U.S. refusal to renew the terms of the International Coffee Agreement in 1989 (Roseberry 1996: 772), all of these conditions are *constraints* that shape the outcome of social practice as much as the agency of local social actors. Moreover, there are *cultural* constraints at work that shape the terms in which Haya action is carried out. An emptied oil tin or a mass-marketed bowl may each be hybrid forms, global consumer products refashioned to suit the projects of rural farmers. Yet, as standard units of measure, each is an anathema in Haya culture, a field of values and relationships that constitutes—and so *constrains*—the way that actions can be realized.

The consequences of social action are always unforeseen. This existential truth is not grounds for insisting that social practice is free to create reality anew with each passing day. The consequences of social action may be unforeseen, but social action *does have consequences*. As such, it establishes the grounds on which ongoing activity will be carried out. Agency matters, not because people are everywhere free to impose their vision of reality on the world they confront, but because, in imposing a vision through their lives' activities, people *make* the world they are a part of. That is, agency *delimits* certain possibilities, which in turn establishes future *conditions* of possibility. Possibility and constraint are both entailed in the contingencies of social action. They are also necessary for defining and recognizing the *efficacy* of concerted practice, for people not only attempt to effect change by their acts, they also hope to make their acts consonant with anticipated results; they evaluate their actions in terms of *prior* expectations. Making a claim for agency in history, then, need not and should not divert us from the dilemmas of those whose agency is a form of unfulfilled struggle as much as completely realized intentions. Our best tack is not to dismiss or even destabilize that struggle, seeing only failure and helplessness when a people's aims are not met. Rather, we might hope to comprehend the force and meaning of the worlds both created through, and so given to social action.

NOTES

1. There is further evidence to suggest that the coercive control of the kings was manifest not only in their control over labor, but in their attempts to increase land alienation for the purposes of establishing *nyarubanja* estates—and perhaps also their interest in controlling young women, as the number of *bazana* seem to have expanded during this decade—even as the White Fathers sought to "liberate" these "enslaved girls."

2. Indeed, coffee trees, unlike other crops, have the capacity to serve as media of value subject simultaneously to uniform standards of measure *and* relative, nonpartible forms of

totalization. Thus, for example, those who inherit coffee trees will both recognize the obligation to pass their trees down to their heirs and take responsibility for providing the labor needed to harvest the yields of the trees they have inherited.

3. Better prices in Uganda reflect a colonial policy that subsidized growers with a "price stabilization fund" (Curtis 1989: 534).

4. In the villages I was familiar with, a standard bowl was roughly three liters in volume. But, like other approximate measures, it is quite likely that bowls of other sizes were taken as standards in those communities that agreed to their use.

5. As I will discuss below, coffee has to be cleaned and dried prior to sale.

6. Note that this practice is different from that described by Cory and Hartnoll for the *ekiibo*/basket. There, the basket was used to measure one's total coffee harvest as a safeguard against being cheated on the trader's scales. Farmers did not sell coffee by the basket; they used baskets to measure the total crop they grew.

Bibliography

UNPUBLISHED SOURCES

Diares des Postes—Rubya, Kashozi, Mugana, Kagondo. Housed in the Archives of the Société des Missionaires d'Afrique (Pères Blancs). Rome, Italy.

PUBLISHED SOURCES

Akyeampong, Emmanuel. 1996. *Drink, Power, and Cultural Change: A Social History of Alcohol in Ghana, c. 1800 to Recent Times*. Portsmouth, NH: Heinemann.

Appadurai, Arjun. 1996. *Modernity at Large: Culture and Globalization*. Minneapolis: University of Minnesota Press.

———. 1986. "Introduction: Commodities and the Politics of Value." In *The Social Life of Things: Commodities in Cultural Perspective*. A. Appadurai, ed., pp. 3–63. Cambridge: Cambridge University Press.

Austen, Ralph. 1968. *Northwest Tanzania Under German and British Rule: Colonial Policy and Tribal Politics, 1889–1939*. New Haven: Yale University Press.

Bakengesa, S.K.S. 1974. "An Historical Survey of the Coffee Industry in Bukoba District, 1932–1954." Master's thesis, University of Dar es Salaam.

Basso, Keith. 1990. *Western Apache Language and Culture: Essays in Linguistic Anthropology*. Tucson: University of Arizona Press.

Bastian, Misty. 1990. "Blood and Petrol. The Dangerous Eroticism of Roads and Transport in South-East Nigeria." Paper presented at the annual meeting of the African Studies Association. Baltimore, MD, November 1990.

Beattie, John. 1970. *The Nyoro State*. Oxford: Oxford University Press.

———. 1958 (a). "The Blood Pact in Bunyoro." *African Studies* 17: 198–203.

Beck, Roger B. 1989. "Bibles and Beads: Missionaries as Traders in Southern Africa in the Early Nineteenth Century." *Journal of African History*, 30: 211–225.

Beidelman, Thomas O. 1982. *Colonial Evangelism: A Socio-Historical Study of an East African Mission at the Grassroots*. Bloomington: Indiana University Press.

Berger, Iris. 1981. *Religion and Resistance: East African Kingdoms in the Precolonial Period*. Tervuren, Belgique: Musée royal de l'Afrique centrale.

Bhabha, Homi K. 1994. *The Location of Culture London*. New York: Routledge.

Bjerke, Svein. 1981. *Religion and Misfortune: The Bacwezi Complex and the Other Spirit Cults of the Zinza of Northwestern Tanzania*. Oslo: Universitetsforlaget.

Brumfit, Anne. 1980. "The Rise and Development of a Language Policy in German East Africa." *SUGIA: Sprache und Geschichte in Afrika*, 2: 219–331.

Bunker, Stephen G. 1987. *Peasants Against the State: The Politics of Market Control in Bugisu, Uganda, 1900–1983*. Urbana: University of Illinois Press.

Burke, Timothy. 1996. *Lifebuoy Men, Lux Women: Commodification, Consumption, and Cleanliness in Modern Zimbabwe*. Durham: Duke University Press.

Burton, Richard Francis, Sir. 1860. *The Lake Regions of Central Africa*. New York: Harper.

Cameron, Donald. 1939. *My Tanganyika Service and Some Nigeria*. 2d ed. Washington, DC: University Press of America.

Carlson, Robert. 1989. "Haya Worldview and Ethos: An Ethnography of Alcohol Production and Consumption in Bukoba, Tanzania." Ph. D. diss., Anthropology Department, University of Illinois, Champaign-Urbana.

Casey, Edward S. 1996. "How to Get from Space to Place in a Fairly Short Stretch of Time: Phenomenological Prolegomena." In *Senses of Place*. Steven Feld and Keith H. Basso, ed. Santa Fe, NM: School of American Research Press.

Cesard, Edmund. 1939. "Le Muhaya (L'Afrique Orientale)" *Anthropos* 32, nos. 1 and 2, pp. 15–60.

———. 1938a. "Le Muhaya (L'Afrique Orientale)" *Anthropos* 31, no. 4, pp. 821–849.

———. 1938b. "Le Muhaya (L'Afrique Orientale)" *Anthropos* 31, no. 3, pp. 489–508.

———. 1937. "Le Muhaya (L'Afrique Orientale)" *Anthropos* 30, no. 1, pp. 75–114.

Cohen, David William. 1989. "The Undefining of Oral Tradition." *Ethnohistory* 36: 1.

Comaroff, Jean, and John Comaroff. 1997. *Of Revelation and Revolution: The Dialectics of Modernity on a South African Frontier*. Vol. 2. Chicago: University of Chicago Press.

———. 1991. *Of Revelation and Revolution: Christianity, Colonialism, and Consciousness in South Africa*. Vol 1. Chicago: University of Chicago Press.

Coronil, Fernando. 1996. "Beyond Occidentalism: Toward Nonimperial Geohistorical Categories." *Cultural Anthropology* 11 no. 1, p. 51(37).

Cory, Hans. 1949. *Historia ya Bukoba*. Mwanza Tanganyika.

Cory, Hans, and M.M. Hartnoll. 1945. *Customary Law of the Haya Tribe, Tanganyika Territory*. Mwanza Tanganyika.

Cronon, William. 1991. *Nature's Metropolis: Chicago and the Great West*. New York: W.W. Norton.

Curtis, Kenneth. 1989. "Capitalism Fettered: State, Merchant and Peasant in Northwestern Tanzania, 1917–1960." Ph. D. diss., History Department, University of Wisconsin–Madison.

Curtis, Kenneth R. 1992. "Cooperation and Cooptation: The Struggle for Market Control in the Bukoba District of Colonial Tanganyika." *The International Journal of African Historical Studies* 25, no. 3, pp. 505–540.

Daniel, E. Valentine. 1993. "Tea Talk: Violent Measures in the Discursive Practices of Sri Lanka's Estate Tamils." *Comparative Studies in Society and History* 35, no. 3, p. 568(33).

De Boeck, Filip. 1994. "Of Trees and Kings: Politics and Metaphor Among the aLuund of Southwestern Zaire." *American Ethnologist* 21, no. 3, pp. 451–473.

de Certeau, Michael. 1984. *The Practice of Everyday Life*. Berkeley: University of California Press.

de Heusch, Luc. 1982. *The Drunken King, or, The Origin of the State*. Translated and annotated by Roy Willis. Bloomington: Indiana University Press.

Eggert, Johanna. 1970. *Missionsschule und sozialer Wandel in Ostafrika; der Beitrag der deutschen evangelischen Missionsgesellschaften zur E.nganyika 1891–1939.* Bielefeld: Bertelsmann.

Fabian, Johannes. 1991. *Language and Colonial Power: The Appropriation of Swahili in the Former Belgian Congo 1880–1938.* Berkeley: University of California Press.

Fanon, Franz. 1967. *Black Skin, White Masks.* Translated by Charles Lam Markmann. New York: Grove Press.

Feeley-Harnik, Gilian. 1985. "Issues in Divine Kingship." *Annual Review of Anthropology* 14: 273–313.

Feld, Steven, and Keith H. Basso. 1996. *Senses of Place.* Santa Fe, NM: School of American Research Press.

Foster, Robert. 1990. "Value Without Equivalence: Exchange and Replacement in a Melanesian Society." *Man* (N.S.) 25(1): 54–69.

Friedman, Jonathan. 2000. "Globalization, Class and Culture in Global Systems." *Journal of World-Systems Research* 6 no. 3, pp. 636–656.

———. 1994."The political economy of elegance: An African cult of beauty." In *Consumption and Identity.* J. Friedman, ed. Chur, Switzerland: Harwood.

Geiger, Susan. n.d. "Engendering and Gendering African Nationalism: Rethinking the Case of Tanganyika (Tanzania)." Paper presented at the annual meeting of the African Studies Association (Chicago).

Glassman, Jonathon. 1995. *Feasts and Riots: Revelry, Rebellion, and Popular Consciousness on the Swahili Coast, 1856–1888.* Portsmouth, NH: Heinemann.

Graeber, David. 2001. *Toward an Anthropological Theory of Value: The False Con of Our Own Dreams.* New York: Palgrave.

———. 1996. "Beads and Money: Notes Toward a Theory of Wealth and Power." *American Ethnologist* 23, no. 1, pp. 4–24.

Gregory, C.A. 1982. *Gifts and Commodities.* London, New York: Academic Press.

Gregory, Christopher. 1996. "Cowries and Conquest: Towards a Subalternate Quality Theory of Money." *Comparative Studies in Society and History* 38, no. 2, p. 195 (23).

———. 1980. "Gifts to Men and Gifts to Gods: Gift Exchange and Capital Accumulation in Contemporary Papua." *Man* 15: 626–652.

Guyer, J.I. 1993. "Wealth in People and Self-realization in Equatorial Africa," *Man* 28: 243–265.

Hanks, William F. 1996. Language & Communicative practices. Boulder, CO: Westview Press.

Hannerz, Ulf. 1996. "The Local and the Global: Continuity and Change." In *Transnational Connections: Culture, People, Places,* U. Hannerz, ed. 17–29. New York: Routledge.

Hansen, Karen Tranberg. 1999. "Second-hand Clothing Encounters in Zambia: Global Discourses, Western Commodities, and Local Histories." *Africa* 69 no. 3, p. 343.

Hartwig, Gerald. 1976. The *Art of Survival in East Africa: The Kerebe and Long-Distance Trade, 1800–1895.* New York: Africana.

Hellberg, Carl-J. 1965. *Missions on a Colonial Frontier West of Lake Victoria; Evangelical Missions in North-West Tanganyika to 1932.* Translated by Eric Sharpe. Uppsala, Swedish Institute of Missionary Research.

Hendrickson, Hildi, ed. 1996. *Clothing and Difference: Embodied Identities in Colonial and Post-Colonial Africa.* H. Hendrickson, Durham: Duke University Press.

Hocart, A.M. 1927. *Kingship.* London: Oxford University Press.

Hogendorn, Jan S., and Marion Johnson. 1986. *The Shell Money of the Slave Trade.* Cambridge: Cambridge University Press.

Howes, David, ed. 1996. *Cross-cultural Consumption: Global Markets, Local Realities* London: New York: Routledge.

Hutchinson, Sharon. 1996. *Nuer Dilemmas: Coping with Money, War, and the State.* Berkeley: University of California Press.

Hyden, Goran. 1969. *Political Development in Rural Tanzania: Tanu Yajenga Nchi.* Nairobi: East African Publishing House.

Iliffe, John. 1979. *A Modern History of Tanganyika.* Cambridge; New York: Cambridge University Press.

Inter-territorial Language Committee for the East African Dependencies. 1969. *Swahili-English Dictionary.* New York: Saphograph Co.

Ishumi, Abel. 1980. Kiziba: *The Cultural Heritage of an Old African Kingdom.* Syracuse, NY: Syracuse University.

Jervis, T.S. 1939. "A History of Robusta Coffee in Bukoba." *Tanganyika Notes and Records* 8: 47–58.

Kaijage, Frederick. 1971. "Kyamutwara." *Cahiers D'Histoire Mondiale* 13: 542–574.

Kajomolo-Tibaijuka. 1985. "Factors Influencing the Cultivation of Firewood Trees on Peasant Farms: A Survey on Smallholder Banana-Coffee Farms, Kagera Region, Tanzania." *Rural Development Studies,* no. 18. Uppsala: Swedish University of Agricultural Sciences.

Kajubi, W. Senteza. 1965. "Coffee and Prosperity in Buganda: Some Aspects of Economic and Social Change." *Uganda Journal* 29, no. 2, pp. 135–147.

Katoke, Israel. 1975. The *Karagwe Kingdom: A History of the Abanyambo of Northwest Tanzania.* Nairobi: East African Publishing House.

Kelly, John, and Martha Kaplan. 1990. "History, Structure and Ritual." *Annual Review of Anthropology* 19: 119–150.

Kenny, Michael G. 1977. "The Powers of Lake Victoria." *Anthropos* 72: 715–733.

Koponen, Juhani. 1988. *People & Production in Late Precolonial Tanzania.* Philadelphia: Coronet Books.

Larsson, Birgitta. 1991. *Conversion to Greater Freedom? Women, Church and Social Change in North-Western Tanzania under Colonial Rule.* Uppsala: Uppsala Universitet.

Lass, Andrew. 1988. "Romantic Documents and Political Monuments: The Meaning-Fulfillment of History in 19th-Century Czech Nationalism." *American Ethnologist* 15: 456–471.

Lefebvre, Henri. 1991. *The Production of Space.* Translated by D.N. Smith. Cambridge: Blackwell.

Lienhardt, Godfrey. 1961. *Divinity and Experience: The Religion of the Dinka.* London: Oxford University Press.

Lwamgira, F.X. 1969. *Amakuru ga Kiziba. The History of Kiziba and Its Kings,* 2d ed. Translated from Luziba by E.R. Kamuhangire. [Makerere] Department of History, Makerere University College.

Mamdani, Mahmoud. 1976. *Politics and Class Formation in Uganda.* New York: *Monthly Review.*

Maquet, Jaques. 1954. "Le system des relations sociales dans le Ruanda ancien. Annales du musée royal du Congo Belge." Serie in-8. Sciences de l'Homme. *Ethnologie* Vol. 1. Tervuren.

Martin, Phyllis. 1996. *Leisure and Society in Colonial Brazzaville.* Cambridge: Cambridge University Press.

Marx, Karl. 1906. *Capital, A Critique of Political Economy*. New York: Charles H. Kerr and Co.

Masquelier, Adeline. 1992. "Encounter with a Road Sign: Machines, Bodies and Commodities in the Imagination of a Mawri Healer." *Visual Anthropology Review* 8: 56–69.

Merleau-Ponty, Maurice. 1962. *The Phenomenology of Perception*. London: Routledge and Kegan Paul.

Middleton, John. 1992. *The World of the Swahili: An African Mercantile Civilization*. New Haven: Yale University Press.

Miller, Daniel. 1995a. *Worlds Apart: Modernity through the Prism of the Local*. London: Routledge.

———. 1995b. *Modernity: An Ethnographic Approach*. London: Berg Press.

———. 1987. *Material Culture and Mass Consumption*. Oxford: Basil Blackwell.

Mintz, Sidney. 1985. *Sweetness and Power: The Place of Sugar in the Modern World*. New York: Viking.

Mukurasi, Peter W. 1970. "The Bukoba Cooperative Union as an Instrument of Agricultural Innovation: The Problem of Transforming the Peasant Mode of Farming in Bukoba." Master's thesis, Department of Political Science, University College, Dar es Salaam.

Munn, Nancy. 1986. *The Fame of Gawa*. London: Cambridge University Press.

———. 1983. "Gawan Kula: Spatiotemporal Control and the Symbolism of Influence." In *The Kula New Perspectives in Massim Exchange*, J. Leach and E. Leach, eds. Cambridge: Cambridge University Press.

Mutahaba, Gelase. 1969. "Problems in Effective Social Reform: A Case Study of Land Tenure Reform in Bukoba." Master's thesis, Department of Political Science, University College, Dar es Salaam.

Niesel, Hans-Joachim. 1971. *Kolonialverwaltung und Missionen in Deutsch Ostafrika 1890–1914*. Berlin: Freie Universität.

Parkin, David. 1991. *Sacred Void: Spatial Images of Work and Ritual among the Giriama of Kenya*. Cambridge: Cambridge University Press.

Parry, J., and M. Bloch. 1989. *Money and the Morality of Exchange*. Cambridge: Cambridge University Press.

Pels, Peter. 1999. A *Politics of Presence: Contacts Between Missionaries and Waluguru in Late Colonial Tanganyika*. Amsterdam: Harwood Academic Publishers.

Peters, Carl. 1891. *New Light on Dark Africa*. Translated by H.W. Dulcken, PH. London, New York, and Melbourne: Ward, Lock, and Co.

Pietilä, Tuulikki. n.d. *Gossip, Markets, and Gender: The Dialogical Construction of Morality in Kilimanjaro*. Department of Social Anthropology, University of Helsinki.

Piot, Charles. 1999. *Remotely Global: Village Modernity in West Africa*. Chicago: University of Chicago.

Rald, Jorgen, and Karen Rald. 1975. *Rural Organization in Bukoba District, Tanzania*. Uppsala: The Scandinavian Institute of African Studies.

Rehse, Hermann. 1910. *Kiziba: Its Land and People*. Translated by Mrs. Denne. n.p. Herskovitz Collection, Northwestern University. Evanston, IL.

Reining, Priscilla. 1973. "The Haya of Northwest Tanzania." In *Cultural Source Materials for Population Planning in East Africa*. A. Molnos, ed., pp. 204–210. Nairobi: East African Publishing House.

———. 1972 "Haya Kinship Terminology: An Explanation and Some Comparisons." In *Kinship Studies in the Morgan Centennial Year*, P. Reining, ed. Washington, DC: Anthropological Society of Washington.

———. 1967. "The Haya: The Agrarian System of a Sedentary People." Ph. D. diss., Anthropology Department, University of Chicago.

———. 1962. "Haya Land Tenure: Land Holding and Tenancy" *Anthropological Quarterly* 35: 58–73.

Richards, Audrey, and Priscilla Reining. 1954. "Report on Fertility Surveys in Buganda and Buhaya." In *Culture and Human Fertility*, F. Lorimer, ed. New York: UNESCO.

Roseberry, William. 1996. "The Rise of Yuppie Coffees and the Reimagination of Class in the United States." *American Anthropologist* 98, no. 4, p. 762(14).

———. 1995 (ed). *Coffee, Society, and Power in Latin America.* Baltimore: Johns Hopkins.

Sahlins, Marshall. 1999. "Two or Three Things That I Know about Culture" *Journal of the Royal Anthropological Institute* 5 no. 3, p. 399.

———. 1993. "Good-bye Tristes Tropes: Ethnography in the Context of Modern World History." *Journal of Modern History* 65: 1–25.

———. 1989. "Cosmologies of Capitalism: The Trans-Pacific Sector of 'The World System.' " *Proceedings of the British Academy* 76: 1–51.

———. 1985. *Islands of History.* Chicago: University of Chicago Press.

Sartre, Jean-Paul. 2001. Introduction to *The Colonizer and the Colonized*, by Albert Memmi. New York: Beacon Press.

Schama, Simon. 1988. *The Embarrassment of Riches: An Interpretation of Dutch Culture in the Golden Age*. New York: Knopf.

Schmidt, Peter. 1978. *Historical Archeology : A Structural Approach in an African Culture*. Westport, CT: Greenwood Press.

Schoenbrun, David Lee. 1998. A *Green Place, A Good Place: Agrarian Change, Gender and Social Identity in the Great Lakes Region to the 15th Century.* Portsmouth, NH: Heinemann.

Schutz, Alfred. 1967. *The Phenomenology of the Social World.* Translated by George Walsh and Frederick Lehnert. Introduction by George Walsh. Evanston, IL: Northwestern University Press.

Seitel, Peter. 1986. "The Bachwezi in Art and History: Who Is Mugasha in Hayaland?" Paper presented at the annual meeting of the African Studies Association. Madison, WI, October 1986.

———. 1980. *See So That We May See.* Bloomington: Indiana University Press.

———. 1977. "'Blocking the Wind': A Haya Folktale and Interpretation." *Western Folklore* 36: 189–207.

Seligman, C. G. 1966. Races of Africa, 4th ed. London: Oxford University Press.

Shipton, Parker. 1994. "Land and Culture in Tropical Africa: Soils, Symbols, and the Metaphysics of the Mundane." *Annual Review of Anthropology Annual* 23: 347(31).

———. 1992. "Debts and Trespasses: Land, Mortgages, and the Ancestors in Western Kenya." *Africa* 62, no. 3, pp. 357–387.

Simmel, Georg. 1978 [1900]. *The Philosophy of Money.* Translated by T. Bottomore and D. Frisby. London: Routledge and Kegan Paul.

Smith, C., and P. Stevens. 1988. "Farming and Income-Generation in the Female-headed Smallholder Household: The Case of a Haya Village in Tanzania." *Canadian Journal of African Studies* 22:552–566.

Société des Missionaires d'Afrique (Pères Blancs). 1905–1910. Rapports Annuels. Première-Sixième Années. Maison-Carrée (Alger): Imprimerie des Missionaires d'Afrique.

Speke, John. 1863. *Journal of the Discovery of the Source of the Nile*. Edinburgh: Blackwell.

Spyer, Patricia, ed. 1998. Border Fetishisms: Material Objects in Unstable Spaces. New York: Routledge.

Strathern, Marilyn. 1991. "Partners and Consumers: Making Relations Visible." *New Literary History* 22: 581–601.

———. 1988. *The Gender of the Gift: Problems with Women and Problems with Society in Melanesia*. Berkeley: University of California Press.

Stuhlmann, Franz. 1894. *Mit Emin Pascha ins herz von Afrika. Ein reisebericht mit beiträgen von dr. Emin Pascha, in seinem auftrage geschildert von dr. Franz Stuhlmann. Im amtlichen auftrage der Kolonial-abtheilung des Auswärtigen amtes herausgegeben*. Berlin: D. Reimer.

Sundkler, Bengt. 1980. *Bara Bukoba: Church and Community in Tanzania*. London: C. Hurst & Co.

Taylor, Christopher. 1991. *Milk, Honey and Money*. Washington, DC: Smithsonian Institution Press.

Tosh, John. 1970. "The Northern Interlacustrine Region." In *Pre-Colonial African Trade: Essays on Trade in Central and Eastern Africa before 1900*. R. Gray, and D. Birmingham, eds. London: Oxford University Press.

Tripp, Aili Mari. 1996. *Changing the Rules: The Politics of Liberalization and the Urban Informal Economy in Tanzania*. Berkeley: University of California Press.

Turner, Terry. 1984. "*Value, Production and Exploitation in Non-capitalist Societies*." Manuscript presented at the American Anthropological Association annual meeting.

Turner, Victor. 1967. *The Forest of Symbols*. Ithaca: Cornell University Press.

Uzoigwe, G.N. 1974. "Pre-Colonial Markets in Bunyoro-Kitara." *Comparative Studies in Society and History* 16: 422–455.

Valerio Valeri. 1985. *Kingship and Sacrifice: Ritual and Society in Ancient Hawaii*. Translated by Paula Wissing. Chicago: University of Chicago Press.

Waters, Malcolm. 1995. *Globalization*. New York: Routledge.

Weiss, Brad. 1999. "Good-for-Nothing Haya Names: Powers of Recollection in Northwest Tanzania." *Ethnos* 64, no. 3., pp. 397–420.

———. 1997a. "Forgetting Your Dead: Alienable and Inalienable Objects in Northwest Tanzania." *Anthropological Quarterly* 70, no. 4, pp. 164–172.

———. 1997b. "Northwestern Tanzania on a Single Shilling: Sociality, Embodiment, Valuation" *Cultural Anthropology* 12, no. 3, pp. 335–362.

———. 1996a. *The Making and Unmaking of the Haya Lived World: Consumption, Commoditization and Everyday Practice*. Durham and London: Duke University Press.

———. 1996b. "Dressing at Death: Haya Adornment and Temporality." In *Clothing and Difference: Embodied Identities in Colonial and Post-Colonial Africa*. H. Hendrickson, ed., pp. 133–154. Durham: Duke University Press.

———. 1996c. "Coffee Breaks and Coffee Connections: The Lived Experience of a Commodity in Tanzanian and European Worlds." In *Cross-Cultural Consumption*. D. Howes, ed., pp. 93–105. London: Routledge and Kegan Paul.

White, Luise. 1994. "Blood Brotherhood Revisited: Kinship, Relationship, and the Body in East and Central Africa." *Africa* 64, no. 3, p. 359 (14).

———. 1993. "Vampire Priests of Central Africa: African Debates about Labor and Religion in Colonial Northern Zambia." *Comparative Studies in Society and History* 35, no. 4, p. 746 (27).

———. 1990b. *The Comforts of Home: Prostitution in Colonial Nairobi*. Chicago: University of Chicago Press.

Zelizer, Viviana A. 1994. *The Social Meaning of Money: Pin Money, Paychecks, Poor Relief and Other Currencies*. New York: Basic Books.

Index

About the Author

BRAD WEISS is Associate Professor of Anthropology at the College of William and Mary. He is the author of the book, *The Making and Unmaking of the Haya Lived World: Consumption and Commoditization in Everyday Practice.*

www.ingramcontent.com/pod-product-compliance
Ingram Content Group UK Ltd.
Pitfield, Milton Keynes, MK11 3LW, UK
UKHW020843290926
15470UKWH00004B/1527